COGNITIVE
LINGUISTICS

To Sheila, Vicky, Debbie, and Cathy

COGNITIVE LINGUISTICS
AN INTRODUCTION

David Lee

OXFORD
UNIVERSITY PRESS

OXFORD

UNIVERSITY PRESS

253 Normanby Road, South Melbourne, Victoria 3205, Australia

Oxford University Press is a department of the University of Oxford.
It furthers the University's objective of excellence in research, scholarship,
and education by publishing worldwide in

Oxford New York

Auckland Bangkok Buenos Aires Cape Town Chennai
Dar es Salaam Delhi Hong Kong Istanbul Karachi Kolkata
Kuala Lumpur Madrid Melbourne Mexico City Mumbai Nairobi
São Paulo Shanghai Taipei Tokyo Toronto

OXFORD is a trade mark of Oxford University Press
in the UK and in certain other countries

National Library of Australia
Cataloguing-in-Publication data:

Lee, David, 1939–.
   Cognitive linguistics: an introduction

   Bibliography.
   Includes index.
   ISBN 0 19 551424 6.

   1. Cognitive grammar. 2. Meaning (Psychology). I. Title.

415

Typeset by Modern Art Production Group
Printed through Bookpac Production Services, Singapore

CONTENTS

PREFACE

A major problem with many contemporary linguistic theories is that they confront the outsider with a difficult, arcane formalism. It will probably come as a welcome surprise to most readers of this book that Cognitive Linguistics is an exception to this rule. This is not to say that the model lacks a complex theoretical apparatus. On the contrary, some advanced readings in the theory pose a major intellectual challenge and are based on subtle arguments invoking a wide range of concepts interacting with each other in intricate ways. But, at least, the nature of the theory is such that it poses no major formal hurdles to those outside the field who wish to gain some familiarity with the approach in the hope that it will add a useful dimension to their perspective on language.

In this book I have attempted to make the theory accessible to a wide audience without sacrificing some of the subtleties of the approach. As it happens, this has been an inevitable consequence of the fact that the project emerged from teaching a course in Cognitive Linguistics for undergraduates in the early stages of their studies. Consequently, the book assumes no prior knowledge of the field, though it is hoped that those who do have some knowledge—particularly those who have some familiarity with generative grammar—will be able to appreciate some of the special characteristics of the approach. To a certain extent Cognitive Linguistics has tended to define itself historically with respect to generative grammar and thus set itself up as a rival to that theory. However, the model does not have to be seen in this way and, as the theory matures, it is becoming less appropriate to do so. In any event, it seems most unlikely that any one theory will be able to deal adequately with every aspect of a phenomenon as complex as human language.

One of the most attractive features of Cognitive Linguistics is its focus on meaning. The relatively impoverished treatment of meaning in some theories of language must be a source of puzzlement to many non-linguists. But it is the nature of the cognitive treatment of the area that makes it particularly attractive in these postmodern times. In particular, the centrality of the notion of *construal* in the model makes it refreshingly different from earlier approaches to meaning. In emphasising the role of construal, cognitive linguists have moved away from earlier treatments of semantics in linguistics, based on the assumption that meaning is independent of human perceptions and human cognition and that it can therefore be objectified and potentially formalised. What unites cognitive linguists (no matter how much they may differ in other ways) is a commitment to the principle that linguistic expressions code a particular way of perceiving the relevant scene. This means that linguistic coding involves such factors as selectivity, perspective, focus, backgrounding, framing, modes of categorisation, and so on. Clearly, this puts the approach much more in tune with current trends in neighbouring disciplines—particularly Literary Theory and Cultural Studies Theory—than many other theories of language. For this reason, if for no other, the cognitive model deserves to be made accessible to scholars in other disciplines.

One of my own enduring areas of interest has been the analysis of texts (both spoken and written) with reference to the question of the relationship between language and perspective. From the outset of my career I have attempted to apply linguistic theory to discourse analysis, even when the nature of the theory did not lend itself particularly well to this task. From my point of view, therefore, the advent of Cognitive Linguistics was a most welcome development. The importance of the notion of construal in the model makes it a tool with enormous potential for analysing the ways in which human beings use language in everyday social interactions, given that these are characterised by ongoing adjustments by participants to each other's moves and given the occasional communication difficulties and (sometimes subtle) misunderstandings that arise in these settings. This interest of mine surfaces explicitly in the later sections of the book, particularly in the last three chapters, though it is a thread that runs through the book as a whole.

In the first instance, however, a linguistic theory must justify itself in terms of its ability to deal with the nature of the relationship between form and meaning. The first ten chapters of this book are therefore devoted to various aspects of this topic. Chapter 1 introduces basic concepts in Cognitive Linguistics: construal, perspective, foregrounding, metaphor, and frame. Chapter 2 investigates the coding of spatial relationships, and chapter 3 discusses extended and metaphorical uses of spatial expressions. Issues concerned with the nature of categorisation arising out of this discussion are dealt with in chapter 4. The following five chapters cover a range of topics that are of crucial interest to all linguists: the nature of constructions (chapter 5), mental spaces (chapter 6), language change (chapter 7), aspects of nominal and verbal structure (chapters 8 and 9), agentivity and causation (chapter 10). I then turn to my own special areas of interest. In chapter 11 I invoke most of the concepts discussed in earlier chapters in the analysis of family argument, and in chapter 12 I consider constructivism in language, focusing in particular on the way in which speakers use categorisation creatively to support their rhetorical stance and construct their social world.

The concluding chapter discusses some general issues arising out of the cognitive approach, including creativity in language and the nature of meaning.

David Lee
May 2001

ACKNOWLEDGMENTS

I owe a debt to a number of people. I am particularly indebted to Ron Langacker who sponsored my visit to the University of California, San Diego, in 1996 and allowed me to attend his course on Cognitive Linguistics. That was an invaluable experience, my only regret being that I have been unable to do full justice to the subtlety and complexity of his ideas in this introductory presentation of the theory. I am also grateful to students in the linguistics program at the University of Queensland and to my linguistics colleagues Lynn Wales, Mary Laughren, John Ingram, and Rob Pensalfini for stimulating discussions of topics covered in this book. I would also like to thank two anonymous readers who made helpful observations and constructive suggestions that have helped to make this a better book than it would otherwise have been. Responsibility for any errors is entirely my own.

Finally, I owe a special debt to my wife, Sheila, for her patience and constant support during the writing of this book.

1

BASIC CONCEPTS

1.1 Introduction

Over the past two decades the Cognitive Linguistics enterprise has developed to the point where a university linguistics program is now arguably incomplete without a significant component devoted to this model. In the early years cognitive grammarians tended to define their model in opposition to what was then the dominant paradigm in the discipline—the theory of generative grammar, associated with Noam Chomsky. This is no doubt because the leading scholars in the movement were themselves trained as generative grammarians and elaborated the cognitive model out of what they perceived to be shortcomings of generative theory. However, Cognitive Linguistics has now developed to the point where it can be considered a mature, autonomous theory of language in its own right.

The main feature that distinguishes Cognitive Linguistics from generative grammar has to do with the place of meaning in the theory. In the generative model the structure of linguistic expressions is deemed to be determined by a formal rule system that is largely independent of meaning. By contrast cognitivists argue that linguistic structure is a direct reflex of cognition in the sense that a particular linguistic expression is associated with a particular way of conceptualising a given situation. This leads to a quite different view of the relationship between language and cognition in general. Whereas generative grammarians claim that there exists a rich set of principles of language design (Universal Grammar) that are specific to language, the cognitivists believe that, although universal principles governing the design of all languages may well exist, they will eventually be found to be rooted in cognition. This leads cognitivists to be sceptical about the view current in generative grammar that there is a specific 'organ' in the human brain devoted exclusively to language.

In this chapter I will attempt to elaborate on the claim that there is an interrelationship between thought, meaning, and linguistic structure by examining the major concepts in the theory. I will focus on the notions of construal, perspective, foregrounding, metaphor, and frame.

1.2 Construal

There is a long tradition in linguistics encapsulating the belief that the role of language is to map elements of the external world onto linguistic form. According to this view, situations can be dissected into a number of component parts, each of which corresponds to some element of language, so that mapping from the external world to language is a relatively straightforward operation. Essentially, it involves a one-to-one encoding of the elements of the situation into linguistic structure, this process being governed by formal rules of grammar.

In contrast, cognitive linguists argue that there is no such direct mapping. Instead, they claim, a particular situation can be 'construed' in different ways, and that different ways of encoding a situation constitute different conceptualisations. Consider, for example, the contrast between (1) and (2).

(1) *John gave the book to Mary.*

(2) *John gave Mary the book.*

The traditional view is that these sentences express the same meaning—that the syntactic (structural) difference has no correspondence in semantics. One reflex of this view is the fact that in some variants of generative grammar the two sentences are 'derived' (by formal rules) from the same underlying structure, implying that the difference between them is one of form rather than substance. However, there are a number of indications that this view is incorrect. One such piece of evidence has to do with the fact that in some cases only one of these constructions is natural. For example, although *John gave the fence a new coat of paint* is unremarkable, it would be odd to say *?John gave a new coat of paint to the fence* (Langacker 1990: 14). Conversely, whereas *He brought the wine to the table* is fine, the sentence *?He brought the table the wine* is strange.[1] These differences suggest that the two constructions illustrated in (1) and (2) involve different ways of construing 'the same situation' and that in certain cases only one mode of construal is appropriate or natural. These examples and others illustrating the same point will be discussed in detail in chapter 5.

1.3 Perspective

One factor involved in alternative construals has to do with perspective. Consider:

(3) *The path falls steeply into the valley.*

(4) *The path climbs steeply out of the valley.*

Although these sentences could be used to describe the same scene, we would hardly want to say that they express the same meaning. The difference between them has to do with perspective. In (3) the viewpoint is that of someone looking down into the valley, whereas in (4) it is that of someone looking up from the valley floor.

Interestingly, the actual position of the speaker in cases of this kind is irrelevant. One does not have to be looking down to say (3), nor is one necessarily looking up when uttering (4); one might be looking at a painting, viewing the scene sideways-on. Another illustration of this point is the fact that, if I am talking to someone on the phone, I would normally say *I'll come over and see you tomorrow* in preference to *I'll go over and see you tomorrow*, even though the verb *come* is oriented to the perspective of the addressee rather than to that of the speaker. In other words, in cases such as (3) and (4) a particular viewing position is **constructed** as part of the process of producing meaning through language. Each sentence involves a particular construal of the scene in question, with contrasting perspectives producing distinct interpretations.

As a second example, consider the contrast between (5) and (6).

(5)   *John bought the car from Mary.*

(6)   *Mary sold the car to John.*

Here too we have a pair of sentences which refer to 'the same event' but they could hardly be said to express the same meaning. Again the contrast has to do with perspective (in a rather more abstract sense than in (3) and (4)). Sentence (5) construes the situation from John's point of view, whereas (6) is an expression of Mary's viewpoint. As a small piece of evidence that this is so, consider:

(7)   *John bought the car from Mary for a good price.*

(8)   *Mary sold the car to John for a good price.*

In (7) we infer that the price was relatively low, whereas (8) suggests that it was high. This must mean that (5) and (7) are oriented to the buyer's point of view, whereas (6) and (8) are oriented to that of the seller.

One important aspect of perspective concerns the question of what we take as the reference point in a given scene. Consider, for example, the contrast between:

(9)   *The lamp is above the table.*

(10) *The table is below the lamp.*

In (9) we take the table as the reference point and relate the position of the lamp with respect to it, whereas the reverse is the case in (10). Following Langacker (1988b: 75–9, 1990: 9–10), I will use the term 'landmark' to refer to the entity that is construed as the reference point, and 'trajector' to refer to the element that is located with respect to it. In many cases pragmatic factors impinge on the choice of trajector and landmark, as illustrated in (11) and (12).

(11) *The pen is on the table.*

(12) *?The table is under the pen.*

Whereas both of these are possible ways of describing the same situation, the fact that pens are normally placed with respect to tables rather than tables with respect to pens makes (11) the more natural way of coding this particular scene. In situations such as those described in (9) and (10), however, there are no such inherent pragmatic factors at work, so that either the table or the lamp can be construed as the landmark, with the other as trajector.

1.4 Foregrounding

A second factor involved in contrasting construals has to do with the relative prominence of the various components of the situation. For example, suppose when I am mowing the lawn, one of the blades strikes a stone, causing it to fly into the air and break a window. I could use either (13a) or (13b) to refer to this event.

(13) (a) *I've broken the window.*

     (b) *A stone has broken the window.*

Again, these codings involve different construals. Example (13a) foregrounds my role in the event, whereas (13b) foregrounds that of the stone, thereby backgrounding my involvement in the scenario. The following examples illustrate a similar point.

(14) (a) *You won't be able to open this door with that key.*

     (b) *That key won't open this door.*

Either of these examples could be used in a situation where the addressee is about to try to open a door with a particular key, but (14a) gives slightly greater prominence to the involvement of the addressee than does (14b). Here are some further illustrations of the point.

(15) (a) *I'm standing on the street.*

     (b) *I'm standing in the street.*

(16) (a) *The fish is in the water.*

     (b) *The fish is under the water.*

(17) (a) *The cloth is on the table.*

     (b) *The cloth is over the table.*

The members of each pair can be used to refer to the same situation, but they highlight different aspects of it. For example, in (15a) the street is conceptualised as a roadway (and therefore as a supporting surface), whereas in (15b) it includes the buildings on either side (and is therefore construed as a container). In (16a) and (16b) the contrast has to do with whether the water is thought of as a volume (container) or as a surface. And (17a) suggests much more strongly than (17b) the fact that the cloth is not only 'on' the table but that it covers it.

Similar contrasts show up in other cases. For example, we would normally interpret *They are demolishing our street* to mean that they are knocking down the houses (possibly leaving the road surface untouched), whereas we interpret *They are resurfacing our street* to mean that they are putting a new surface on the roadway rather than on the houses. This tendency for the interpretation of an expression to vary slightly from one context to another is known as (contextual) 'modulation' (Cruse 1986: 52; Taylor 1995: 124). As another example of the phenomenon, note that the expression *the window* is interpreted rather differently in *He cleaned the window* and *He opened the window*, in that the former draws attention to the glass in the window, whereas the frame is more salient in the latter (see Langacker 1990: 189–201 for discussion of the related concept of 'active zone').

Perspective and salience are not totally independent parameters. Instead of identifying the contrast between (5) and (6) as one of perspective, we could equally well say that (5) highlights John's role in the event, whereas (6) gives special prominence to Mary's role. In other words, the entity from whose perspective we view a situation is often also the most salient participant.

Perspective and foregrounding connect linguistic coding closely to visual perception. Just as a particular construal of a situation highlights certain elements in a scene and backgrounds others, so the process of visual perception involves focusing on certain elements and relegating others to the periphery of our visual field. In some cases there is a direct correspondence between visual focus and linguistic coding. If I say to my wife *The cat wants something to eat*, this utterance normally stems directly from a visual experience of mine, involving focus on a particular feature of an inherently complex scene, any one feature of which might have claimed my attention. Moreover, it typically has the effect of shifting the attention of my addressee to a new focus. Associated with such a shift in visual focus is a shift in cognitive focus. If my wife is reading a book when I make this remark, the utterance may cause her to shift her cognitive focus (if she decides to pay any attention to it).

This observation can also be applied more generally to word meanings. One way of thinking about the meaning of words is to see them as tools for causing speakers to access specific parts of their knowledge base (Moore & Carling 1982: 11). At any given moment, individuals have a huge store of knowledge available to them. The function of the noun *cat* in the utterance *The cat wants something to eat* is to cause the addressee to home in on a very specific region of that knowledge base—specifically on those neural structures that constitute her store of knowledge concerning cats in general and the family cat in particular. These connections between language and vision provide grounds for the view that the relationship between language and the cognitive processes associated with other areas of human perception may be closer than has traditionally been thought. This point is developed in the discussion of frames below (1.6).

1.5 Metaphor

The concept of construal is closely linked to another important feature of Cognitive Linguistics that differentiates it from other theories of language—namely, a concern with metaphor. Metaphor used to be thought of as a rather unusual form of discourse, characteristic of the literary language. However, important pioneering work by Lakoff and Johnson (1980) showed that metaphor is in fact a fundamental property of the everyday use of language.

Metaphor is linked to the notion of construal by virtue of the fact that different ways of thinking about a particular phenomenon (that is, different construals of that phenomenon) are associated with different metaphors. For example, we sometimes think about the concept of intimacy in terms of heat (*I couldn't warm to her, He is such a cold person, He has a very cool manner*) and sometimes in terms of distance (*I felt really close to him, I found his manner rather distant, He is quite unapproachable*). Similarly, an argument can be thought of as a building (*That supports what I'm saying, Your argument has crumbled, You need something to buttress that claim*), or as a journey (*What are you driving at?, This point takes us a little further, That leads me to the following conclusion*), so that understanding an argument is sometimes construed as following someone (*I don't follow you, You've lost me, I'm not with you*). Alternatively, it can be thought of in terms of seeing (*I don't see your what you are getting at, Your explanation isn't clear, It was a really obscure lecture*).

A metaphor is essentially a device that involves conceptualising one domain of experience in terms of another. Thus, for any given metaphor, we can identify a source domain and a target domain. In examples such as *He's a really cold person, She gave us a warm welcome*, the source domain is the sense of touch and the target domain is the more abstract concept of intimacy. It is not difficult to find other aspects of interpersonal behaviour that can be conceptualised similarly in terms of physical properties—*I'll be really blunt with you, There's no need to be so sharp with him, That was a cutting remark*. In examples such as *He has a high reputation in the department, He has just risen to deputy manager, John occupies a relatively low position in the firm*, the source domain is the vertical dimension of physical space and the target domain is social status. As these examples show, source domains tend to be relatively concrete areas of experience and target domains to be more abstract.

Lakoff and Johnson emphasise that metaphors involve not only ways of talking about phenomena but also ways of thinking about them. In some cases this can have significant social implications. For example, investigations into the language used about nuclear weapons over the last half century suggest that different modes of discourse have been employed at various times in an attempt to make them palatable to the public (Kress 1985). Part of this process involves the names that have been applied to such weapons. In the early days of intercontinental ballistic missiles, names such as *Jupiter*, *Titan*, *Zeus*, and *Atlas* were used.[2] This process is metaphorical in that it invokes all the connotations of the source domain of classical mythology. When British atomic tests were carried out in Australia in the 1950s, weapons were named after Australian birds and animals (for example, *Wombat*) in an attempt to 'indigenise' the program and make it more acceptable to the Australian public.[3]

In the United Kingdom official pamphlets from the British Ministry of Defence and in speeches in the House of Commons, a rather different range of metaphors has been employed. One of the most common practices is for nuclear weapons to be constructed in terms of economic, industrial, and technological processes, as if these weapons were part of the nation's machinery for the production of wealth (Beedham 1983; Lee 1992: 86). This makes it possible for the radioactivity generated by a nuclear explosion to be thought of in terms of 'yield' (certain weapons being 'low-yield, enhanced radiation warheads'). Alternatively, the metaphor 'Nuclear weapons are ideas' can be invoked, so that terms such as concept, capability, system can be applied (the Cruise Missile concept, our nuclear capability, the final launch of our ultimate capability, land-based system, submarine system, land-based support system).

In some cases metaphors are large-scale structures that influence our thinking about whole areas of human experience. For example, Johnson (1987: 127–37) discusses in detail a shift in ways of thinking about the human body that took place as a result of the research of Hans Seyle into the nature of stress research. Prior to Seyle's work, the predominant metaphor in the practice of medicine was the metaphor of the body as a machine. Seyle's discovery that there was a general reaction in the body to a variety of stimuli (in addition to specific reactions to specific diseases) led to a new metaphor of the body as a homeostatic organism. Whereas the 'body as machine' metaphor had caused medical practitioners to ignore certain bodily reactions because they did not fit the accepted models of disease and bodily functions, Seyle gradually came to realise that these reactions required a whole new way of thinking about the body, which included considerations of overall balance. This has led to new ways of thinking about disease and, more importantly, new ways of treating disease. Johnson argues that this case is simply one example of the general idea that 'vast domains of our experience, understanding, reasoning, and practice are metaphorically structured' (Johnson 1987: 137). Metaphor is in fact a prime manifestation of the cognitive claim that language and thought are inextricably intertwined.

1.6 Frame

The concept of 'frame' in cognitive linguistics can best be illustrated by an example. If one were asked by a non-native speaker of English what the word *wicket* meant, one might consult a dictionary for help. The Concise Oxford Dictionary gives the following definition: 'wicket: one set of three stumps and two bails'. But how much would this mean to a non-native speaker of English who knew nothing of the game of cricket?

If one were asked to **explain** the meaning of the word *wicket*, it would be natural to say not only what a wicket is but also something about its overall role in the game. For example, one might explain that one person (known as the 'bowler') tries to knock the wicket down by throwing a ball at it in a special way, while another person (known as the 'batsman') stands in front of the wicket and tries to prevent the ball from hitting it by using a wooden instrument known as a 'bat'. This could be the beginning of quite a long explanation. In other words, a good understanding of the word *wicket* requires a significant amount of knowledge that extends well beyond the dictionary definition. We refer to this background knowledge as the 'frame'.

The frame is not in itself what is generally thought of as 'the meaning' of a word but it is nevertheless crucial to an understanding of it. For example, the word *uncle* makes sense only in the context of an understanding of kin relations in general—in particular how *uncle* relates to terms such as *father, mother, aunt,* and so on These words share the same frame, even though they have different meanings.

There is a close connection between the concept of frame and that of foregrounding. Consider, for example, a word such as *hypotenuse* (Langacker 1990: 6). This word derives its meaning from the concept of a right-angled triangle (even though it does not mean 'right-angled triangle'). The word *hypotenuse* designates (or 'profiles' in Langacker's terminology) one element of a right-angled triangle, specifically the side opposite the right angle. So, like *wicket* and *uncle*, the word *hypotenuse* foregrounds an element in a larger frame.

The term 'frame' should not be taken to imply that there is necessarily a well-defined boundary between those elements that form part of the frame for the meaning of a particular word and those that do not. For example, in explaining the term *wicket* to someone who does not understand cricket, it is a matter of subjective choice as to how much detail one gives. Where does one stop in explaining about wicketkeepers and fielders and stumpings and run-outs and so on? In principle everything that a speaker knows about the world is a potential part of the frame for a particular term, even though some aspects of that knowledge base are more immediately relevant to a particular term than others (and therefore more strongly activated when the term is used).

A corollary of this is that the concept 'frame' is multidimensional. The word *mother*, for example, belongs to a number of different frames, including most saliently the genetic frame and the social frame. If I say *Did you know that Sue is John's mother?* I am using the term *mother* to refer to a biological relationship, so that it is principally the genetic frame that is in play. On the other hand, if I say *Sue is not really cut out to be a mother* I do not mean that Sue lacks the biological equipment to be a mother. Rather, I am thinking of a mother as someone who behaves in a particular way, so here it is principally the social frame that is in play. This explains an example such as (18).

(18) *Mary adopted John when he was a baby so she's not his real mother—but in fact she has been a wonderful mother to him.*

At first sight this sentence seems to assert (a) that Mary is not John's mother and (b) that she is. However, the sentence is not a contradiction, because the first occurrence of the word *mother* is located in the genetic frame, whereas the second is located in the social frame.

So the notion of frame has both a conceptual and a cultural dimension. On the conceptual dimension the meaning of *mother* is defined by the fact that it contrasts with words such as *father, daughter, aunt, sister,* and so on, and there are relatively concrete semantic features that differentiate it from these other words, located in the same frame. On the cultural dimension the word carries a complex range of associations that would be difficult to define precisely but that often feed into the way the word is interpreted and that therefore contribute to its meaning.

As a further example, consider the word *weekend* (Fillmore 1982: 119). An understanding of this term involves knowledge that it refers to the days that we call Saturday and Sunday rather than to the days we call, for example, Monday and Tuesday. In other words, the term profiles a certain part of the seven-day cycle. This could be regarded as conceptual knowledge. But that knowledge is overlaid with other aspects of knowledge that are also part of the frame. A visiting Martian might wonder why we have a term that refers specifically to Saturday and Sunday but no term for just Monday and Tuesday—until we explain that Saturday and Sunday have a special status as non-working days for most people in our culture. In other words, part of the knowledge base for *weekend* involves an understanding of certain very specific cultural patterns.

This means that the concept of frame embraces the traditional concept of 'connotation'. For many people the word *weekend* conjures up pleasant images of relaxation, sport, camping, trips to the beach, and so on, just as the term *mother* conjures up images of warmth, affection, and care. In later chapters we will see how important these elements are to word meaning (see in particular chapter 7 on language change, and chapters 11 and 12 on discourse analysis).

This point leads to a further observation. Although there is clearly a great deal of overlap between the frames of different members of the same speech community for specific words, it is also obvious that there are individual differences in this respect. If one person devotes her weekends to fishing, while another devotes his to sailing, then there is a difference between their respective frames. In certain circumstances, the term *weekend* will conjure up different images (that is, have different connotations) for them. To this extent they understand the term in different ways. This does not normally lead to a communication problem, since the differences in question are small in relation to the degree of common ground and they are largely irrelevant to most situations in which the word is used. Nevertheless, there is some potential here for minor or even major communication problems. This issue is taken up in chapter 11.

What is essentially 'the same phenomenon' is sometimes referred to by different words when it is located in different frames. For example, the words *roe* and *caviar* refer to the same entity but they are differentiated according to whether the context of use is the anatomical or gastronomic frame (Langacker 1987: 164–5). Similarly, if I approach the boundary between land and sea from the land, I refer to it as 'the coast', whereas if I approach it from the sea, I call it 'the shore', so that a journey from coast to coast is a journey over land, whereas one from shore to shore is over water (Fillmore 1982: 121).

Conversely, the same term may be associated with rather different meanings in different frames. For example, the word *knife* normally conjures up for me an image of the instrument I use for eating food, but if I hear that someone has been killed with a knife, then I construct a different image. In this sense, the meaning of the word *knife* is in part a function of the frame in which the word is used.

The concept of frame also has implications for language change. When new frames arise, existing words are often carried over into the new domain, thereby undergoing some change of meaning. Much of the terminology that relates to aircraft and air travel, for instance, is derived from the nautical domain. The process of entering a plane is called 'boarding', the main passenger area is called the main 'deck', the kitchen is called the 'galley', and the left and right sides of the plane are sometimes referred to (by the crew) as 'port' and 'starboard' (terms that are never used in relation to cars and trucks). In some cases the nature of the referent is very different from the corresponding entity in the source domain (for example, the deck), so that there is a significant shift in meaning.

As another case in point, consider the word *bug* as it applies to a fault in a computer program. This term was reportedly first used when a problem with one of the early computers was found to be due to the presence of a dead insect in its innards. When the person who made this discovery said *There's a bug in it*, he was using the term *bug* in its original sense. However, this situation involved the activation of a new frame (computer programming)— a development that established a new semantic potential for the word.

One interesting issue relating to such examples has to do with the question of whether the new meaning (and the frame in which it is located) has separated completely from the original meaning. In other words, the question is whether the insect frame is still activated (no matter how weakly) when someone refers to a 'bug' in a computer program. Chafe (2000: 115–16) has used the term 'shadow meaning' to refer to this kind of phenomenon. For example, Chafe reports that in the Native American language Seneca the word for *horse* is a compound noun made up of the morphemes *pull* and *logs* and that the word for *strawberries* is made up of the morphemes *embers* and *attached*. It is easy enough to see the motivation for each of these examples. Speakers of Seneca first encountered horses when they were being used to pull logs for making houses, and there is an obvious connection between the appearance of strawberries on the ground and glowing embers. However, the question is whether current speakers of Seneca are aware of the internal structure of these items. (One might ask the same question of English speakers with respect to nouns such as *breakfast* and *cupboard* as well as *bug*). Chafe reports that speakers of Seneca are aware that their word for *horse* does have the internal structure that he describes, but this is not so for all speakers in the case of the word for *strawberry*.

The concept of frame has implications for our understanding of such notoriously problematic terms as 'meaning' and 'concept'. It is conventional in linguistics to say that a particular word corresponds to a particular 'concept' and to assume that concepts are essentially identical across speakers. Some linguists have gone so far as to attempt to characterise these 'concepts' in objective terms—by constructing lists of features that represent 'the meaning' of particular words. But the notion of frame challenges this assumption, if we accept that the frame for a particular word can vary across speakers as a function of their particular life experience.

I have already suggested that, instead of thinking in terms of words as expressing 'concepts', we should think of them as tools that cause listeners to activate certain areas of their knowledge base, with different areas activated to different degrees in different contexts of use. This approach to an understanding of meaning has a number of advantages over the concept-based model. First, as noted above, it accommodates the notion of 'connotation'. This term has generally been relegated to the periphery of studies in semantics. Yet connotational meaning is central to many areas of language use, including our enjoyment of literature, and possibly plays a much larger part in everyday communication than has sometimes been realised. Second, this model accommodates recent work in crosscultural communication (including cross-gender communication) much more easily than the alternative model. It is well known that crosscultural communication is often plagued by misunderstandings that have nothing to do with the meaning of linguistic forms in the narrow sense (Gumperz 1982; Scollon & Wong Scollon 1995). A model based on the view that communication involves the exchange of shared 'concepts' between individuals would have considerable difficulty in accounting for this phenomenon. In a frame-oriented approach, however, knowledge differences based on an individual's life experiences (including growing up in a particular culture) can be built into the model. If this kind of experiential knowledge informs our use of language and our understanding of specific linguistic forms, as the frame-based approach claims, then we have the beginnings of an explanation for some of these findings. In chapter 11 we will consider a specific manifestation of this phenomenon, involving cross-generational communication.

1.7 Conclusion

The concepts introduced in this chapter do not constitute an arbitrary set. Their interrelationship stems from the central role in Cognitive Linguistics of the notion of construal. The notions of perspective, highlighting, and framing constitute different aspects of that process, while metaphor is an important medium through which a particular 'imaging' (Langacker 1990: 5) is imposed on a given scene. In interaction with each other, these notions have significant implications for an understanding of the nature of communication. In particular, they suggest that meaning is not a property of utterances but a product of the interaction between an utterance and a human being's 'knowledge base'—an idea that introduces an important relativist dimension to the process of interpretation. This view of language and interpretation brings linguistic theory much closer to related disciplines such as ethnography and cultural studies than do formally based approaches.

Relativism is by no means a new phenomenon in linguistics. The notion is closely associated with the American linguists Edward Sapir and Benjamin Lee Whorf, whose work on Native American languages in the early years of the twentieth century led them to propose the idea that learning our first language causes us to acquire a particular world view, distinct from that of native speakers of other languages (Whorf [1945] 1971). What makes the notion of relativism different in Cognitive Linguistics is the idea that there is variation across different speakers of **the same language** with respect to the interpretation and coding of particular situations. This claim will be developed in subsequent chapters.

Exercises[4]

Construal

I Give alternative codings for each of the situations coded by the following sentences and say what factor or factors would trigger the alternative coding.

(a) *The post office is next to the bank.*
(b) *The red car is behind the tree.*
(c) *The red car is behind the blue one.*
(d) *Jim married Mary in 1960.*

2 Consider the sentence *John went to London in 1998*. An alternative coding may be *John came to London in 1998*. What alternatives might there be for the expressions *John, went, to London, in 1998*, and what contextual factors would trigger such alternative codings?

3 *Ed has been hurt in an accident.* Give several examples of ways in which this could be coded at greater levels of specificity.

4 The words *each* and *every* are obviously very close in meaning but do they express identical meanings? Is there any difference between *I could see every star in the sky quite clearly* and *I could see each star in the sky quite clearly*?

5 Why can nouns such as *committee*, *crowd*, and *team* take either a singular or plural verb form (*The committee has considered the question*, *The committee have considered the question*)? Are there any other grammatical reflexes of this contrast between 'singular construal' and 'plural construal'? Are there any contexts in which it would be more natural to use one or another of these forms?

6 Is there any difference in meaning between *Drinking and singing is fun* and *Drinking and singing are fun*?

Foregrounding

7 Explain the ambiguity of the expression *a red pen* and say how this relates to the process of foregrounding.

8 In some parts of Australia a foldable baby carriage is called a *stroller* whereas in other parts it is called a *pusher* (Bryant 1985: 60). How might this difference be related to the notion of foregrounding?

9 How do the following examples relate to the notions of foregrounding and backgrounding?

(a) *I hit the stick against the fence.*

(b) *I hit the fence with the stick.*

Does your answer help to explain why *I hit Harry with the stick* is a more natural sentence than **I hit the stick against Harry*?

Metaphor

10 Make a list of metaphors that are in play in the (randomly ordered) examples below. Some examples contain more than one metaphor and the same metaphor may be present in more than one example. For each metaphor noted, give a couple of illustrative examples.

> *He broke under cross-examination.*
> *How can we get out of this mess?*
> *I can't get through to him.*

I can't bring myself to tell him.
I can't give you any more time.
He's coming around (regaining consciousness).
I could see the joy in his eyes.
I couldn't take my eyes off her.
It's difficult to put my idea into words.
I don't buy his story.
The experience shattered him.
My eyes were glued to the screen.
I feel quite drained of emotion.
This gadget will save you hours.
I gave you that idea.
He's gone a long way towards solving this problem.
It's hard to get that idea across to him.
I feel full of happiness.
We're heading for a disaster.
Christmas is coming.
Nothing I say gets through to him.
We're in a tight spot.
You are on the right track with that suggestion.
She is easily crushed.
I just couldn't take it all in.
You're going nowhere in this job.
Don't let him get you down.
Don't let yourself be sidetracked.
Stick to your guns.
He looked straight at me.
My mind is a bit rusty today.
He's not really with us (doesn't understand).
It was a stunning performance.
I'm on top of the world.
It was a gripping movie.
I'm mulling it over.
He's suffering from stress.
He's out for the count.
He caught a cold from standing out in the rain.
He's getting into debt.
I'm trying to digest what you've just said.
She is under a lot of pressure.
It was a moving ceremony.

Anger was welling up inside me.
I was touched by his offer.
He was churning out ideas.
You're wasting my time.
Do you think you'll be able to sell that idea to the boss?
Would you run your eyes over this draft?

Frame

11 Consider the following sentences.

(a)   *The haystack was important because the cloth ripped.*

(b)   *The journey was not delayed because the bottle shattered.*

Does each of these sentences become more meaningful to you if you place it within one of the following frames?

- washing clothes
- launching a ship
- typing a letter
- making a parachute jump
- playing in a football game

Can you give any examples of communicative problems you have experienced with someone else because of some discrepancy in your mutual knowledge or mutual focus of interest at that moment?

12 Suppose we lived in a society where children were taken away from their mothers at birth and reared in institutions supervised by professional caretakers. Why would such a society have little use for the word *orphan*? If the word did exist, how might its connotations differ from those it has in our society?

13 In what kind of situation might one utter (a) below and how might this differ from the situation in which one would say (b)?

(a)   *I can see the ground.*

(b)   *I can see (the) land.*

14 Why are expressions such as *a fake gun, a fake van Gogh* quite natural, whereas *a fake biscuit* and *a fake pencil* are rather odd?

15 In some places it is possible to get 'breakfast' at any hour of the day or night. What aspect of our eating habits does this usage depend on? (To put the question another way, how would our eating habits have to be different for the notion 'breakfast at any time' to be meaningless?)

16 Explain the concept 'tamper-evident packaging' to a visiting Martian. How much cultural information do you feel it appropriate to convey?

Further reading

Each article listed below gives a useful overview of the cognitive approach. The collections of papers listed are for more advanced study. Details of books on Cognitive Linguistics are of various levels of difficulty: Lakoff 1987, Taylor 1995, and Ungerer & Schmid 1996 are suitable for beginning students; Langacker 1999 is for more advanced study, as are the two foundational texts, Langacker 1987 and 1991.

- The journal *Cognitive Linguistics*, published by Mouton de Gruyter, is the major forum for ongoing research in the field.
- The website address of the International Cognitive Linguistics Association is <www.siu.edu/~icla>.
- There is a University of California, Berkeley, website on metaphor at <http://cogsci.berkeley.edu/MetaphorHome.html>.

Overview articles

Lakoff, G. 1982, 'Categories: an essay in cognitive linguistics', in Linguistic Society of Korea (ed.), *Linguistics in the Morning Calm*, Hanshin, Seoul, pp. 139–93.

Langacker, R. W. 1988, 'An overview of cognitive grammar', in B. Rudzka-Ostyn (ed.), *Topics in Cognitive Linguistics*, John Benjamins, Amsterdam, pp. 3–47.

——1988, 'A view of linguistic semantics', in B. Rudzka-Ostyn (ed.), *Topics in Cognitive Linguistics*, John Benjamins, Amsterdam, pp. 3–47, 49–51.

——1990, *Concept, Image and Symbol*, chapter 1: Introduction, Mouton, Berlin, pp. 1–32.

——1994, 'Cognitive grammar', in R. E. Asher (ed.), *The Encyclopaedia of Language and Linguistics*, Pergamon, Oxford, pp. 590–3.

——1999, 'Assessing the cognitive linguistic enterprise', in T. Janssen & G. Redeker (eds), *Cognitive Linguistics: Foundations, Scope and Methodology*, Mouton, Berlin, pp. 13–60.

Newmeyer, F. J. 1999, 'Bridges between generative and cognitive linguistics', in L. de Stadler & C. Eyrich (eds), *Issues in Cognitive Linguistics*, Mouton, Berlin, pp. 3–19.

Radden, G. 1992, 'The cognitive approach to natural language', in M. Pütz (ed.), *Thirty Years of Linguistic Evolution*, John Benjamins, Amsterdam, pp. 513–41.

Collections of papers

Casad, E. H. (ed.) 1996, *Cognitive Linguistics in the Redwoods*, Mouton, Berlin.

Geiger, R. A. & Rudzka-Ostyn, B. (eds) 1993, *Conceptualizations and Mental Processing in Language*, Mouton, Berlin.

Goldberg, A. (ed.) 1996, *Conceptual Structure, Discourse and Language*, CSLI Publications, Stanford.

Janssen, T. & Redeker, G. (eds) 1999, *Cognitive Linguistics: Foundations, Scope and Methodology*, Mouton, Berlin.

Rudzka-Ostyn, B. (ed.) 1988, *Topics in Cognitive Linguistics*, John Benjamins, Amsterdam.

Stadler, L. de & Eyrich, C. (eds) 1999, *Issues in Cognitive Linguistics*, Mouton, Berlin.

Books

Lakoff, G. 1987, *Women, Fire and Dangerous Things: What Categories Reveal About the Mind*, University of Chicago Press, Chicago.

Langacker, R. W. 1987, *Foundations of Cognitive Grammar*, vol. 1, *Theoretical Prerequisites*, Stanford University Press, Stanford.

——1991, *Foundations of Cognitive Grammar*, vol. 2, *Descriptive Applications*, Stanford University Press, Stanford.

——1999, *Grammar and Conceptualization*, Mouton, Berlin.

Taylor, J. R. 1995, *Linguistic Categorization*, Clarendon, Oxford.

Ungerer, F. & Schmid, H.-J. 1996, *Introduction to Cognitive Linguistics*, Longman, London.

Notes

1 A question mark or asterisk in front of an example marks it as odd or deviant in some way.

2 I owe this point to Paul Chilton (ABC interview, 'Background Briefing', Australian Broadcasting Commission, Sydney 1985).

3 Noel Sanders made this observation in the radio interview referred to in the previous note.

4 Many of the examples used in the exercises at the end of each chapter are based on examples discussed in the literature. However, in general I have refrained from citing the source of the example in order to discourage students from looking up 'the answer' instead of thinking it out for themselves. I hope this will prove acceptable to scholars whose work I have used in this way. I should, however, give a general list of sources that have provided me with ideas for exercises used in the book. I am conscious of having drawn particularly on the following sources: Bransford & Johnson 1972; Fauconnier 1994; Fillmore 1977, 1982; Herskovits 1986; Hopper & Thompson 1985; Johnson 1987; Lakoff 1972, 1996; Lakoff & Johnson 1980; Langacker 1982, 1987 (chapter 7), 1988a, 1990 (chapter 11); Levin & Rappaport Hovav 1991; Schiffrin 1987; Sweetser 1996; Talmy 1988; Taylor 1995; Traugott 1993; Wierzbicka 1985.

2

SPACE

2.1 Introduction

One of our earliest and most basic cognitive achievements as infants is to acquire an understanding of objects and of the way in which they relate to each other in physical space. The kind of concepts represented by words such as *up*, *down*, *in*, *out*, *on*, *off*, and so on are the building blocks on which we construct our mental models of the physical world. The Swiss psychologist Jean Piaget ([1936] 1952) recognised the fundamental importance of these concepts when he characterised the first stage of cognitive development as 'sensorimotor knowledge'. In other words, infants come to understand the world through grasping things, picking them up, dropping them, pulling them—and generally watching what happens when objects are manipulated by themselves and by others. Infants spend hours placing objects on top of each other or inside one another, so that these relationships are well established conceptually before the corresponding words are used.

It is no doubt because spatial relationships are so fundamental that we use space as a domain for structuring other less concrete aspects of our experience. For example, when we say that someone occupies a 'high' position in society, we are using the up–down axis as a means of talking about social status. If someone says that they are 'in trouble', they are treating 'trouble' as a container and themselves as a contained object. If I say that I have a 'close' relationship with someone, I am constructing the notion of intimacy in terms of physical proximity. The next chapter is devoted to a detailed discussion of this kind of application of spatial concepts to more abstract domains. Before this discussion is undertaken, we need to consider the ways in which we talk about space itself, since even in this very basic area, the relationship between language and reality is surprisingly complex. To illustrate this claim, three basic locative prepositions—*in*, *on*, and *at*—will be considered.

2.2 Example: *in*

The basic function of *in* is to refer to a situation where one object (the 'trajector') is contained within another (the 'landmark'). However, even if we focus only on those uses of *in* that are concerned with relations between objects in physical space (as opposed to examples such as *in trouble*), we find that *in* is used in a whole range of situations where there is only an approximation to this ideal meaning. Consider the following examples (Herskovits 1986).

(1)   *the cat in the house*

(2)   *the bird in the garden*

(3)   *the flowers in the vase*

(4)   *the bird in the tree*

(5)   *the chair in the corner*

(6)   *the water in the vase*

(7)   *the crack in the vase*

(8)   *the foot in the stirrup*

(9)   ?*the finger in the ring*

Example (1) is a prototypical use of *in*, referring to a situation in which the trajector (TR) is wholly contained within the landmark (LM). Example (2) is similar, except that a garden is a less prototypical example of a container than a house, since it has no clearly defined upper boundary. Nevertheless, there is some notional boundary, since a sparrow can be 'in' a garden if it is flying around at a relatively low height, but we would not say that a hawk hovering at 200 metres above the garden was 'in' it. Already in this example, then, we see another example of the notion of 'construal'. Objectively speaking, a garden is not a well-defined three-dimensional container, but in our everyday use of a word such as *in*, it is construed as one.

Examples (3), (4), and (5) show that there is a good deal of flexibility in the way we apply the notion of containment to the real world. In (3) the fact that the flowers are not inside the vase does not prevent us from using *in* to refer to this situation (figure 2.1).

Figure 2.1 *The flowers in the vase*

In (4), in order to conceptualise a tree as a container, we have to construe it as a three-dimensional object, the boundaries of which are defined by the ends of the branches. In (5) the question of whether a chair is 'in' a corner is a particularly ill-defined issue, given the indeterminate nature of 'a corner'. The question can also be affected by the presence of other objects in the scene—we are much more likely to identify the chair in the diagram on the left of figure 2.2 as being in the corner than we are in the diagram on the right, even though it is in exactly the same position in both (Herskovits 1986: 47).

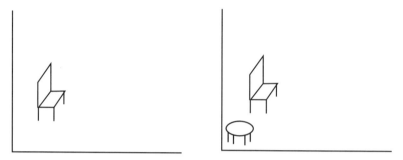

Figure 2.2 *The chair in the corner*

Examples (6) and (7) illustrate a rather different point—namely, the fact that the concept of 'containment' itself manifests a certain degree of flexibility. Example (6) constitutes a prototypical example of the concept, where a three-dimensional entity (the water) is entirely contained within the confines of a three-dimensional container, which surrounds it on all sides. But in (7) we interpret the notion of containment differently. Here, TR (the crack) is embedded in the surface of LM rather than in some hollow space inside it. In other words, there is some variation in the way LM is construed—as a volume in one case and an area in another. Similar examples of this latter use of *in* are found in such examples as *the weeds in the lawn, the wrinkles in his skin*.

Examples (8) and (9) are different again. The spatial configuration is similar in both cases (figures 2.3 and 2.4), yet there is a difference in how we identify the relationship between the two entities.

Figure 2.3 *The foot in the stirrup*   **Figure 2.4** *The ring on the finger* (*The finger in the ring*)

In (8) we see the relationship as one of containment (even though only a small part of the foot is contained within the stirrup). In (9), it would be odd to conceptualise the situation in terms of the finger being 'in' the ring. The reasons for this have to do with a pragmatic asymmetry between TR and LM in each case. Since the function of a stirrup is to hold the foot in a particular position, it is naturally construed as LM, with the foot as TR. A ring does not have this function. The relationship here is the converse, with the finger functioning as a fixed entity (LM), with respect to which the ring is placed as TR. These examples show that, in order to explain the forms that we use to code these situations in language, we need to go beyond the level of surface topographical relationships. Background knowledge involving the relevant functional relationships is crucial to an understanding of the forms of coding, which reflect subtle aspects of everyday human experience.

The same point can be made about the following pair (Herskovits 1986).

(10) *the bulb in the socket*

(11) **the jar in the lid*

The topographical relationships are similar in each case (figures 2.5 and 2.6), but only in (10) is the relationship construed in terms of containment, since only in this case is the uppermost entity naturally construed as a fixed reference point. Again, our background knowledge concerning the functional relationships involved is crucial to an understanding of the relevant linguistic patterns.

Figure 2.5 *The bulb in the socket*

Figure 2.6 *The lid on the jar*
(***The jar in the lid*)

2.3 Example: *on*

Similar points can be made about examples containing *on*. If native speakers are asked to give an example of a sentence containing the word *on*, they tend to give one such as (12), in which two entities are in physical contact with each other, with one positioned above the other and supported by it.

(12) *the pen on the desk*

However, consider the following examples.

(13) *the writing on the paper*
(14) *the poster on the wall*
(15) *the wrinkles on the face*
(16) *the fly on the ceiling*

The situation described in (13) is different from that in (12). Since writing is not a physical object, the relationship between TR and LM in (13) is not one of physical support. From the point of view of a human conceptualiser, however, it seems entirely natural to see this situation as analogous to (12). Since the writing is applied to the paper in a manner that bears some similarity to the way in which a pen is placed on a desk, the objective differences between the two situations can be ignored for coding purposes.

Example (14) is judged by most speakers to be a slightly unusual use of *on*, because the wall is behind the poster rather than beneath it. (Other languages typically do not use the word corresponding to *on* in this case; French, for example, uses *à*, meaning 'at' in English, rather than *sur*, 'on' in English, in this case.) This example is perhaps closer conceptually to (13) than to (12) in that the wall, like the paper, forms a background, with the writing and the poster as foregrounded or displayed entities. Something similar can be said of (15), where the face is construed as a background against which the wrinkles are displayed, as opposed to *the wrinkles in his face*, which suggests that the wrinkles are etched more deeply into the skin and thus foregrounds the notion of embedding.

Example (16) is unusual in that the topological relationship between the ceiling and the fly is precisely the opposite of that which holds in the normal situation coded by *on*. As we move from the prototypical situation to cases such as (13), the notion of display seems to assume as prominent a role in the situation as that of support, and it is perhaps this factor that motivates the incorporation of (16) into the 'on' category (though the fact that the ceiling functions as a resting place for the fly is clearly also relevant). What this shows is that members of the same category may differ from each other quite markedly with respect to the characteristics that qualify them for their membership. This poses a critical problem for the traditional (Aristotelian) theory of category membership, according to which there is a necessary feature or features that all members of a category share (see Lakoff (1987: 161) for discussion). In chapter 3 it is noted that members of a particular category may in fact express meanings that are diametrically opposed to each other, since they connect to central (or 'prototypical') members by virtue of quite different features.

2.4 Example: *at*

The preposition *at* provides a particularly clear example of the flexibility and abstraction involved in the coding of spatial relationships. Herskovits (1986: 128–40) argues that the function of *at* is to locate two entities at precisely the same point in space and construe them as geometric points. This provides an elegant account of various characteristics of the use of *at*, but it clearly involves a considerable degree of abstraction and idealisation.

Consider (17) as a case in point.

(17) *John is at the supermarket.*

This sentence would be an entirely natural utterance if I were at home telling someone where John was at that moment. However, I would be much less likely to say this if I were actually in the supermarket (or even just outside it), reporting the same situation. If I am close to or in the supermarket, it is difficult for me to conceptualise it as a geometric point in space. Given its size and salient materiality, it is much more natural to think of it in these circumstances as a container, as in (18).

(18) *John is in the supermarket.*

As one moves away from the supermarket, however, it becomes progressively easier to conceive of it as a point. This may well have something to do with the fact that, as we move away from objects in our visual field, their image on the retina grows smaller, so that at a given distance they begin to approximate to a point.

A second piece of evidence supporting Herskovits's characterisation of the meaning of *at* is the fact that if I arrange with someone to meet me 'at the library', this can cause difficulties when the time of meeting actually comes, since it does not specify whether the meeting is to take place inside or outside the building. This distinction is lost when the building is construed as a point.

A third piece of evidence has to do with the situations in which it would be natural to use (19) rather than (20).

(19) *The café is at the highway.*

(20) *The café is on the highway.*

At first sight, (19) appears to constitute a counterexample to the claim that *at* involves the construal of the two elements involved in the relationship as geometric points, since this seems incompatible with the fact that a highway is a long, straight object, more naturally conceptualised as a line in geometric terms. In fact, the typical context of use for (19) is when I am moving along a path (for example, driving a car) and I say that the café is located at the place where my path intersects with the highway at some point ahead—a location that is quite naturally conceptualised as a point. Similarly, there is an implicit notion of path in each of the following.

(21) *The bomb exploded at 1000 feet.*

(22) *We'll hold a lifeboat drill at the equator.*

(23) *The horse fell at the water jump.*

In (21) the point at which the bomb exploded is the point at which its trajectory (path) intersects with the 1000 feet altitude level; in (22) the lifeboat drill will be held at the point where the ship's path intersects with the line of the equator; and in (23) the conceptualiser tracks the progress of the horse to the water jump, where it falls.

The concept of path is also present in the following examples, but in a more abstract form.

(24) *The bird has a white band at its neck.*

(25) *The bird is at the top of the tree.*

(26) *There are bubbles at the surface.*

Whereas in (19)–(23) an actual physical movement is involved (that is, cars, ships, bombs, and horses follow paths through physical space), in (24)–(26) there is no such physical trajectory. Nevertheless, the cognitive claim is that there is movement in the following sense. What (24) implies is that the conceptualiser scans the body of the bird and comes across a white band when this scanning process reaches the neck;[1] similarly, in (25) the scanning process moves across the tree, finding a bird when it reaches the top; and in (26) there is implicit movement through the liquid, encountering bubbles when it reaches the surface.

Further evidence for the notion that *at* involves some abstract notion of path in examples such as these is that the only circumstance in which a sentence such as *John is at London* is natural is if London is one of a series of points on a journey. Otherwise, it is more natural to conceive of London as a container than as a point.

2.5 Construal of objects and spatial relationships

In the discussion of *in*, *on*, and *at* above a number of cases were noted in which the choice of one preposition over another is a matter not of the objective properties of the observed situation but of the way in which the various elements of the situation and the relationships between them are construed. Let us consolidate this observation with a few more examples.

Consider (27) and (28).

(27) *the words on the page*

(28) *the words in the margin*

From one point of view the selection of *on* in (27) seems somewhat arbitrary. After all, in both these situations the words are located in a two-dimensional area. In (27), however, this topographical relationship is overridden by pragmatic factors. The fact that the paper is construed as a background serving to display the (foregrounded) words makes the concept of support more salient than that of containment, strongly motivating the use of *on* (see the discussion of (13) above). The function of a margin, however, is not to display text but to define a particular area of the page, so that in cases such as (28) it is the notion of containment that is salient.

Consider next those cases noted above where *in* is used to refer to a situation where one entity is embedded within another.

(29) *the weeds in the lawn, the wrinkles in his skin, the cracks in the vase*

These examples contrast with those, such as (30), that contain *on*:

(30) *the spots on his nose, the bruises on his face*

There is no reason in principle why *in* could not be used in (30), and there are undoubtedly some languages that do not differentiate between the two cases. In English, however, the use of *on* foregrounds the similarity between the situations in (30) and the one referred to in (27) (*the words on the page*) at the expense of the similarity with the situations in (29). In other words, the relationship between body parts such as noses, faces, arms, legs, and so on, and entities such as spots and bruises is construed as one involving support and display rather than embedding.

Consider next the contrast between (31) and (32).

(31) *John is in the bus/train/plane/boat.*

(32) *John is on the bus/train/plane/boat.*

These examples show that vehicles such as trains, buses, planes, and boats can be construed either as containers or as supporting surfaces. (Cars are an exception that will be dealt with directly.) Why is this so? After all, buses, trains, planes, and boats are prototypical containers and people generally sit inside them. So, the fact that *on* is as natural as *in* here (more so in some circumstances) requires explanation.

The differences between (31) and (32) again involve salience, framing, and construal. The use of *in* is favoured if the vehicle is stationary (and therefore analogous to a house, a shed, a garage, or any other prototypical container). I might say *John is in the train*, for example, in reporting his position to someone who was looking for him on the platform where the train was standing. However, if I am waiting at the station for his train to arrive, I am much more likely to say *He's on the next train* rather than *He's in the next train*. This is because the role of the train as a transport vehicle is more salient in this context than its role as a container. In construing the train as a transport vehicle, I conceptualise it as a rather abstract device for conveying people from one place to another. The fact that people are inside it (rather than outside it) is less important than the fact that they are attached to it and supported by it. In this sense *on* involves a greater degree of abstraction than *in*. This also shows up in the fact that we say *John is on the 8.45* rather than *John is in the 8.45*. In referring to a particular train as 'the 8.45', I construe it as a transporter rather than as a material object—that is, in relatively abstract terms.

This helps to explain why there is no comparable use of *on* with cars (*John is on that car* cannot normally be used in a situation when he is inside it). This seems to have to do with the fact that cars are not normally used to provide scheduled services for transporting people in the way that trains and planes are. In a situation where they are being used in that way (for example, a fleet of cars ferrying a large number of people from A to B), the statement *He'll be on the next car* would perhaps be slightly less surprising.

The motivation for the choice between *in* and *on* with boats is probably governed by rather different factors. It is certainly possible to say *John is on that boat over there* when the boat is not being used as a transporter. The fact that the function of boats is to keep people on top of the water makes 'support' a particularly prominent notion in this context. (For the same reason *on* is used with bridges, even though most bridges would lend themselves, by their nature, to being construed as containers.) Interestingly though, *in* is more natural if the boat is a rowing boat—perhaps because its small size makes the notion of containment particularly salient.

Another set of situations in which the choice between contrasting prepositions has more to do with psychological factors than with objective properties is illustrated by the following examples.

(33) *He hit the ball through the outfield.*

(34) *He rolled the ball across the pitch.*

(35) *He pushed the mower over the lawn.*

Through is like *in* in that it involves construal of LM as a container, whereas with *across* and *over* (as with *on*) it is construed as a supporting surface. The large area constituted by the outfield surrounding a cricket pitch makes it a natural container—fielders as well as balls are located 'in' it. The pitch is an area too, but in this case, since it is smaller and the grass on it is short, it is more naturally seen as a surface. Lawns are also conceptualised as supporting surfaces for similar reasons, except when we refer to entities embedded in them (*There are a lot of weeds in this lawn*).

Another situation in which the length of grass is relevant to the choice of preposition is illustrated by the contrast between (36) and (37).

(36) *I walked across the grass* (short grass).

(37) *I walked through the grass* (longer grass).

Note that the use of *through* here does not presuppose that the grass is taller than the person walking through it (it may only be knee-high). In other words, the path of the walker is conceptualised not as the three-dimensional space traversed by the entire body but rather as a virtual path emanating from the feet. Again, there is a good deal of abstraction in the conceptualisation of these relationships.

As a final example of the general point, consider the following contrast.

(38) *John was at a fight/football game.*

(39) *John was in a fight/football game.*

As we have noted above, *at* involves construal of both TR and LM as geometric points. In (38) this degree of abstraction tends to background those aspects of the event involving action, so that the main effect is simply to express a locative relationship between TR and LM. By contrast, the construal of a fight or football game as a container in (39) seems to characterise LM as an event rather than as a place, causing the idea to emerge that TR was an active participant in LM.

The claim that the choice between different prepositions in cases of this kind is associated with different construals needs to be reconciled with the idea that there is often some degree of arbitrariness or conventionality in such cases. The fact that different languages often make different choices in these cases shows that convention does indeed play a significant role. In fact, the notion of construal itself predicts that there should be some degree of conventionality (or arbitrariness) at work, since in situations that lend themselves to different construals, it is to be expected that different languages will make different choices for their preferred coding.

2.6 Conclusion

In this chapter we have considered a range of uses of three basic English prepositions. The analysis shows that, even in this very basic area of linguistic coding, there is often no straightforward relationship between properties of the situation and the linguistic forms used to refer to them. A particular situation can be construed in more than one way with respect to such basic topographical relationships as containment and support, for example. The way in which a particular situation is conventionally encoded can be heavily influenced by functional considerations deriving from everyday human experiences. Moreover, even a preposition as basic as *at* requires us to postulate a considerable degree of abstraction in order to explain the ways in which it is used in everyday discourse.

The application of basic topographical notions such as containment and support to observed situations is characterised by a significant degree of flexibility or plasticity. The significance of this observation is that it helps to explain the fact that basic spatial notions can be applied to a wide range of non-spatial situations. Such uses will be discussed in the following chapter.

Exercises

1 What difference in meaning do you find between the following examples?

(a)   *The marchers converged on Times Square.*

(b)   *The marchers converged at Times Square.*

What is it about the meaning of *at* that produces this contrast?

2 What is the difference between the interpretations of the expression *all over the floor* in *He walked all over the floor* and *There were toys all over the floor*?

3 If the preposition *at* codes a situation in which TR and LM are construed as points, why can we say *There's a queue at the counter*, when both a queue and a counter are more naturally conceptualised as lines rather than as points?

4 What is the difference in meaning between *He was sitting by his desk* and *He was sitting at his desk*? Why is it natural to say *He was sitting by the fridge* but odd to say *He was sitting at the fridge*?

5 The sentence *The bike is in front of the car* is ambiguous in a way that *The bike is in front of the tree* is not. Explain.

6 Imagine a situation in which a table is lying on its side and a cat is lying on the floor between the legs of the table. This means that the cat is lying under two of the legs of the table. Could we code this situation as *The cat is under the table*? If not, why not? How might this be related to the fact that we can refer to 'the rabbit under the bush' even though the rabbit is not under the roots of the bush and to the fact that we can refer to 'the house on top of the hill', even though the foundations and cellar of the house are not (quite) on top of the hill?

7 In identifying how two entities are related to each other in space, we tend to select large, fixed objects as landmarks and smaller moveable objects as trajectors. For example, *The bike is next to the post office* rather than *The post office is next to the bike*. Why then is it just as natural to say *The town hall is quite near us* as it is to say *We are quite near the town hall*?

8 Comment on the bolded expressions in the following examples.

(a)   *There are farms **every so often** through the valley.*

(b)   *Coolangatta is **still** in Queensland, but Tweed Heads is **already** in New South Wales.*

(Note: Coolangatta is a town in Australia on the Queensland side of the border with New South Wales; Tweed Heads is just across the border in New South Wales.)

9   If someone travelled from Manchester to London, we could say that they went 'down to London' or 'up to London'. Why are both of these possible?

Further reading

Aurnague, M. & Vieu, L. 1999, 'A modular approach to the semantics of space in language', in L. de Stadler & C. Eyrich (eds), *Issues in Cognitive Linguistics*, Mouton, Berlin, pp. 23–34.

Hawkins, B. 1988, 'The natural category MEDIUM: an alternative to selection restrictions and similar constructs', in B. Rudzka-Ostyn (ed.), *Topics in Cognitive Linguistics*, John Benjamins, Amsterdam, pp. 231–70.

Herskovits, A. 1985, 'Semantics and pragmatics of locative expressions', *Cognitive Science* 9: 341–78.

——1986, *Language and Spatial Cognition: An Interdisciplinary Study of the Prepositions in English*, Cambridge University Press, Cambridge.

——1988, 'Spatial expressions and the plasticity of meaning', in B. Rudzka-Ostyn (ed.), *Topics in Cognitive Linguistics*, John Benjamins, Amsterdam, pp. 271–97.

Langacker, R. W. 1990, 'Inside and outside in Cora', in B. Rudzka-Ostyn (ed.), *Topics in Cognitive Linguistics*, John Benjamins, Amsterdam, pp. 33–57.

Ogawa, R. H. & Palmer, G. B. 1999, 'Langacker semantics for three Coeur d'Alene prefixes glossed as "on" ', in L. de Stadler & C. Eyrich (eds), *Issues in Cognitive Linguistics*, Mouton, Berlin, pp. 165–224.

Pütz, M. & Dirven, R. (eds) 1996, *The Construal of Space in Language and Thought*, Mouton, Berlin.

Talmy, L. 1980, 'How language structures space', in H. L. Pick Jr & L. P. Acredolo (eds), *Spatial Orientation: Theory, Research and Application*, Plenum Press, New York, pp. 225–82.

Vandeloise, C. 1994, 'Methodology and analyses of the preposition *in*', *Cognitive Linguistics* 5: 157–84.

Note

1   Alison Pottinger (pers. comm.) observed that this kind of sentence tends to be found in books on birds, where visual scanning is particularly relevant.

3

EXTENSIONS FROM SPATIAL MEANINGS

3.1 Introduction

This chapter focuses on the ways in which we use spatial terms and spatial concepts to structure non-spatial domains. The fact that our encoding of spatial relationships involves the kind of processes of abstraction and idealisation discussed in the previous chapter provides some explanation for the facility with which spatial concepts are applied to more abstract domains. It means that there is in fact no sharp dividing line between spatial and non-spatial concepts.

We begin by considering some apparently puzzling aspects of the non-literal use of spatial expressions (Lindner 1982). Consider:

(1) (a) *The sun is out; The stars are out.*

    (b) *The light is out; The fire is out; He blew the candles out.*

(2) (a) *He threw out a suggestion to the meeting.*

    (b) *They threw out Bill's suggestion.*

It may seem rather odd to non-native speakers of English that when the sun or stars are 'out' they are visible, but when lights, fires, or candles are 'out', they are invisible. If a suggestion is 'thrown out' to a meeting, it is introduced for discussion, whereas if it is simply 'thrown out' it is dismissed. Similarly, in (3) the word *up* is part of an expression that refers to an object getting bigger, whereas in (4) the object gets smaller.

(3) *He blew up the balloon.*

(4) *He rolled up the carpet.*

However, opposite meanings are sometimes expressed by prepositions that are apparently unrelated to each other. For example, the opposite of *They rolled up the carpet* is *They rolled out the carpet* rather than *They rolled down the carpet,* and the opposite of crumpling 'up' a letter involves smoothing it 'out' rather than smoothing it 'down'.

Moreover, prepositions that normally express opposite meanings sometimes express similar meanings—

(5)   *She filled in the form.*

(6)   *She filled out the form.*

(7)   *They shut up the theatre.*

(8)   *They shut down the theatre.*

—and sometimes such prepositions express meanings that seem to be quite unrelated to each other:

(9)   *The students dropped in* (paid a visit).

(10) *The students dropped out* (gave up their courses).

In other cases, similar meanings are expressed by prepositions (*up* and *out*) that are not closely related to each other in their basic locative uses.

(11) *Lots of people turned up for the party.*

(12) *Lots of people turned out for the party.*

In other words, the relationships between prepositions and meanings manifest all of the following possibilities:

• The same preposition can express opposite meanings.
• Opposite meanings can be expressed by unrelated prepositions.
• Prepositions that normally express opposite meanings can express similar meanings.
• Prepositions that normally express opposite meanings can express unrelated meanings.
• Similar meanings can be expressed by unrelated prepositions.

These observations suggest that prepositional usage is simply chaotic in English, and such a claim has indeed been made. For example, Swan (1980: 19) says of these expressions:

> There aren't many rules to help you choose correctly so you have to learn each expression separately.

Yet a careful analysis, invoking some of the central concepts in cognitive linguistics, shows that the situation is considerably less unruly than it appears at first sight.

3.2 Example: *out*

The core meaning of *out* involves an image schema such as that represented in figure 3.1, where an entity (trajector) is located outside a container or containing space (landmark).[1] The *out* relationship is sometimes static (*The cat is out of the house*) and sometimes dynamic (*The cat went out of the house*), and is extended to a wide range of situations, both physical and abstract, that can be construed in terms of exteriority.

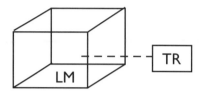

Figure 3.1 Image schema for *out*

One form of extension from the dynamic situation involves situations in which an entity expands in size (*The lava spread out*) or comes to occupy a greater area (*Roll out the carpet, Hand out the brochures*). The link with exteriority is that increase in size is naturally conceptualised in terms of parts of the entity moving 'out' from the space that it originally occupied (figure 3.2). In such cases the trajectory is 'reflexive', since the movement is construed with respect to a previous state of the same entity.

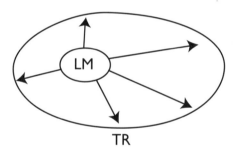

Figure 3.2 *The lava spread out*

Another (related) semantic extension involves a process whereby an entity (or part of an entity) moves away from a landmark (LM) without any obvious notion of exit, illustrated by examples such as *She set out for Nepal, He reached out to grab it*. Both increase in size and movement away from LM can be expressed in ways that do not involve the notion of exteriority, as we see from such verbs as *increase, enlarge, move away, leave*, so that the imposition of the notion of exteriority on these situations is a form of construal.

Examples such as *The sun is out* and *The stars are out* involve applications of the basic notion of exit from location, but there is a further factor at work here. In these cases, LM is a container that is inaccessible to an observer and TR is an entity that is deemed to have emerged from this area into the observer's perceptual field. One piece of evidence supporting this claim is the fact that we say *The sun came out* and *The stars came out*, where the use of the verb *come* expresses movement towards the speaker or conceptualiser. Conversely, sentences in which *out* is associated with invisibility (*The fire is out*, *The light is out*) involve metaphorical movement of an entity away from the observer into the hidden area, as evidenced by the fact that we use *go* rather than *come* to refer to the process whereby these situations come about (*The fire went out*, *The light went out*). These examples illustrate the relevance of the notion of perspective (compare 1.3) to the process of conceptualisation and coding. The apparently puzzling fact that *out* is sometimes associated with visibility and sometimes with invisibility can be accounted for by supposing that the two usages involve locating an observer in different parts of the image schema (figures 3.3 and 3.4).

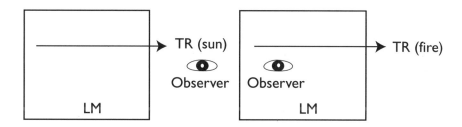

Figure 3.3 *The sun came out*   **Figure 3.4 *The fire went out***

Strongly associated with the example *The sun is out* are expressions such as *The news is out*, *The secret is out*, *The cat is out of the bag*, where it is a matter of presence in someone's **cognitive** field rather than their **perceptual** field. Things that were previously not known are now known and therefore 'out'. Related examples are *He spoke out*, *He threw out a few ideas*, *I worked out a solution to the problem*, *I found out the truth*, *We sounded him out*. Also related are the expressions *Everything turned out okay*, *I've sorted it out*, in which the result (or outcome) of a process comes to be known.

Conversely, expressions such as *The noise drowned out the music*, *He tried to blot out the memory*, *The criminal is hiding out* are related to *The fire is out*, since these situations involve metaphorical movement of the phenomenon into an area that is removed from the conceptualiser's perceptual or cognitive field.

The process whereby a particular phenomenon becomes inaccessible is pragmatically linked to the idea of a particular phenomenon or resource becoming unavailable. Examples such as *The fire is out* and *The light is out* can be interpreted in either way. When the fire dies, we no longer see it and it is no longer available as a resource. It is therefore not surprising to find *out* being used to code situations where physical (or indeed mental) resources become unavailable (*We're out of petrol*, *Our supplies have run out*, *I'm tired out/burnt out*).

There is also a conceptual link between some of the notions mentioned above and that of change from a normal to an abnormal state, including a move from consciousness into unconsciousness. Hence the use of *out* in such expressions as *black out, knock out, pass out, psych out, freak out, flip out, space out, bomb out*.

The examples above show that the range of meanings expressed by *out* constitute a structured semantic network, with each element in the network connected to another element (or elements) by some kind of cognitive relationship or association. Since the network is structured around a core meaning (in this case the notion of exit from a container), it is appropriate to call it a 'radial category'—that is, to conceptualise the various meanings expressed by *out* as a web radiating out from a central point. Metaphor is centrally involved in semantic extension of this kind, since even examples that are close to the core (for example, *The stars came out*) do not involve exit (or indeed movement) in the literal sense. At the periphery of the network, we find the notion of exit being applied to increasingly abstract phenomena:

- exit from perceptual field
- exit from cognitive field
- exit from area of control or availability
- change from normal state.

Observations of this kind help to construct the cognitive map of speakers of English. (Figure 3.5 represents an attempt to sketch the nature of the cognitive network for *out* in English.) To the extent that these linguistic connections also exist in other languages, we can take it that they represent natural cognitive associations.

3.3 Puzzle: *fill in* and *fill out*

We noted earlier that *fill in a form* and *fill out a form* can be used by many native speakers of English to refer to the same process. This is because the action in question can be conceptualised in two different ways (Lindner 1982: 316). We can think of it as a process whereby material is inserted into spaces in the form, in which case we 'fill it in'; alternatively, it can be construed as a process that causes the form to increase in size as material is added, which motivates the expression *fill out* (compare *She spread out the tablecloth, The sail billowed out, They rolled out the carpet, The budget has blown out*, and similar expressions).

This example provides a further illustration of the role of the notion of salience in the process of construal. Neither *fill in* nor *fill out* expresses all the

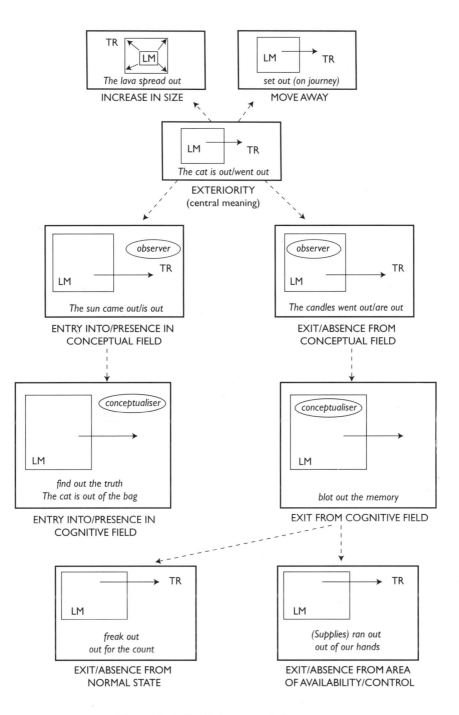

Figure 3.5 Radial network for *out*

characteristics of the process. Each coding constitutes a particular construal, such that certain aspects of the process are foregrounded and others backgrounded in each case. Each coding, incidentally, also constitutes a particular mode of categorisation. The process is construed either as one in which material is inserted into a container or as one in which an entity increases in size.

As another example illustrating the point that *in* and *out* can refer to the same situation but involve different construals, consider the contrast between *His hair grew in* and *His hair grew out*. In one case the process is thought of as one in which the new hair fills in some gaps, whereas in the other case the process is one in which the hair moves 'out' from the bald patches.

3.4 Example: *up*

The preposition *up*, like *out*, is associated with an extensive semantic network. There is in fact some overlap between the two, in that *up* (like *out*) can involve increase in size (*She blew up the balloon*). However, whereas the notion of exit remains relatively salient with *out* (even in extended uses), the notion of upward vertical position or movement that constitutes the basic meaning of *up* is often not present in extended uses. There seems to be no notion of verticality in *They scaled up the map*, for example.

This is not to say that the use of *up* to express increase in size is unmotivated. On the contrary, there is an obvious pragmatic connection between increase in size and upward movement, just as there is an obvious connection between increase in size and outward movement. It is simply that the basic locative meaning associated with *up* has been bleached out more significantly in some uses than is the case with *out*.

In many domains increase in size is conceptually related to increase in scale, and it is *up* rather than *out* that has come to express many of these meanings (*Prices went up, Her temperature shot up, The car speeded up, My blood pressure is up*). As a further extension, it is often used to express activity (or heightened activity) in various physical and mental domains: *start up, pep up, perk up, pick up* (as in *Business is picking up*), *key up, tense up, brighten up, cheer up*.

There are a number of expressions in which *up* expresses the rather different notion of 'approach' (*move up, sneak up, sidle up, walk up, run up*). This usage is presumably motivated by the fact that, as an object moves towards an observer, the retinal image enlarges, with increase in the vertical dimension being particularly salient. In other words, there is an experiential connection between approach, on the one hand, and both increase in size and upward movement, on the other.

These perceptual relationships help to explain why, paradoxically, *up* is also involved in some situations involving decrease in size (*roll up the carpet, crumple up the paper, fold up the sheet*). This meaning connects with the concept of approach in that, as an object contracts upon itself, the various parts of the entity move nearer to each other—that is, the process is 'reflexive'. This also explains why the opposite of *up* in these situations tends to be *out* rather than *down* (*roll out*, *smooth out*), given that the process whereby parts of an object move away from the core is naturally coded in terms of exit from location.

The fact that *up* codes both heightened activity and the notion of approach helps to explain why it is also associated with the notion of completion of a process (*settle up a bill, cut up the meat, even up, balance up, square up, use up, It's all up with us*). These cases involve the continuation of an activity towards a culmination—a process naturally conceptualised in spatial terms as movement towards a goal.

Many expressions involving *up* are associated with processes involving the coming into existence of an entity (*make up a story, print up some invitations, run up a dress, whip up a meal*), appearance in the perceptual field of an observer (*When did he show up?, Where will she pop up next?, look someone up, hunt up a reference*), or increased salience in someone's perceptual field (*speak up, pipe up, turn up the lights, brighten up, liven up, play up (a piece of evidence)*). There are obvious connections here with those uses of *up* involving activity and also some connections with the notion of approach (especially in expressions such as *show up, pop up*).

Since *out* is also used to code some of these situations (for example, 'appearance in perceptual field', as in *The sun came out, The stars came out*), it is legitimate to ask why *out* is not used for some of the other situations that we are claiming to be conceptually related. Why, for example, do we not find any uses of *out* coding the coming into existence of an entity? Part of the reason may have to do with differences between *out* and *up* with respect to the process of 'bleaching'. As noted above, the basic locative meaning of *up* seems to have been bleached out of many of its uses, whereas this is not so in the case of *out*. The continuing salience of the locative schema in *out* makes it unsuitable for coding the concept of coming into existence, since the schema suggests that the object had some prior existence in a hidden area before it appeared in the observer's perceptual field.

Of course, this account only puts the question of explanation one step back, since the question now arises as to why *up* has been bleached more strongly than *out*. There may be deep perceptual or cognitive reasons for this of which we are as yet unaware, but it may simply be a matter of conventionalisation. In other words, it may be a matter of chance that *up* has acquired a more extensive semantic network than *out* and undergone bleaching in the process. In general cognitivists argue that many facets of language are not susceptible to the kind of rigorous, predictive explanations that we expect in the hard sciences, given that language is a sociocognitive phenomenon that is at least to some extent subject to convention and conventionality (Lakoff 1987: 96).

3.5 Puzzle: *hunt up* and *hunt down*

Certain puzzles associated with *up* and *down* are similar to those associated with *in* and *out*. Although there are many uses of *down* that code opposite meanings to *up*, even in extended uses (compare the use of *down* to express reduced activity in *pipe down, play down, turn down,* and so on), there are some cases in which *up* and *down* code similar meanings, even with the same verb. For example, *hunting something up* is close in meaning to *hunting something down*. As in the case of *fill in a form* and *fill out a form,* the explanation for the contrast between *hunt up* and *hunt down* has to do with alternative construals, involving differences of focal prominence. The process of *hunting something up* involves hunting for something until it is brought within our area of access or control (compare *chase up, follow up*). To *hunt something down* on the other hand is to hunt something to the point where it is no longer active (compare *track down, chase down*) (Lindner 1982: 319). These are different ways of thinking about the same activity and, as in the case of *fill in* and *fill out*, they each highlight different aspects of the same process.

A similar explanation suggests itself for the contrast between the following examples.

(13) *They closed up the business/shut up shop.*

(14) *They closed down the business/closed down the game.*

In (13) we find the *up* that denotes a reflexive path defined relative to a goal. In other words, the business is closed 'up' on itself in much the same way that a carpet is rolled 'up' on itself. The difference is that rolling up a carpet (or crumpling up a piece of paper) involves physical movement, whereas the 'movement' involved in closing up a business is metaphorical. Example (14), on the other hand, involves an alternative construal, with *down* coding transition from activity to inactivity.

3.6 Puzzle: *speak up* and *speak out*

In the case of *speak up* and *speak out* we have different codings of 'the same situation' with prepositions that are unrelated in their basic uses. If we suggest to someone that they should *speak up*, we may simply want them to speak louder (so that *up* refers to heightened acoustic activity). Alternatively, we may mean that we want them to make certain facts known. On this second interpretation the process is similar to that of 'speaking out'. There may nevertheless be a subtle difference of interpretation. The process of speaking 'up' involves bringing certain facts within the mental field of the audience, whereas 'speaking out' highlights rather more strongly the idea that these facts are taken from a hidden location (that is, there is a danger of them being suppressed).

3.7 A case study: *through*

In order to examine in some depth the role of locative concepts in structuring our thinking in more abstract domains, let us consider a particular case in some detail: the preposition *through*.

The image schema for *through* involves the path of an entity (TR) in physical space as it enters a container and then moves from the point of entry to a point at the opposite side of the container, where it exits (figure 3.6).

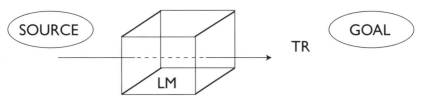

Figure 3.6 Image schema for *through*

For example, in (15) the train is the TR, and the tunnel is the LM.

(15) *The train rushed through the tunnel.*

TR may be the referent of the grammatical subject, as in (15), or it may be that of the object, as in (16), which involves an AGENT (the postman) causing TR (the letter) to traverse LM (the letterbox).

(16) *The postman pushed the letter through the letterbox.*

In an example such as (17) there is also an explicit SOURCE (Sydney) and an explicit GOAL (Cairns).

(17) *They* [AGENT] *built a motorway* [TR] *from Sydney* [SOURCE] *through Brisbane* [LM] *to Cairns* [GOAL].

In some cases LM may be understood, as in *I managed to get through to Pat.*

There are a number of variants of this basic locative situation. For example, there is a difference between *The train rushed through the tunnel* and *The brick smashed through the window* involving the dimensionality of LM. The essentially two-dimensional nature of LM in the latter tends to reduce the salience of the notion of containment—a process that is taken a little further when the LM is one-dimensional (*She drew a line through five points*). The semantic elements that are preserved in this case are the notions of movement to LM and movement from LM that are part of the basic image schema.

Other cases manifest further degrees of divergence from the basic meaning. In *John was looking through the window* there is no object that moves through physical space and therefore no trajectory in the literal sense. There is, however, a virtual trajectory—a notional line emanating from the eyes.[2] Less obviously, in *John was walking through the grass,* the conceptualised trajectory is arguably not the actual space traversed by John's body (since this would not normally be fully contained within LM, unless the grass was unusually long). Rather, it seems once again to be a notional line, in this case emanating from John's feet.

In (18) a similar process of abstraction applies to LM.

(18) *One of the buses, its windows draped in black, drove in through the massive green gates of the cemetery ramparts.* (ACE: A26: 5657)[3]

Here, the bus does not actually drive through 'the gates' in the literal sense (as would be the case if the verb were *smashed*); rather it drives through the space between the gates. Other examples of this kind include the following.

(19) *As the 45 000 tonne warship sailed through the Heads and towards its mooring place, smaller boats, greatly outnumbering protest boats, hovered around it.* (ACE: A25: 5450)

(20) *Yeah, they just fall on top of the ball and then you know they kick it back through the legs and off they go again.* (BSS)

(21) *There have been many since who have carried out their jobs sufficiently and successfully, like Richie Benaud and Ian Chappell, and some whose names will drop through the bottom of the basket without leaving a trace.* (ACE: A37: 7903)

In (19), 'the Heads' is an imaginary plane between two promontories of land at the entrance to Sydney Harbour; in (20) LM is not 'the legs' themselves but the plane between them; and in (21) the notion 'bottom of the basket' is again construed in a non-material way.

Although these examples can all be thought of as belonging to the basic image schema, it is clear that there is already a good deal of variation along the concrete–abstract dimension involving the various elements in the schema. This potential for abstraction and idealisation paves the way for extension to more abstract domains.

3.7.1 Impact on landmark

It was noted above that one factor in the growth of semantic networks is the activation of elements in the knowledge base associated with the core meaning. In the case of *through* one such element is the fact that the traverse of TR through LM has the potential to change LM in some way. This aspect of the knowledge frame associated with *through* is activated in (22).

(22) *Just as he leaves for Australia, Pope John Paul II has been handed a book that is sending shockwaves through the Australian Catholic Church.* (ACE: C09: 1749)

This example would make little sense if we thought of the process simply in terms of traverse. The semantics of *shockwaves* activates the notion that TR impacts on and changes LM. The same connotations are invoked in examples such as (23) and (24)—

(23) *Sue has gone through all the chocolate* (eaten it all).

(24) *John has gone through all his savings* (spent them all).

—where LM is in effect destroyed or made unavailable by the process of traverse (now metaphorical). Closely related to these examples are those such as (25) and (26), where the focus is on the fact that TR impinged on **every part** of LM in the process:

(25) *The customs officer went through John's suitcase with a fine toothcomb.*

(26) *Since Amanda charmed Perth audiences as the voluptuous Josie in 'Steaming', she has made three movies, and travelled through South-East Asia and China.* (ACE: A42: 8925)

In (26), for example, the suggestion is not that Amanda made a single journey from one end of South-East Asia to the other but that she visited many parts of it.

3.7.2   Landmark as obstacle

Another component of the knowledge frame activated in many tokens of *through* is the idea that TR traverses LM only with difficulty—that is, that LM constitutes some kind of obstacle (Rudzka-Ostyn 1988: 523). This is a reflex of the association between the concept of containment, which is part of the basic image schema, and the notion of constraint. These examples contrast with those in the previous section, in that the focus here is on the impact of LM on TR rather than the converse. The example may be situated in the locative domain, as in (27):

(27) *My spy deep within the fusty portals of LO tells me the honeyed tones of Mary Adams are favoured to greet us as we somnambulate around the kitchen and bathroom and headache our way through peak-hour traffic next year.* (ACE: B22: 5059)

Or there may be some metaphorical or metonymic element in play:

(28) *The premier wants his industrial relations minister to hack his way through the state bureaucracy.* (ACE: B17: 3950)

In some examples of this kind, there is interaction with other metaphors, particularly a ubiquitous metaphor of communication known as the 'conduit metaphor', according to which communication is thought of as involving the transportation of meanings from speaker to hearer (Reddy 1979; Lakoff & Johnson 1980: 11–13; Langacker 1988b: 58; Moore & Carling 1982: 149–75; Lakoff 1987: 67–74; Lee 1992: 79–83; Radden 1992: 523). The fact that communication can be problematic makes the *through* schema a particularly natural one to invoke here, given our experiential knowledge that the passage of TR through LM often involves difficulty. Hence, we find expressions such as *Sue just can't get through to John* (on the interpretation that Sue finds it difficult to communicate her point of view). A corpus example involving the conduit metaphor is (29).

(29) *The ghost in the tower of a deserted house has a message to convey and the long-dead Adelaide eventually gets through to Paul, who is able to solve a half-century-old mystery.* (ACE: C10: 2165)

3.7.3 Achievement

The notion of difficulty of passage is a negative aspect of the experience of traverse, but positive connotations are also potentially available. This potential is activated in an example such as (30).

(30) *Mary came through with flying colours.*

Here, the notion of difficulty of traverse is less salient than is that of achievement—a reflex of the fact that the basic image schema involves not only the passage of TR through LM but also emergence from it. Related examples from the corpora include the following.

(31) *It also was pushing for the urgent establishment of a register of companies with proven expertise and financial backing to carry through contracts.* (ACE: A33: 7007)

(32) *The commission has given the unions carte blanche to force schemes through whether the economy can afford them or not.* (ACE: B03: 668)

(33) *The government, in its enthusiasm to stop tax-dodging rorts, failed to think through administrative simplicity, as well as general equity, before bringing in this tax.* (ACE: B14: 3146)

There is some variation across these examples in that in (30) TR (Mary) is agentive, whereas in (31)–(33) the trajectors ('contracts', 'schemes', 'administrative simplicity') are non-agentive. In other words, (30) is a reflex of the structure exemplified by *The train* [TR] *went through the tunnel* [LM], whereas (31)–(33) are mappings from the structure exemplified by *John* [AGENT] *pushed the letter* [TR] *through the letterbox* [LM], with 'companies', 'the unions', 'the government' mapping onto the AGENT role. The fact that the notion of achievement necessarily involves focus on TR or on AGENT causes LM to be unspecified in these cases.

3.7.4 Landmark as instrument

Whereas the examples in the two previous sections involve the notion of the landmark as an obstacle, there are other cases where it is a facilitator. Consider (34) and (35).

(34) *John sold the house to Mary through Smith's.*

(35) *John bought the house from Mary through Smith's.*

The motivation for this mapping is the fact that there are many situations in the real world where substances are funnelled to a particular place by means of a pipe or similar tool. Corpus examples are:

(36) *John said he could get all the VAB semen he wanted through other sources.* (ACE: A44: 9449)

(37) *Through Phoenix Holidays a special offer gives the tourist two weeks of air-conditioned accommodation at the Sanur village club.* (ACE: A30: 6493)

(38) *The services are available through public hospitals.* (ACE: A43: 9214)

(39) *The initial wave of widely based US buying of Australian bonds either directly or through retail vehicles such as the first Australia prime income fund was triggered by a wide yield spread between Australian and US government securities.* (ACE: A02: 402)

3.7.5 Causatives and resultatives

In all the examples cited in previous sections, both LM and GOAL are entities rather than processes, so that the interpretation is primarily (albeit rather loosely) spatial. In other examples, however, one or both of these elements is a process or situation. Consider (40).

(40) *Hooker's growing overseas involvement was part of a conscious fundamental policy of minimising risk through geographic diversification.* (ACE: A18: 3925)

Here both LM and GOAL are processes, LM being the (reified) process of geographic diversification, leading to the GOAL of minimised risk. This mapping of processes and situations onto LM and GOAL gives such examples a more strongly temporal character than those in which LM is an instrumental entity (for example, (36)–(39)). The *through* schema here is being used in effect to express causation—a concept that is present, though somewhat less salient, in (36)–(39).

Examples of this type divide into two subcategories. In some examples, TR is agentively involved in creating the LM situation with the intention of achieving the GOAL situation.

(41) *The Herald and Weekly Times's strategy of increasing assets* [GOAL] *through major acquisitions* [LM] *will help future growth.* (ACE: A18: 3733)

(42) *Through the acquisition of regional and suburban papers* [LM], *HWT established itself for the first time as a publisher in NSW* [GOAL]. (ACE: A18: 3755)

(43) *Through the acquisition of Gordon and Gotch Ltd* [LM], *the group has an effective 50 per cent share in Crawford Productions Holdings Pty Ltd.* [GOAL] (ACE: A18: 3793)

In other cases, however, TR is non-agentive, so that the GOAL situation is a result, not an aim.

(44) *Whether his suicide* [GOAL] *was the result of a moment of insanity, or whether it was through his frustration at not being able to physically emulate truly the deeds of his heroes* [LM] *remains open to question.* (ACE: C03: 472)

(45) *The boys, who have lost a couple of drummers* [GOAL] *through spontaneous combustion* [LM], *are on the decline after reaching their peak in the days of flower power.* (ACE: C07: 1381)

The absence of agentivity in these examples means that LM lacks the instrumental character it has in (36)–(43), though in both cases the LM situation is causatively linked to GOAL.

The examples in this section are motivated by our experiential knowledge involving paths. If someone intends to move to location A by taking a path that runs through location B, then moving to B becomes the means of fulfilling that intention. If we have been taken along such a path involuntarily, then the process of being taken to B is perceived as the event that eventually caused us to find ourselves in A. The complex interaction of concepts such as intentionality, instrumentality, and result in our experience of space is the basis of the mapping processes at work here. One way of putting this is to say that 'events are places' (King 1988: 585); however, it would be just as appropriate to say that places are events, since the experience of being in a particular place is as much an experience as any other kind of experience. The overlap between space and time in these cases is total. Movement through space is inherently also movement through time and the notions of intentionality, instrumentality, and result also straddle both the locative and temporal domains.

3.7.6 Subjectification

In all the examples cited above, the participants in the GOAL situation are also participants in the LM situation. In (40), for example, 'Hooker' engaged in the process of 'geographic diversification', as a result of which it experienced 'risk minimisation'. In (41) 'the *Herald and Weekly Times*' made major acquisitions, thereby experiencing 'increased assets'.

It is not difficult, however, to find examples in which there is no entity that participates overtly in both the LM and GOAL situations. Such cases pose a problem for the claim that the use of *through* to express causation and result involves mapping onto the basic image schema. For example, consider (46) and (47).

(46) *It was through John knowing Sue that Harry met Alice.*

(47) *It was through John's stupidity that Max didn't get the contract.*

Since there is no single individual who participates in both situations here ('John knowing Sue' and 'Harry meeting Alice' in (46), 'John being stupid' and 'Max not getting the contract' in (47)), there is no apparent candidate for the role of TR. At first sight, therefore, there is no obvious trajectory in the situation and therefore no mapping onto the image schema.

A solution to this difficulty can be found in the concept of 'subjectification', which was originally invoked by Langacker (1990: 315–44) to deal with examples such as (48) and (49).

(48) *Vanessa walked across the road.*

(49) *Vanessa is sitting across the table from John.*

In (48) the conceptualiser occupies an 'objective' position, observing the path followed by Vanessa from an external vantage point. However, since the situation in (49) involves a static configuration, there is no 'objective' movement of this kind. Instead, there is 'subjective' movement in the sense that the preposition *across* is a reflex of the conceptualiser's mental scanning of the situation along a path starting from the position occupied by John, moving across the table, and ending at the position occupied by Vanessa. This shift from 'objective construal' to 'subjective construal' is called 'subjectification' by Langacker. The concept of subjectification provides an elegant solution to the difficulty posed by (46) and (47)—namely, the absence of a trajectory followed by one of the participants in the scene through the relevant situations. The (abstract) motion involved here is the process of conceptualisation itself, with the conceptualiser performing a mental scan through the LM situation, emerging into the GOAL situation. Since the trajectory through LM is interpreted as leading directly to GOAL, this serves as the basis for the mapping from space/time to causality.

3.7.7 Basic temporal uses

We turn now to a number of examples situated exclusively in the temporal domain. This shift from the domain of causation to that of time is associated with the absence of a GOAL component. In this circumstance, LM is interpreted either as a straightforward period of time (examples (50) and (51) below), or as a period of time associated metonymically with a life experience such as a term of government, a cricket innings, or a maths class (examples (52)–(55)).

(50) *Wendy saw all of this getting worse through the 1990s.*

(51) *Half way through the night Michael wakes me up and he goes, 'There's someone there!'* (BSS)

(52) *The other immortal occasion happened in Adelaide when Woodfull batted through the second innings total of 193 for 73 not out.* (ACE: A37: 7868)

(53) *Through one-and-a-half terms of government Bob Hawke and company have been telling of all the great things they have done to put Australia to rights.* (ACE: B15: 3379)

(54) *This all happens through maths.* (BSS)

(55) *The Pope said that the only strong bases for civilisation were reverence for human life from the moment of conception and through every stage of life.* (ACE: A24: 5143)

The precise nature of the mapping onto the locative situation in these examples deserves some attention. As far as the landmark is concerned, the mapping is straightforward. Since periods of time are naturally conceptualised as spaces, they are prototypical landmarks for *through*. The same point applies to some trajectors. In (50)–(55), there is a prototypical trajector in the form of an explicit human participant (for example, 'Wendy in (50), 'Michael' in (51), 'Woodfull' in (52)), who moves through the relevant period of time or life experience. Indeed, in some examples the movement of a human trajector along such a trajectory is explicitly coded by the verb *go*.

(56) *You know, your school can be really good in something and then you go through years where they're kind of at the bottom of the heap.* (BSS)

(57) *I reckon we're going through a second childhood.* (BSS)

(58) *Hawke, he added, is 'a guy who is separate from the pack and who goes through life being a stranger.'* (ACE: C04: 848)

However, in some examples involving temporal LMs, the nature of the mapping process is much less clear. Consider:

(59) *It rained all through Monday.*

(60) *It rained all through the concert.*

The problem here is that there is no clear candidate for the TR role, since the example involves no explicit reference to a specific participant. One possible interpretation is that TR here is a process rather than an entity—in other words, that the process 'It rained' moved through the relevant temporal LM. However, this analysis is open to question, since there is no independent motivation for it—that is, there are no other examples in which TR is a process. Moreover, there are certain discrepancies between the basic image schema for *through* on the one hand, and the situation expressed by (59) and (60), on the other, which makes the idea of the mapping of a process onto TR problematic. For example, the discrepancy between the size of TR and LM in the image schema and the asymmetrical nature of the relationship between them (the fact that one is contained within the other) is ill-adapted to cases where there are two temporally coextensive situations, equal in duration and status.

Again, Langacker's notion of subjectification provides a solution. The motion involved in this case is not that of an objective entity but the process of conceptualisation itself, with the conceptualiser scanning through the relevant situations and time periods and observing that they are temporally coextensive. In other words, for any segment of the scanning process in which a conceptualiser is located within the period of time or life experience designated by LM, the focal situation (TR) also obtains.

The examples in this section can be divided into three subsets with respect to the interpretation of TR as a participant in the relevant situation (objective construal) or as the conceptualiser (subjective construal). Examples (56)–(58), in which we find the verb *go*, involve objective construal, with the subject of *go* explicitly construed as TR. By contrast, (59) and (60) involve subjective construal, since there is no overt mover. Examples (50)–(55) are intermediate in that they allow either analysis. TR can be interpreted either as a participant in the relevant process or as the conceptualiser scanning through the relevant time periods and situations.

As far as these intermediate examples are concerned, there is no question of having to decide which interpretation is 'correct'. To attempt to do so would be to fall into what Langacker (1987: 28) calls the 'exclusionary fallacy'—that is, to insist that every issue of this kind be resolved definitively in favour of one analysis or the other. Situations where there is a continuum from clear examples of one kind to clear examples of another kind are expected by cognitive linguistics to involve intermediate cases characterised by properties found at each end of the spectrum. It is precisely the potential for such ambiguities that underlies the process of semantic extension.

3.7.8 Landmark as ordeal

The transposition from space to time exemplified by the items in the previous section is relatively unencumbered by elements of our knowledge frame associated with the process of traverse. Such elements do, however, come into play in other examples, where LM is some kind of trial or ordeal (an experience that we sometimes describe as a 'difficult' time). In other words, the fact that LM can impose physical constraint on TR in the locative domain is a natural source for the mapping to unpleasant experiences, given the metonymic association between physical and mental discomfort. Hence, we find a slight contrast between (61), which is entirely natural, and (62), which is odd.

(61) *I went through a terrible week last week.*

(62) *?I went through a wonderful week last week.*

The corpora provide many examples of ordeals as LM.

(63) *The people of this area have been put through a very bad ordeal over the past week.* (ACE: A17: 3489)

(64) *Through the criticism, Jan, said to have a standing offer of $150,000 to pose for Penthouse, remains unmoved.* (ACE: A20: 4324)

(65) *Yet through numerous personal crises she has played superb golf—winning a US open, US PGA and becoming the first woman to break 200 for a 54-hole tournament.* (ACE: A20: 4331)

(66) *A small child could not be expected to sit through a four-hour dinner.* (ACE: A27: 5719)

(67) *Federal cabinet cruises through a stormy session.* (ACE: A32: 6942)

(68) *A lot of women are going through exactly the same things she's experiencing.* (ACE: A42: 8946)

(69) *Have you thought about that yet or are you thinking of getting through exams?* (BSS)

These examples tend to be characterised by objective rather than subjective construal in that the focus is on the impact of LM on the participant in the relevant process rather than on the conceptualiser.

3.8 Conclusion

The range of situations mapped onto the *through* schema provides a good illustration of the descriptive and explanatory power of Cognitive Linguistics. The basic cognitive claim that meaning is conceptualisation (rather than a straightforward encoding of the objective properties of the situation) is illustrated, in the first instance, in the basic locative domain, where each of the major components of the schema can be subject to processes of abstraction and idealisation. This helps to explain why there is a natural extension to situations involving such notions as instrumentality and result. In other words, there is strong evidence here for the claim that semantics is topology (King 1988: 585).

The view that there is no principled boundary between semantics and pragmatics also derives support from this analysis. There are many cases in which pragmatic knowledge associated with the basic *through* schema is strongly activated in producing the relevant meaning. Prominent among these is our real-world knowledge that the traverse of a trajector through LM can involve constraints on the former and/or change to the latter. This meaning potential is activated in various ways, transposing into such notions as destruction, ordeal, achievement, survival, and so on.

Other elements activated in some but not all uses are roles and circumstances such as AGENT and GOAL—the latter, for example, being exploited for the notion of 'target' in instrumentals, for that of 'resultant situation' in causatives, and for 'achievement' and 'survival' in the temporal domain. The emergence and activation of specialised meanings of this kind makes perfect sense in a model in which language is rooted in human experience of the physical world and where our understanding grows from basic sensorimotor knowledge and associated experiences. This helps to explain why almost opposite interpretations can come to be associated with a single schema. Theories that treat languages as formal systems divorced from human experience of the world have little light to throw on phenomena of this kind.

In general, the semantic network associated with *through* provides a compelling example of the nature of the cognitive map of speakers of English. Moreover, although there is a good deal of variation across languages with respect to the question of the degree to which they exploit the *through* schema to express extended meanings, there is no doubt that much of the radial network associated with *through* in English is duplicated in other languages. This is to be expected, if the nature of the network is motivated by strong experiential connections, as cognitivists claim. To that extent, an analysis of this kind contributes to an understanding of human cognition in general, without committing itself to the claim that the specific features of the network are necessarily found in all languages.

This chapter has provided a range of examples illustrating the rich and varied ways in which human beings use basic locative schemas as devices for conceptualising more abstract domains. This process involves the construction of extensive semantic networks around a basic, core meaning. The nature of such networks is considered in more detail in the next chapter.

Exercises

1   Construct radial networks for *up* and *through* like the one given in the text for *out* (figure 3.5, page 35).

2   The fact that the verb *rely* collocates with the preposition *on* rather than with some other preposition does not seem to be arbitrary. The meaning of *rely* involves the notion of moral or mental 'support' and is thus related to the concept of physical support associated with *on*. Consider each of the verb–preposition combinations below in relation to this issue. Does the choice of preposition in each case seem motivated or arbitrary? What does the choice of preposition tell us about the way in which we conceptualise the situation in each case?

(a)   *I differ from you on this issue.*
(b)   *I discouraged Ed from talking to Mary.*
(c)   *I agree with you.*
(d)   *I agreed to the proposal.*
(e)   *That idea just does not appeal to me.*
(f)   *They shared out the food.*
(g)   *That won't prevent me from speaking my mind.*

(h) *He asked us to refrain from talking about what we had seen.*

(i) *Please desist from smoking.*

(j) *The pressure drove us to desperation.*

3 How would you interpret someone's meaning if they said *He talked at me rather than to me*? Does this have anything to do with examples such as *He's been at the chocolate again, She's been at me again about fixing the roof*?

4 What meaning do you associate with *on* in the following examples?

(a) *The engine just died on me.*

(b) *The car broke down on me.*

(c) *He went bankrupt on me.*

(d) *The stapler's run out on me.*

5 Comment on the bold items in the following expressions:

(a) *That's quite **out of** character.*

(b) *He did it **out of** spite.*

(c) *That's true **up to a point**.*

(d) ***On the other hand** she could be wrong.*

(e) ***From** what you tell me, it's obvious that Ed's a fool.*

(f) *She came **out** in spots.*

(g) *[Are you trying to be funny?] **Far from** it.*

(h) *There's nothing **remotely** funny about that.*

(i) *There's a **further** difference between these two people.*

(j) *He deceived us **into** thinking that he could help.*

6 Why does *come* collocate with the word *good*, whereas *go* collocates with words such as *wrong, haywire* (*I think Jenny will come good in time, It all went wrong/haywire*)? Is there any connection between these expressions and the choice of *come* or *go* in each of the following?

(a) *He's coming around* (regaining consciousness).

(b) *I think she'll come round to our point of view.*

(c) *She just went berserk.*

(d) *He went crazy.*

(e) *He's going to pieces.*

(f) *She went to sleep.*

(g) *He's gone native.*

(h) *She's gone walkabout.*

7 What connection is there between the *out* in *The sun came out, The roses came out* (on the one hand), and *We need to sort out this problem, We can work this out, I've found something out* (on the other)?

8 While looking at a painting, someone comments, *You need to bring out the highlights a bit more.* Comment on the use of *out* in this example.

9 Comment on the use of *between* in the following.

(a)   *There isn't much to choose between them.*

(b)   *There's only you between this woman and ten years in jail* (said to a lawyer defending a woman in a court case).

10 Comment on the use of *over* in *There's some disagreement over whether John should be invited.*

Further reading

Brugman, C. 1988, *The Story of 'Over'*, Garland, New York.

Hilferty, J. 1999, '*Through* as a means to metaphor', in L. de Stadler & C. Eyrich (eds), *Issues in Cognitive Linguistics*, Mouton, Berlin, pp. 347–65.

Janda, L. A. 1988, 'The mapping of elements of cognitive space onto grammatical relations: an example from Russian verbal prefixation', in B. Rudzka-Ostyn (ed.), *Topics in Cognitive Linguistics*, John Benjamins, Amsterdam, pp. 327–43.

Johnson, M. 1987, *The Body in the Mind: The Bodily Basis of Meaning, Imagination, and Reason*, chapter 2: 'The emergence of meaning through schematic structure', pp. 18–40, and chapter 4: 'Metaphorical Projections of Image Schemata', pp. 65–100, University of Chicago Press, Chicago.

King, R. T. 1988, 'Spatial metaphor in German causative constructions', in B. Rudzka-Ostyn (ed.), *Topics in Cognitive Linguistics*, John Benjamins, Amsterdam, pp. 555–85.

Langacker, R. W. 1985, 'Observations and speculations on subjectivity', in John Haiman (ed.), *Iconicity in Syntax*, John Benjamins, Amsterdam.

——1990, *Concept, Image and Symbol*, chapter 5: 'Abstract motion', Mouton, Berlin, pp. 149–63.

——1990, *Concept, Image and Symbol*, chapter 12: 'Subjectification', Mouton, Berlin, pp. 315–44.

Lee, D. A. 1998, 'A tour through *through*', *Journal of English Linguistics* 26: 333–51.

Lindner, S. 1982, 'What goes up doesn't necessarily come down: the ins and outs of opposites', *Papers from the 18th Regional Meeting of the Chicago Linguistics Society*, pp. 305–23.

Radden, G. 1995, 'Spatial metaphors underlying prepositions of causality', in W. Paprotté & R. Dirven (eds), *The Ubiquity of Metaphor*, John Benjamins, Amsterdam, pp. 177–207.

——1996, 'Motion metaphorized: the case of *coming* and *going*', in E. H. Casad (ed.), *Cognitive Linguistics in the Redwoods: The Expansion of a New Paradigm in Linguistics*. Mouton, Berlin, pp. 423–58.

Rice, S. 1999, 'Aspects of prepositions and prepositional aspect', in L. de Stadler & C. Eyrich (eds), *Issues in Cognitive Linguistics*, Mouton, Berlin, pp. 225–47.

Rudzka-Ostyn, B. 1988, 'Semantic extensions into the domain of verbal communication', in B. Rudzka-Ostyn (ed.), *Topics in Cognitive Linguistics*, John Benjamins, Amsterdam, pp. 507–53.

Schulze, R. 1993, 'The meaning of (a)round', in R. A. Geiger & B. Rudzka-Ostyn (eds), *Conceptualizations in Mental Processing in Language*, Mouton, Berlin, pp. 399–431.

Vandeloise, C. 1991, *Spatial Prepositions: A Case Study from French*, University of Chicago Press, Chicago.

Notes

1   It is difficult to gloss the meaning of *out* without using the word *out* itself (or some synonym thereof). This is because it refers to a basic image-schematic relationship derived from our experience of physical space (Johnson 1987; Lakoff 1987: 271–83). The same point applies to *in*, *up*, *down*, *through*, *over*, and so on.

2   Expressions such as *We looked towards the ship* and *I couldn't see past him* show that seeing is conceptualised quite generally as movement away from the observer.

3   Examples marked 'ACE' are from the Australian Corpus of English, compiled at Macquarie University, Sydney. Examples marked 'BSS' are from transcripts of interviews with students at a number of high schools in Brisbane, collected in the course of a sociolinguistic study by a research team from the University of Queensland (Ingram 1989; Lee 1989).

4

RADIAL CATEGORIES

4.1 Introduction

In the previous chapter the nature of the semantic networks associated with such words as *out*, *up*, and *through* was considered. A crucial property of such networks is that they are structured around a central or core meaning (often referred to as the 'prototype'), located in these cases in the domain of physical space. This property of 'radiality' is now known to be characteristic of many types of linguistic and conceptual category—indeed, it is arguably the most common type of category structure. The notion of radiality stands in direct opposition to the traditional (Objectivist) view of the nature of categories derived from Aristotle, which holds that members of any category share a set of necessary and sufficient features that define the category. According to this traditional view, category membership is an all-or-nothing matter, such that any entity that possesses the requisite defining features is a fully fledged member of the category, whereas any entity that lacks one or more of these features is excluded.

By contrast, the prototype-based model recognises that category membership is a gradient phenomenon, such that some members of a category are more central members than others. The opposition between these two positions is discussed at length in Lakoff (1987) and is a dominant theme in Taylor (1995).

Early work in category theory was carried out by the psychologist Eleanor Rosch in the 1970s. One of her studies involved asking 200 American college students to judge the extent to which certain household items could be regarded as a 'good example' of a particular category. Categories investigated were 'furniture', 'fruit', 'vehicle', 'weapon', 'vegetable', 'tool', 'bird', 'sport', 'toy', and 'clothing' (Rosch 1975). Prototype effects were found in all cases. For example, chairs, sofas, tables, and beds were generally agreed to be prototypical examples of 'furniture', with radios, clocks, vases, and ashtrays deemed to be peripheral examples.

The notion of radiality is central to cognitive linguistics. In later chapters, the phenomenon will be seen to be relevant to the meanings of constructions (chapter 5), the process of language change (chapter 7), the structure of the noun and verb categories (chapters 8 and 9) and the concept of agency (chapter 10). It has a particularly important contribution to make to the analysis of discourse, since it is shown in chapters 11 and 12 that certain constructivist moves by participants in everyday conversations depend on the fact that categories are characterised by prototype structure.

Radial networks shed a good deal of light on how specific concepts and conceptual areas relate to each other in the minds of speakers of a particular language. As cognitive descriptions of different languages are developed, we can use radial category structures to identify natural cognitive relationships. In this chapter this idea is illustrated with examples from various areas of the linguistic system and from various semantic domains.

4.2 Example: the suffix -*able*

The suffix -*able* that we find in such words as *likeable, washable, readable, solvable* is typically attached to a verb to produce the corresponding adjective—an adjective meaning 'able to be verbed'. For example, *solvable* means 'able to be solved', *washable* means 'able to be washed', and so on. This meaning can be regarded as the core meaning of the form.

One does not have to look very far, however, to find some degree of variability in this meaning. If I describe a book as *readable*, I do not mean that it is 'able to be read' (presumably all books are able to be read by someone), but that it is easy or interesting to read. The book could in fact be described as *very readable*, an expression that would make little sense if *readable* meant simply 'able to be read'. In adjectives such as *comparable* and *payable*, we move further away from this core meaning of 'able to be verbed'. When I receive a bill from the electricity company or the phone company with a note to the effect that 'This bill is now payable', this does not necessarily mean that the bill is able to be paid (from my point of view). What it means is that payment is due. As for *comparable*, I once asked a (linguist) friend of mine who was in the process of moving from Sydney to London whether house prices were 'comparable'. His reply was, 'Yes, they can be compared'. But this was a (linguist's) joke, of course.[1]

It is worth asking why words such as *payable* and *comparable* have come to acquire specialised meanings of this kind. It seems reasonable to surmise that this derives from the fact that *comparable* would not be a very useful word if it meant simply 'able to be compared'. Since anything can be compared with anything else, it would make little sense to tell someone that X and Y were 'comparable'. The point is that, when we compare two things, we do so for a particular purpose—to assess to what degree they resemble each other (in the case of prices, to see if they are of similar magnitude). This is therefore another example of foregrounding. In this case, a part of the situation as a whole—namely, the **purpose** of the relevant process—has been semantically foregrounded at the expense of those aspects of the situation that relate to the process itself.

As far as *payable* is concerned, if we ask why this word means 'due to be paid' rather than 'able to be paid', the answer that suggests itself is slightly different in detail (but not in principle). A word that meant 'able to be paid' could in principle be useful, since to say that a bill is or is not 'able to be paid' is informative. However, only the payer of the bill is in a position to make such a statement. The payee cannot normally know whether it is able to be paid or not. The aspect of the situation that a payee is normally interested in is the need to be paid rather than the financial status of the payer. But since there is a close relationship between ability to pay and the payment itself (the latter is contingent on the former), there is an obvious motivation for the notion 'able to be paid' to extend to that of 'due to be paid'.

Again, we see here an illustration of the fact that meaning is an emergent phenomenon. It is the interaction between a given verb and the *-able* suffix that produces a particular meaning. More accurately, the meaning of the combined form is the outcome of an interaction between the **frames** associated with the two forms. The background knowledge associated with the verb modulates the meaning of the suffix in a particular direction—a direction that in many cases is peculiar to that verb. Once we have seen this, we find the process at work in practically every combination. For example, although one might roughly gloss the meaning of *drinkable* as 'able to be drunk', the word actually means rather more than this. Hydrochloric acid is 'able to be drunk' but it is not 'drinkable'. A crucial question for human beings is whether a particular substance can be drunk **safely**—it is this consideration that has coloured the meaning of *drinkable*.

4.3 Example: past tense

We turn now to an example of radiality in the area of inflectional morphology, specifically past-tense marking in English. The prototypical function of the past-tense inflection is to situate an event in a period of time prior to the present moment of utterance. However, there are a number of cases in which its meaning diverges from this prototype.

4.3.1 Counterfactuality

Consider the contrast between

(1) *If John likes Mary, he will help her.*

(2) *If John liked Mary, he would help her.*

The difference between *likes* and *liked* here has nothing to do with time, since in each case the speaker is considering the question of whether John likes Mary at the present time (the time of utterance). The difference between them is that in (1) the speaker is unsure whether John likes Mary, whereas (2) carries the implication that he does not like her. In other words, the difference between the present-tense form *likes* in (1) and the past-tense form *liked* in (2) has to do with the dimension of factuality rather than time. This difference can be described as involving a contrast between a 'real condition' (example (1)) and an 'unreal condition' (example (2)).

In the framework of Cognitive Linguistics, the obvious question to ask is: How is it that a formal contrast that normally expresses a contrast between present time and past time can come to express a contrast between a real condition and an unreal condition? Clearly, the answer has to do with the fact that, by locating a situation in past time, the speaker locates it in a conceptual space that is distinct from the present and it is this property that relates it to counterfactual situations. The link between these two types of situation is by no means unique to English. In French, for example, the distinction between real conditions and unreal conditions is also marked by a contrast between present-tense and past-tense forms: *s'il sait la réponse ...* ' ('if he knows the answer ... ') contains a present-tense form (*sait*), whereas '*s'il savait la réponse ...* ' ('if he knew the answer ... ') contains a past-tense form (*savait*). Other languages, such as German, add a further dimension to this contrast by adding an indicative/subjunctive distinction to the tense contrast. This suggests that we are dealing here with a natural cognitive association.

The situation is complicated by the fact that English uses the contrast between present-tense and past-tense forms to mark the difference between these two types of condition only in present-time situations. Consider:

(3)   *If John knew Mary last year, he didn't tell me.*

Here, the past-tense form *knew* has its normal function—it locates the relevant situation in past time. Example (3) is a real condition in that the speaker does not know whether John knew Mary last year or not. In some circumstances, however, we need to express an unreal condition—for example, to imply that John did not know Mary last year. Since the contrast between present tense and past tense is unavailable in this case to express the contrast between a real condition and an unreal condition (the past-tense form being needed to locate the situation in past time), the speaker has to introduce the perfect auxiliary *have* to express the unreal condition.

(4)   *If John had known Mary last year, he would have told me.*

Since the auxiliary verb *have* normally performs quite a different function (for example, locating a situation in recent past time), we have here another case of radiality.

The past-tense forms of modal auxiliaries provide further examples of the ability of past-tense forms to express counterfactuality. For example, although the contrast between the present-tense form *can* and the past-tense form *could* sometimes expresses a time difference, as in *I can hear it now* and *I could hear it yesterday*, the form *could* often refers not to past time but to hypothetical situations in the present (*I could lift this easily if I were twenty years younger*) or future (*I could do it tomorrow if you like*). In the verbs *will* and *may*, the contrast between the present- and past-tense forms is concerned with differences of factuality much more frequently than with time differences. For example, both (5) and (6) express a present-time willingness to perform a future action. The difference between them is that in (5) the willingness is located in present actuality, whereas in (6) it is located in a hypothetical situation contingent on some condition.

(5)   *I will talk to him.*

(6)   *I would talk to him.*

As far as *may* and *might* are concerned, there is, in many cases, very little difference in meaning—for example, I can use either (7) or (8) to mean 'It is possible that Jenny has hurt herself' ".

(7)   *Jenny may have hurt herself.*

(8)   *Jenny might have hurt herself.*

However, if I wish to express an unreal condition (that is, if I wish to express the meaning that Jenny could have hurt herself if some condition had been met), then I can only use *might*.[2] In other words, the difference between (7) and (8) is another example of the potential of a tense contrast to express a difference involving factuality rather than time.

The following example illustrates another situation where a past tense expresses counterfactuality rather than past time.

(9)   *It's time we left.*

Here, *left* is the past-tense form of the verb *leave* but it clearly does not refer to an occurrence of leaving in past time. Rather, the speaker refers to a possible event of leaving located in the near future. It is therefore a hypothetical situation still to be realised at the moment of utterance.

These counterfactual uses can be interpreted as further examples of the processes of highlighting and bleaching. In its prototypical use, the past-tense form is used to refer to a situation that is (a) located in past time and, therefore, (b) counterfactual at the moment of utterance. The uses discussed above involve bleaching of (a) and foregrounding of (b).

4.3.2 Politeness

Some linguists have suggested that another area of meaning associated with the contrast between present and past tense is that of politeness (Taylor 1995: 150–1). For example, it is arguable that the contrast between (10) and (11) does not relate to time but to a difference of politeness, since in both cases the speaker is (or may be) referring to a present state of wondering.

(10) *I wonder if you would help?*

(11) *I wondered if you would help?*

This claim, however, is more problematic, since the impression of greater politeness (or indirectness) in (11) arguably has to do with the fact that the speaker is purporting to refer to a past mental state rather than to a present one. The point here is that reference to the past existence of a mental state does not preclude the possibility that it continues up to the present. To say *I knew John a long time ago* clearly does not preclude my still knowing him. Certainly, it is arguable that the primary reason for choosing a past-tense form in cases such as (11) has to do with considerations of politeness (or indirectness) rather than with time reference, but this does not entail that the meaning of the past-tense form here is different from its normal usage.

The situation is complicated somewhat by examples such as the following.

(12) *Will you close the door?*

(13) *Would you close the door?*

(14) *Can you close the door?*

(15) *Could you close the door?*

Here too the examples containing the past-tense forms seem to be more polite than those containing their present-tense counterparts, but in this case the contrast does not involve time. The politeness effect here is due to the counterfactuality associated with *would* and *could*. The general point seems to be that removal from the plane of present reality does correlate with politeness and that past-tense forms can be harnessed for this function by virtue of the fact that they either locate a situation in past time or in some counterfactual world.

4.4 Attribute radiality

We turn now to radiality in adjectives, to consider ways in which words denoting attributes of entities manifest this property.

One reason why attributes are characterised by radiality is that the character of an attribute tends to vary according to the nature of the entity with which it is associated. A particularly obvious example of this is colour, given that the kind of red that we associate with blood, for example, is different from the kind of red that we associate with hair. Two common adjectives—*strong* and *good*—will be used as illustrations of radiality in attributes in general.

4.4.1 Example: *strong*

The core meaning of the word *strong* has to do with physical strength. If one asks native speakers to give an example of a phrase or sentence containing the word, they tend to produce examples such as *a strong man* or *a strong horse*. But there are many contexts in which *strong* does not refer to physical strength in this sense—for example, *a strong argument, a strong claim, a strong beer, a strong candidate, a strong smell.*

Although 'a strong argument' is not one that possesses physical strength, it nevertheless has some characteristics that cause us to see it as pragmatically related to entities that are physically strong. Such an argument has the ability to persuade us to a particular point of view or to a particular action. In other words, it has the potential to affect us by changing our mental world, our world of beliefs and intentions. Similarly, an entity possessed of physical strength is one that has the potential to impinge on its surroundings, to overpower other entities, or to move objects that are not easily moved.

Consider now such examples as *a strong cup of tea, a strong coffee, a strong beer, a strong wine.* Whereas 'a strong argument' is one that has a significant influence on our world of beliefs, 'a strong cup of tea' is one that has a significant impact on our perceptual experiences. It is the shift in the **frame** of application that causes the word to acquire a rather different shade of meaning here. Another area in which this notion of 'impact' is invoked is that of the emotions: 'a strong painting' is one that has a marked visual or emotional impact.

There is possibly another motivation for the use of *strong* in examples such as *a strong cup of tea.* In the physical domain, strong entities tend to be characterised by solidity or high density. For example, strong animals and people tend to have solid, muscular bodies. A strong cup of tea also seems to have this characteristic because of its high degree of concentration and dark colour. It is presumably this property that sometimes leads people to say *The tea was so strong you could stand your spoon in it.*

The general point here is that we do not necessarily expect there to be just one dimension of motivation in radial connections. This follows from the fact that there are often parallel clustering patterns across features in different domains—patterns that provide multiple dimensions of motivation for radial structures. The correlation between strength and density in the physical domain is parallelled by a correlation between impact on the senses and degree of concentration in the domain of taste. This provides multiple motivation for the transposition of *strong* from one domain to the other.

The claim that we are dealing with conceptual links in cases of this kind (as opposed to an arbitrary set of meanings) is supported by the fact that related words participate in a similar range of uses. For example, the word *powerful* can be applied not only to entities possessing physical strength but also to such entities as drinks, arguments, and claims. Similarly, the word *weak* can be used to describe the converse range of properties in each of these cases. The claim receives further support from the fact that expressions such as *I couldn't shift him, She wouldn't budge an inch, Would you be prepared to move a little?* can be applied not only to the physical domain but also to the mental domain. (For example, *I couldn't shift him* can mean that I was unable to change his beliefs or intentions.) Clearly, we are dealing here with a pervasive metaphor.

The possibility of multiple motivation provides an explanation for the fact that some expressions are characterised by a certain degree of ambiguity or vagueness. Consider the expression *a strong claim*. Sometimes a strong claim is one that has a lot of evidence to support it—a close physical parallel being a building that is made of strong materials, resting on a solid foundation. However, the expression is sometimes used to mean 'a bold claim', in which case there may in fact be very little evidence to support it. When Noam Chomsky first claimed that fundamental aspects of language were innate, it was a 'strong' claim in this second sense—a claim in which the motivation relates to the notion of 'impact'. Such a claim was bound to make a significant impact on the intellectual community of the time, in spite of its (arguably) rather tenuous evidential basis.

Interestingly, although we use expressions such as *a strong taste*, *a strong smell*, and *a strong light*, we do not apply the epithet to the noun *noise*. There is no obvious reason for this gap.[3] This observation suggests that language is not subject to the kind of inexorable laws that are generally thought to operate in the hard sciences. Linguistic practices are subject to convention. Since language is rooted in human social behaviour, we can expect historical accident to be one of the forces at work in linguistic practice.

Consider finally the expression *a strong woman*. In some contexts, it would be quite natural to use this expression to refer to a woman of great physical strength, in which case *strong* carries its normal meaning. However, the expression *a strong woman* is often interpreted in terms of moral strength: 'a strong woman' is someone who has the potential to endure hardship. This notion of moral strength is not as salient in the expression *a strong man*. Why is this so? The answer clearly has to do with cultural norms. In general, men are physically stronger than women, with the result that tasks that require physical strength are traditionally performed more often by men than by women. Consequently, physical strength is more highly prized in men than in women. Since physical strength belongs primarily to the male rather than the female domain, the word *strong* in *a strong man* is naturally interpreted in those terms.

But the role of women has been somewhat different historically in that in all human societies women have traditionally been the caregivers. In that role the important attribute is not physical strength but the ability to survive adversity. This provides a very different frame for the interpretation of *strong* in the expression *a strong woman*.

This example shows that semantic modulation is often a function of specific cultural models. Such models are part of the frames associated with particular words and concepts. There is a great deal of cultural modelling associated with terms such as *man* and *woman*, and significant parts of such belief systems come into play in the interpretation of expressions containing these words. This presents a very different picture of the meaning of the words *man* and *woman* from accounts in some earlier linguistic approaches. For example, the approach known as 'componential analysis' (Goodenough

1956; Lounsbury 1956; Romney & d'Andrade 1964) attempted to account for the meanings of words in terms of a basic metalanguage, consisting of a limited set of primitive terms. The meaning of *man* in this approach was deemed to be a function of the combination of the features 'male', 'adult', 'human', and the meaning of 'woman' to derive from the features 'female', 'adult', 'human'. Such an account rules out all the cultural knowledge associated with words. But, clearly, such an account could not even begin to approach an explanation of the rather striking meaning differences that emerge from the collocation of each of these words with a word such as *strong*.

4.4.2 Example: *good*

The word *good* provides another illustration of the claim that meaning is an emergent phenomenon. The way in which we interpret the word *good* in the expressions *a good parent*, *a good child*, *a good baby*, *a good dog*, *a good book*, *a good pen*, and so on is predominantly a function of the **frame** associated with the word with which *good* combines, rather than with *good* itself. So notions such as 'well behaved' and 'obedient' are much more strongly associated with 'good' in expressions such as *a good child* and *a good dog* than they are in the other examples. Clearly, this is again due to our cultural models, within which we expect children to obey their parents and dogs to be obedient to their owners. If we imagine a different culture, in which children had no interaction with parents or other adults, it is difficult to imagine what *a good child* might mean. There is even a difference between the interpretation of *good* in *a good child* and *a good baby*. 'A good baby' is normally interpreted not as one who is obedient (given the inappropriateness of this notion in this case) but as one who generally shows signs of contentment, does not cry much, sleeps through the night, and so on.

This observation concerning the emergent nature of meaning provides some explanation for certain gaps in the system. For example, although it is common to refer to a particular dog as *a good dog*, it is rather less common to hear people referring to their cat as *a good cat* and even more unusual to hear them referring to a pet goldfish as *a good goldfish*. Because of its nature, we expect a dog to be friendly, obedient, loyal, and well-behaved, so it will be 'good' to the extent that it lives up to these expectations. We have much lower expectations of cats and goldfish, so the question of how well a particular cat or goldfish behaves is less of an issue. To put it another way, it is difficult to know what *a good cat* or *a good goldfish* might mean, given that neither cats nor goldfish are judged with respect to specific behavioural criteria.

For slightly different reasons it is not obvious what expressions such as *a good door* or *a good window* would mean. Doors and windows have well-defined functions, but there is little variability in the way that they fill these functions. In other words, it is difficult to find a door that performs its primary function less satisfactorily than other doors. The word *good*, however, is useful only when there is such variability. Of course, in a particular context it is possible to use an expression such as *a good window* to express a certain meaning—I might, for example, say *This is a good window* if it looks out on a particularly fine view. Anyone standing next to me would probably interpret my utterance correctly (that is, in the way that I intend), though this is much less likely to happen if the person I am talking to is at the other end of the phone and has never seen the window in question.

4.5 Process radiality

Let us turn now to verbs—that is, to radiality in the area of processes. The nature of processes (events and situations) is such that they are particularly prone to radiality, given that they too—like attributes—interact with entities of many different kinds. For example, the way in which a horse runs is quite different from the way in which a human being runs, but we perceive these processes to be sufficiently similar to assign these event types to the same conceptual category. Again, we will take just two examples of process radiality: *climb* and *turn*.

4.5.1 Example: *climb*

Consider:

(16) *We climbed up the rock face.*

(17) *She climbed up the ladder.*

(18) *The plane climbed into the sky.*

(19) *The spider climbed across its web.*

(20) *We climbed down the rock face.*

(21) *The rose climbed up the trellis.*

If the first three examples represented the full range of uses, we would be inclined to claim that the basic meaning of *climb* was simply 'move upward' and that the various types of movement involved in such motion were irrelevant to the meaning of the word. Examples (19) and (20) pose a problem for this view, however. There are two factors that seem to motivate the presence of (19) in the category. One is the fact that a spider is suspended in the air and the other is the nature of the movement involved—in particular the fact that it involves apparently careful and delicate movement of all limbs, which is also true of the movements described in (16) and (17) (but not (18)). In (19) the notion of upward movement has disappeared altogether. This is even more obvious in (20), where the notions of suspension and careful movement of the limbs are again prominent. If we were to adopt the traditional view of category membership, according to which there is a necessary set of features shared by all members of a category, examples (19) and (20) would force us to the counterintuitive claim that upward movement is not a component of the meaning of *climb*. The notion of radiality allows us to retain this claim, with the qualification that it relates only to prototypical members of the category such as (16)–(18).

Example (21) differs from the others in that it describes a static situation— one in which the rose covered the trellis from top to bottom. Here *climb* is motivated by the fact that the current situation is a **result** of a process of climbing. If nature were organised in such a way that roses grew downwards from very small seeds deposited by the wind, there would be no motivation for (21). In this case aspects of our knowledge frame relating to the process whereby the current situation has come about are built into the way in which the situation is coded.

4.5.2 Example: *turn*

The basic meaning of *turn* involves the rotation of an entity about an axis, as in *The wheels are turning, Mary turned the doorknob*. When the entity has an intrinsic front, the fact that turning causes the entity to face in a different direction is often profiled by explicit mention of the original orientation and the new orientation (*He turned from Mary to John*).

A rather different use shows up in *The car turned into the High Street*, where the change of orientation is accomplished not by rotation but by a change in the direction of forward movement. This contrast between rotation and change of trajectory shows up in the contrast between *John turned round* (rotation) and *John turned back* ('retraced his steps') and provides the basis for a number of distinct metaphorical extensions.

In combination with intransitive prepositions such as *up, out, in, down*, and so on, *turn* produces a set of meanings that cover a continuum from the literal to the highly idiomatic. For example, in *John turned up his collar*, the verb has its literal meaning, in that the collar undergoes a change in physical orientation. In *Susan turned up the volume*, the verb may retain some of its literal meaning if the action involves rotating a knob (for example), but if it involves simply pressing a button, the verb has a more abstract character. This property is more salient in examples such as *Jenny turned up at the party*, where change of orientation has been reduced to that of movement only (with *up* expressing the notion of movement towards a goal).

There is a similar semantic range from the literal to the abstract in expressions involving the collocation *turn out*. In *John turned out his pockets*, the landmark undergoes a literal change of orientation. In *A lot of people turned out for the party*, this notion seems much weaker. In *I wonder how events will turn out*, all that remains of the original meaning is that of movement (or change), with *out* expressing the notion of emergence into the speaker's cognitive field.

This metaphorical connection between movement in physical space, change of orientation, and change of state enables *turn* to be applied to an extensive range of situations involving only the notion of change of state (*It's turning cold, We turned them loose*).

A particularly well-established usage is one in which there is a change in colour (*The liquid turned red, John's face turned quite green*). Many cases involve examples in which the resultant state is expressed by a noun phrase, typically introduced by *to* or *into* (with *from* expressing the original state): *The sparks turned to points of residual light, It turned to ashes, He might turn you into a fish, We'll turn you into a soldier, It turns photographs into computer data, It turned them from waiters into rock singers, It turned to pulp, Everything turned to gold, The laughter turned to tears, The dream turned into a nightmare, He's a Vietnam veteran turned cop, You turned a funny colour.*[4] The resultant state may also involve an emotional condition (*He turned nasty, She turned peculiar*). Interestingly, examples of this kind typically involve situations in which the resultant state involves an undesirable rather than a desirable situation (*She turned vicious/?She turned friendly, She turned stupid/?She turned intelligent*). This bias presumably has to do with an assumption that the default condition of a person or thing is positive (people being well disposed, things being useable), so that a significant change in condition tends to involve a change for the worse (compare *The milk has turned*).

The uses illustrated above exploit the cognitive association between a change of physical orientation (through rotation) and a change of state. By contrast, an example such as *The talk turned to food* derives from the notion of trajectory change (the talk did not turn into food but changed direction). There are two metaphors at work here. The underlying metaphor, 'Conversation is a journey', is a prerequisite for the superimposed metaphor of change of topic as change of direction. Again, we see here not only that metaphors can be interwoven but also that metaphor is basic to the process of meaning-making. Other manifestations of the metaphor of talk as a journey can be seen in such examples as *We've drifted off the topic, I don't get your drift, Where is this conversation heading?, This discussion is getting us nowhere.*

An interactive process of a rather different kind shows up in such examples as *John has turned eighteen, When you turn sixty-five,* and so on. The interesting feature of this usage is that in some contexts it is conventionally associated with ages that have some particular significance in our culture. In other words, we are much less likely to find such examples as *When you turn thirty-two …* or *After you turn fifty-four …* than we are to find examples such as those cited above. Since the age of eighteen is the point at which an individual is generally deemed to make the transition from childhood to adulthood, it can naturally be conceptualised as the point at which one makes a significant change in direction (metaphorically speaking), thus strongly motivating the use of *turn*. Here, then, we see an interaction between three cognitive and sociocultural elements—the metaphor of life as a journey, the cultural notion of different phases of life, and the notion of temporal transition as spatial transition.

4.6 Thing radiality

Radiality in nouns is pervasive, so much so that it is difficult to think of a noun that does not show the property in some form or other. One interesting perspective on this area comes from the process of overextension in children. It has been widely noted that children often go through a stage where they use an adult word to refer to a wider variety of phenomena than those to which the word is properly applied in the adult language. For example, they use the word *dog* to refer to any four-legged animal or the word *Daddy* to refer to any adult male. One child used the word *mooi* to refer not only to the moon but also to cakes, round marks on windows and in books, tooling on leather book covers, round postmarks, and the letter 'O'. Another child applied her word for the bars of her cot (*kotibaiz*) to a large toy abacus, a toast rack with parallel bars, and a picture of a building with a columned façade (Clark & Clark 1977: 493). Overextension is particularly marked on nouns, but it also applies to other word classes. This phenomenon shows that from a very early age, children perceive similarities across the phenomena of experience and expect language to be flexible enough to cope with these similarities. In this respect, the process whereby children learn to narrow their range of reference can be interpreted as a move to restrict the radiality of their lexical system.

There are also cases of underextension. For example, one of my own daughters, at the age of five, was watching a television program on artificial insemination in cows with considerable interest. (She later became a vet.) There were several references to eggs in the course of the program and at the end of it she said *I didn't know that cows laid eggs*, showing that, for her, the concept of 'egg' was considerably more restricted than it is for (most) adults.

This example is instructive from several points of view. In the first instance, it suggests that the vast majority of underextensions in children (unlike examples of overextension) probably go unobserved. This particular example of underextension is one that has probably applied to every learner of English. We have presumably all encountered eggs in the first few years of our lives only in the form of hens' eggs, so that only with a later understanding of biological reproduction in general were we able to construct a cognitive connection between hens' eggs and mammals' eggs. Yet the example would never have been noticed had it not been referred to by the child herself. Presumably what happens in normal circumstances is that when we encounter a novel member of a category in this way, we unconsciously adjust our internal representation of the radial network to accommodate it.

As another small example among thousands that could be cited, consider the word *ring*. It seems likely that most of us first encountered this word in a context where it referred to a gold object worn on a woman's finger. If we were taken to the circus, we may later have come across it as the name for the area in which the performance took place. It is not clear whether we would have judged this new usage to be a homonym of *ring* or whether it would have been associated immediately with the meaning 'finger ornament'. The ease with which young children construct categories of this kind based on similarities of shape (as manifested in overextension) suggests that the connection is often established quickly. When it is, the construction of the radial category is underway.

At a later stage, we would have also come across an application of the word *ring* to a boxing ring. The similarity between a boxing ring and a circus ring is much closer than that between a boxing ring and a finger ornament. A child who encounters a boxing ring before a circus ring may well take considerably longer to construct the relevant network. As for the use of *ring* to refer to a (typically clandestine) group of people (for example, *dope ring*), it is possible that not all speakers of English assign this to the radial category that contains finger ornaments, circus rings, and boxing rings, though expressions such *a circle of friends* and *We move in different circles* probably help to construct such connections.

Each of these examples suggests that even in adult language underextension is rife. For example, there are relatively few people in the world who know that the word *tree* has an application in linguistic theory. In other words, there is a marked difference between the radial category for *tree* of people who have studied linguistics and those who have not. In fact, the process of encountering new category members for the radial structures associated by items in our vocabulary—particularly for nouns—is probably a process that goes on throughout our lives.

4.7 Conclusion

The fact that radiality is such a pervasive property of language has a wide range of consequences. For one thing, it has important implications for the process of language change. Since the semantic networks associated with words and morphemes are open, new phenomena can be assimilated to existing categories on the basis of perceived similarities, without the need to create a new word every time we encounter a new phenomenon. Thus, a (more or less) finite system is able to cope with a world that is infinite and in constant flux.

A further consequence of the fluid nature of linguistic and conceptual categories is that categorisation is often a matter of negotiation and contestation. Courts of law, for example, are typically concerned with issues of categorisation. Was this action a case of murder, manslaughter, or accidental killing? Was that article a case of libel or fair comment? Even at the mundane level, issues of categorisation are pervasive. The activity in which I am currently engaged, as I put this sentence together, is in my view most appropriately described as 'writing', but my wife will occasionally (rather mischievously) refer to it as 'computing' (since I am using a word processor). And yesterday evening I watched a television interview in which the interviewer repeatedly suggested that the interviewee (a representative of a large company that is in dispute with some of its customers) was accusing its customers of 'lying', whereas the interviewee insisted that they were simply 'mistaken'. In all such cases, we are concerned with issues of categorisation and construal.

These issues will be taken up in later chapters. First, however, we need to add an important dimension to the notion of radiality. In this chapter, we have been concerned with the semantic networks associated with words and morphemes. In the next chapter, the same notion will be applied to syntactic constructions.

Exercises

1 Consider the following sentences.

   (a) *A sparrow is a bird par excellence.*
   (b) *?A chicken is a bird par excellence.*
   (c) *Loosely speaking, an ashtray is a piece of furniture.*
   (d) *?Loosely speaking, a chair is a piece of furniture.*
   (e) *Strictly speaking, rhubarb is a vegetable.*
   (f) *?Strictly speaking, beans are vegetables.*

   Why are some of these sentences more natural than others? What do these sentences tell us about the way in which we use the expressions *par excellence*, *loosely speaking*, and *strictly speaking*?

2 For each of the words below, give a range of sentences illustrating semantic variation of the word in question. (In some cases you may need to comment on uses associated with different grammatical classes—*attack*, for example, can be used either as a noun or a verb.) Comment on the relationships between the various meanings for each word in terms of metaphor, metonymy, and so on.

   attack, back, branch, bright, clear, close, cool, cream, cut, dark, deep, drive, flower, fly, full, heavy, hit, hold, hot, keep, light, lose, off, open, run, safe, sharp, side, strange, table, waste, wave, wheel, wild, win, work

3 Comment on the meaning of *cheap* in each of the following sentences.

   (a) *That was a cheap remark.*
   (b) *She won some cheap points* (from a commentary on a tennis match).

4 Comment on the verbs *promise* and *threaten* in the following.

(a) *This theory promises to supplant earlier theories.*

(b) *The situation threatens to get out of hand.*

In what way is the meaning/use of these verbs unusual in these examples? How might these uses relate to the concept of subjectification (3.7.6)?

5 The word *sorry* can be used in a number of different situations. What is the main difference between the following examples?

(a) *I'm sorry to hear about your mother.*

(b) *I'm sorry I made fun of you yesterday.*

What other uses of *sorry* are there?

6 In what way is the adjective in the following examples used in an unusual way?

(a) *a serious elephant*

(b) *a happy outcome*

(c) *a hopeful sign*

How could we account for this type of usage? In what way is the expression *a sad man* ambiguous?

7 How does the meaning of *to* differ in the following examples?

(a) *I turned to speak to John.*

(b) *I turned to see a lion about to spring.*

Further reading

Givón, T. 1986, 'Prototypes: between Plato and Wittgenstein', in C. Craig (ed.), *Noun Classes and Categorization*, John Benjamins, Amsterdam, pp. 77–102.

Lakoff, G. 1982, 'Categories: an essay in cognitive linguistics', in Linguistic Society of Korea (ed.), *Linguistics in the Morning Calm*, Hanshin, Seoul, pp. 139–93.

——1986, 'Classifiers as a reflection of mind', in C. Craig (ed.), *Noun Classes and Categorization*, John Benjamins, Amsterdam, pp. 13–51.

——1987, *Women, Fire and Dangerous Things: What Categories Reveal about the Mind*, University of Chicago Press, Chicago.

Norvig, P. & Lakoff, G. 1987, 'Taking: a study in lexical network theory', *Proceedings of the Berkeley Linguistics Society* 13: 195–206.

Rosch, E. 1978, 'Principles of categorization', in E. Rosch & B. B. Lloyd (eds), *Cognition and Categorization*, Lawrence Erlbaum Associates, Hillsdale, NJ, pp. 27–48.

Smith, M. B. 1993, 'Cases as conceptual categories: evidence from German', in R. A. Geiger & B. Rudzka-Ostyn (eds), *Conceptualizations and Mental Processing in Language*, Mouton, Berlin, pp. 531–65.

Schulze, R. 1993, 'The meaning of (*a*)*round*: a study of an English preposition', in R. A. Geiger & B. Rudzka-Ostyn (eds), *Conceptualizations and Mental Processing in Language*, Mouton, Berlin, pp. 399–431.

Taylor, J. R. 1995, *Linguistic Categorization*, 2nd edn, Clarendon, Oxford.

——1998, 'Contrasting prepositional categories: English and Italian', in B. Rudzka-Ostyn (ed.), *Topics in Cognitive Linguistics*, John Benjamins, Amsterdam, pp. 299–326.

Notes

1 I owe this example to Günther Kress.
2 This statement does not apply to many speakers of Australian English, who can use *may* in this situation.
3 If the existence of *loud* explained this gap, then *a strong light* should be ruled out by the existence of *bright*.
4 I owe some of the examples cited in this section and some details of the analysis to Sands 1996.

5

CONSTRUCTIONS

5.1 Combining words and phrases

There is a widespread tendency in linguistics to assume that the process of sentence construction is largely determined by the grammatical properties of words. A speaker is deemed to have a mental lexicon, in which words are assigned to the appropriate grammatical class (noun, verb, adjective, and so on), and speakers construct phrases and sentences with reference to rules that refer to such word classes. For example, phrases such as *the woman, this house, my cats, which book,* and so on are said to be constructed with reference to a rule that states that members of the grammatical class 'determinative' (*the, this, my, which,* and so on) can combine with members of the class 'noun' (*woman, house, cat, book,* and so on) to form noun phrases. This, however, is a rather misleading view of the constructional process. Arguably, the primary determinant of whether linguistic units can combine with each other is meaning rather than grammar.

Consider, for example, the words *after* and *under* in English. One 'grammatical' difference between these words is that, whereas *after* can take a noun phrase (NP) or a clause as a complement, *under* can take only a noun phrase.

(1) *Mary left after the accident.*
(2) *Mary left after the table collapsed.*
(3) *The cat disappeared under the table.*
(4) **The cat disappeared under the table collapsed.*

Now if one takes the view that the combinatorial potential of words is determined by their grammatical properties, it would be natural to claim that *after* and *under* take different complement patterns because *after* is both a preposition and a subordinating conjunction, whereas *under* is a preposition only. This would explain the patterns illustrated above on the assumption that prepositions take NP complements, whereas subordinating conjunctions (such as *although, because,* and so on) take clause complements. But this would clearly be absurd. The decision to classify *under* as a preposition and *after* as both a preposition and a subordinating conjunction is a **consequence** rather than a **cause** of the patterns in (1)–(4). The reason why *after* and *under* differ from each other with respect to their combinatorial potential has to do with differences in meaning rather than with differences of grammar.[1]

The combinatorial properties of *under* clearly have to do with the fact that it expresses a relationship between two entities (*the cat under the table*) or between a process (state or event) and an entity (*The cat was asleep under the table*) in the domain of space. Since the landmark of *under* is an entity, and since an entity is typically designated by an NP, it follows that the complement of *under* will be an NP. By contrast, the fact that *after* expresses a sequential relationship between two events or situations in the temporal domain means that it can be followed either by a clause (*The fire started after we heard the explosion*), or by an NP (*The fire started after the explosion*)—these properties deriving from the fact that events can be designated by NPs or by clauses. The different behaviour of *under* and *after* with respect to NPs and clauses therefore follows from their semantic rather than their grammatical properties. The role of grammar in these cases is to map the linguistic unit that refers to the relevant semantic entity onto a particular position. The grammar of English requires that words such as *under* and *after* should precede their complement (landmark), whereas the grammar of, say, Japanese, requires that they should follow.

Following this line of argument, we can think of the process of semantic compositionality as involving a process of mapping or blending. For example, let us take it that the word *under* designates (or 'profiles' in Langacker's (1990: 5) terminology) a particular spatial relationship between two entities, such that one is located vertically below the other in physical space. The difference between *under* and *above* is that in the case of *under*, the lower entity is located with respect to the higher entity (the former is the trajector and the latter the landmark), whereas these relationships are reversed in the case of *above*. Figure 5.1 represents the image schema for *under*.

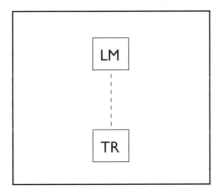

Figure 5.1 Image schema for *under*

The process of combining the concept 'under' with the concept 'the table' to form the expression *under the table* involves mapping 'the table' onto the LM of *under*, as illustrated in figure 5.2. Similarly, the process of combining the concept 'the newspaper' with the concept 'under the table' to form the expression *the newspaper under the table* involves mapping 'the newspaper' onto TR of 'under the table' (figure 5.3). In other words, the meaning of *under* is such that it provides two conceptual slots available for 'elaboration' (Langacker 1988c: 104), the LM slot functioning as an 'elaboration site' for words referring to physical entities (for example, *the table*), and the TR slot functioning as an elaboration site for expressions referring to physical entities (for example, *the newspaper*) or processes (for example, *The cat was asleep*).

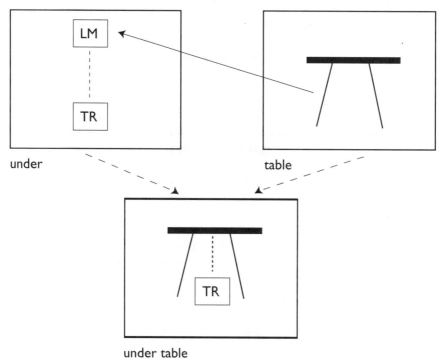

under

table

under table

Figure 5.2 *Under the table*

5.2 Combining frames

The above discussion is misleading in one important respect. It suggests that 'the meaning' of a construction is simply an aggregate of the meanings of its individual constitutive elements. However, we have already seen that this is not the case. As was noted in the previous chapter, the meanings of expressions such as *a strong man, a strong woman, a strong wine, a strong*

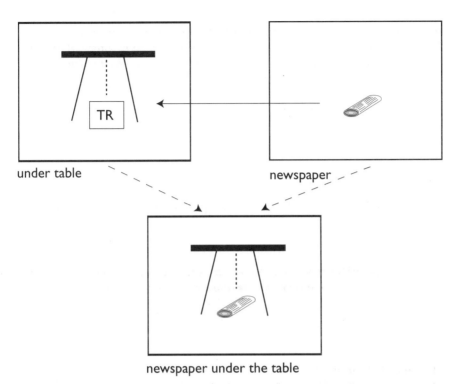

under table

newspaper

newspaper under the table

Figure 5.3 *The newspaper under the table*

argument, and so on, are not straightforward aggregates of the meanings of the words of which they are composed. The fact that *strong* varies semantically from one example to another, and the fact that aspects of encyclopaedic (including cultural) knowledge come into play in the interpretation of each expression, shows that meaning is the product of a complex interaction between the **frames** associated with the relevant words rather than with their 'meanings' (in some narrow sense).

As a further example of this point consider such noun compounds as *windmill, watermill, steel mill, flour mill, paper mill, pulp mill,* and so on. A grammar-oriented approach to compositionality has little to say about such constructions. But in fact the same general principles apply to these cases as to constructions such as *the newspaper under the table.*

The word *mill* refers to an industrial building in which power (of various kinds) is used to drive tools (of various kinds) to produce a variety of outcomes, such as generating electricity, pumping water, or manufacturing a product. This means that (as in the case of *under*) a number of unspecified semantic slots are available as targets for the mapping of appropriate concepts. In *windmill* and *water mill* the concepts 'wind' and 'water' map onto the TYPE-OF-POWER-SOURCE slot; in *steel mill, flour mill, paper mill, pulp mill* the concepts 'steel', 'flour', 'paper', and 'pulp' map onto the PRODUCT slot; in *sawmill* the concept 'saw' maps onto the TYPE-OF-TOOL slot.

Compound expressions of this type typically involve extensive frame knowledge. For example, tins of tuna are sometimes marked *dolphin-safe*, but it takes more than an understanding of the words *dolphin, safe,* and *tuna* to understand the meaning of the expression *dolphin-safe tuna.*[2] Similarly, in order to interpret a construction such as *top-rack dishwasher safe*, one needs to know that certain types of container can suffer damage in a dishwasher but that they are more likely to do so in the bottom rack (which is nearer the heating element) than in the top rack.

5.3 Constructional meaning

We turn now to a consideration of the meanings of a number of syntactic constructions, beginning with the contrast between the prepositional construction illustrated in (5) and the ditransitive construction illustrated in (6), a contrast generally known as 'the dative alternation'.

(5)   *Mary gave the book to him.*

(6)   *Mary gave him the book.*

Since the prototypical meaning of *give* involves the transfer of ownership of an entity from one person to another, the fact that it occurs in (5) needs no explanation. All the properties of this construction (including the fact that the preposition phrase contains the preposition *to*) follow from general principles of English grammar; however, the fact that *give* can also enter into construction with two NPs in the ditransitive structure illustrated by (6) does call for an explanation.

Historically, the existence of the ditransitive structure is due to the fact that English used to have a case system, involving a distinction between an accusative form and a dative form. In Old English, the NP or pronoun filling the slot occupied by the word *him* in (6) was marked by the dative case (expressing directionality), and the noun or pronoun filling the slot occupied by the phrase *the book* was marked by the accusative case.[3] In Modern English the distinction between these two case forms has been lost, so that we now find only an accusative form (*me, him, us, them,* and so on) in the postverbal position in this construction. The fact that the meanings previously expressed by the dative case have been taken over by the preposition *to* has given us the structure illustrated in (5), but the older structure has also survived in the form of (6).

In Modern English, although there are many cases such as (5) and (6), where either construction can be used, there are some situations in which only one of these structures seems natural. For example, although (7a) is entirely natural, (7b) is decidedly odd; similarly, (8a) is more natural than (8b) (Langacker 1990: 14).

(7)   (a)   *John gave the fence a new coat of paint.*

       (b)   *?John gave a new coat of paint to the fence.*

(8)   (a)   *John taught me all I know.*

       (b)   *?John taught all I know to me.*

In these examples it is the ditransitive structure that is more natural than the prepositional structure. The following pairs illustrate the converse situation.

(9)   (a)   *Brian sent a walrus to Antarctica.*

       (b)   *?Brian sent Antarctica a walrus.*

(10)   (a)   *He brought the wine to the table.*

       (b)   *?He brought the table the wine.*

(11)   (a)   *John cleared the floor for Bill.*

       (b)   *?John cleared Bill the floor.*

And although a verb such as *bake* occurs easily in either construction (*He baked me a cake, He baked a cake for me*), verbs such as *open* and *mow* generally do not.

(12)   (a)   *He opened the door for me.*

       (b)   *?He opened me the door.*

(13)   (a)   *He mowed the lawn for me.*

       (b)   *?He mowed me the lawn.*

These contrasts suggest that the two constructions have slightly different meanings. Langacker (1990: 13) argues that the ditransitive structure (for example, (7a) and (8a)) gives focal prominence to the result of the process, whereas in the prepositional construction with *to* (for example, (9a) and (10a)) it is the notion of **movement** that is foregrounded. Thus, (7a) is well formed because the coat of paint comes into existence as the end result of the process; (8a) is well formed because the outcome is a situation in which I know what I know. On the other hand, (7b) is unnatural because it suggests that a coat of paint is a moveable object; (8b) is unnatural because it is odd to think of 'all I know' as an object that can be moved from someone else's mind into mine. This claim provides a neat explanation for the fact that *I taught them French* carries a suggestion that they came to know French, whereas *I taught French to them* does not (Goldberg 1995: 33).

An associated characteristic of the ditransitive structure is that the direct-object referent (henceforth the 'patient') must be construable as a recipient rather than simply as the place to which the transferred object moves (Goldberg 1995: 38). Thus, (9b) is odd because it would be strange to construe Antarctica as the recipient of a walrus; (10b) is strange because, when wine is brought to a table, it is not the table itself but the people sitting there who are naturally construed as the recipients. As for (11b), the oddity of this example may have to do with some incongruity in the notion of the relationship between a person and a floor as one involving a recipient and a received object. The example can be improved by substituting *a place to sleep on the floor* for *the floor* (*John cleared Bill a place to sleep on the floor*), since one can use a particular part of the floor for a specific purpose (for example, sleeping on it) and therefore be construed as a recipient (Langacker 1990: 14–15).

5.4 Constraints on generalisation in child language

Supporting evidence for the claim that there is a difference in meaning between these structures also comes from the process of generalisation in child language. It is well known that children make generalisations on the basis of structures they know and that sometimes such generalisations are 'incorrect' (from the viewpoint of the adult language). For example, children produce sentences such as *I goed out, I seed it, I taked it down,* involving past-tense forms that are generalisations from regular forms such as *liked, walked, played,* and so on. What is puzzling is that there are cases where children do not tend to overgeneralise in cases where one might expect them to do so. For example, given that they hear adults saying *I opened the door for Mary* and *I mowed the lawn for Mary,* one might expect them to produce sentences such as **I opened Mary the door* and **I mowed Mary the lawn,* by analogy with pairs such as *I baked a cake for Mary* and *I baked Mary a cake.* Interestingly, however, children do not tend to overgeneralise in these cases.

This observation can be explained if we assume that children understand that different constructions express different meanings. The reason why children do not say things such as **I opened Mary the door* and **I mowed Mary the lawn* is that it is unnatural in these cases to construe the result of the process designated by these sentences in terms of Mary as the recipient of the door or the lawn. In other words, if we assume that children understand the general principle that formal differences express semantic differences and the specific fact that the patient in a ditransitive structure is construed as a recipient, then the absence of overgeneralisation in these cases is readily explained. It follows quite naturally from the assumption that children will express only those meanings that are cognitively natural in terms of their experience of the world.

5.5 Naturalness and grammaticality

In the preceding discussion a number of cases were noted in which a particular lexical substitution affects the acceptability of the sentence. For example, *I cleared Bill a place on the floor* is more natural than *?I cleared Bill* *the floor.* We might also observe that *Brian sent the zoo a walrus* is more natural than *?Brian sent Antarctica a walrus* and that *He opened me a can of sardines* is better than *?He opened me the door.* Contrasts of this kind pose serious problems for theories that hypothesise that speakers of a language distinguish sharply between grammatical and ungrammatical sentences, and assume that the primary goal of the theory is to explain such an ability. On that view relatively minor lexical substitutions of this kind should not produce significant differences of 'grammaticality'.

These contrasts, however, are entirely consistent with the general principles of cognitive grammar. If a language is conceptualised as a symbolic system, designed to express meanings produced by the cognitive processes of human beings, with human experiences of the world feeding into these cognitive processes, then we would expect precisely the kind of gradation and variability illustrated by the data above. Sentences will be maximally natural if the meanings they express correspond to natural ways of conceptualising the relevant situation. Conversely, they will exhibit various degrees of unnaturalness to the extent that this correspondence does not hold. Judgments about particular sentences are grounded firmly in our everyday experience of the relevant situations rather than in some abstract set of rules that refer only to the formal properties of sentences.

5.6 Iconicity

A further general observation emerging from this discussion has to do with the concept of 'iconicity'. A relationship between a symbol and its referent (for example, between a form and a meaning) is 'iconic', if there is some structural or formal correspondence between them. For example, a map is iconically related to the landscape it represents, since the positions of the places in the landscape match directly with the positions of the corresponding 'places' on the map. (On the other hand, not all aspects of this relationship are iconic, since the map is not a three-dimensional model of the landscape.) If there is no such correspondence, the relationship is arbitrary. There is nothing about the word *dog*, for example, that corresponds to the nature of the concept it represents.

The traditional view of language is that most relationships between linguistic units and the corresponding meanings are arbitrary (one exception being onomatopoeic words). But the cognitive claim is that the degree of iconicity in language is much higher than has traditionally been thought to be the case. The meanings attributed to the ditransitive and prepositional structures in the above discussion are a case in point. Since the ditransitive structure comprises two syntactically juxtaposed NPs, it makes sense to suggest that it profiles a particular kind of conceptual juxtaposition (the notion of 'receipt') between the relevant entities, given the principle of iconicity. Conversely the fact that the prepositional construction contains a word expressing either a directional meaning (*to*) or a benefactive meaning (*for*) is iconically related to the fact that it gives prominence to meanings such as movement or benefit. In general, cognitivists expect the relationship between forms and meanings to exhibit a higher degree of iconicity than do traditional models.

5.7 Raising constructions

5.7.1 Object-raising

We turn now to a different set of constructions as a further illustration of the claim that the relationship between form and meaning is more iconic than has previously been thought to be the case. (This discussion follows Langacker 1995.) Consider the following sentences.

(14) *To solve the crossword is difficult.*

(15) *The crossword is difficult to solve.*

In syntactic terms (14) consists of a clausal subject (*To solve the crossword*) and a predicate (*is difficult*). The mapping of this structure onto meaning is straightforward. Just as a sentence such as *Mary is tall* is interpreted to mean that the property of 'tallness' is predicated of Mary, so we interpret (14) to mean that the property 'difficult' is predicated of the process 'to solve the crossword'.

Sentence (15), however, is problematic. The grammatical subject here is not a clause but an NP: *the crossword*. The problem is that, at the semantic level, the property 'difficult' is generally not applicable to the referents of NPs. For example, it would not be easy to interpret sentences such as *This hypotenuse is difficult* or *That chair is difficult* (except in special circumstances, to be discussed below). Moreover, in spite of the syntactic differences between (14) and (15)—specifically, the fact that the subject of (14) is a reduced clause, whereas that of (15) is an NP—we nevertheless assign roughly the same interpretation to both sentences. That is, we interpret (15) to mean that the process of solving the crossword is difficult, even though *to solve the crossword* is not the subject of the sentence.

In generative approaches, the normal way of dealing with sentences such as (15) is to postulate a movement rule that 'raises' the object of the subordinate clause into the subject position in the main clause. This involves postulating two levels of structure (deep and surface), linked by a movement rule, as illustrated in figure 5.4.

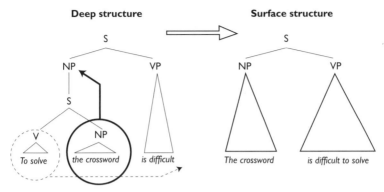

Figure 5.4 *Raising*

The cognitive framework suggests a different approach, which involves treating the difference between (14) and (15) in a similar way to the contrast between the ditransitive and prepositional structures discussed above. For example, it was argued that the constructions illustrated by (5) and (6) are characterised by a semantic distinction involving different foregrounding choices. The same claim can be made with regard to (14) and (15). Since both of these sentences attribute the property 'difficult' to the process of solving a crossword, we can suggest that they share a common cognitive structure, illustrated in figure 5.5, in which the process of some unidentified person solving the crossword ('X———►C') is located towards the upper end of a scale of difficulty.

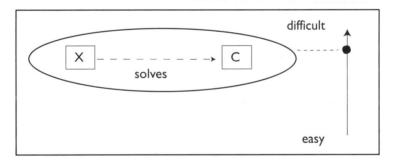

Figure 5.5 *To solve the crossword is difficult/*
The crossword is difficult to solve

The semantic difference between them is accounted for by postulating that in (14) it is the whole process ('X solves the crossword') that is foregrounded, whereas in (15) the LM of that process ('the crossword') is given focal prominence, the process itself being backgrounded. This contrast is illustrated in figures 5.6 and 5.7 (in which the heavy ellipses represent foregrounding and the dotted ellipse backgrounding).

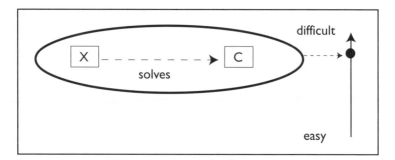

Figure 5.6 *To solve the crossword is difficult*

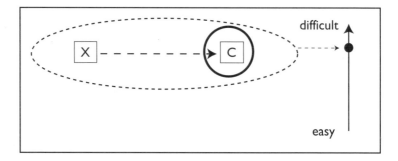

Figure 5.7 *The crossword is difficult to solve*

In one sense the structure illustrated in figure 5.5 corresponds to the 'deep structure' of the generative analysis, with figures 5.6 and 5.7 corresponding to the surface structures. The difference between the two approaches is that, whereas the generative analysis involves movement, the cognitive analysis involves the imposition of a particular 'imaging' on the various components of meaning in the form of differences of focal prominence, associated with the different constructions. While this operation is conceived of as a purely syntactic operation in the generative approach, in the cognitive framework it is primarily a semantic distinction with syntactic consequences.

Support for the cognitive analysis comes from various sources. If we ask why there should be a structure in English (and other languages) in which the patient of a process is foregrounded, with concomitant backgrounding of the process itself (as in figure 5.7), the answer has to do with the fact that in some situations a particular process is easy or difficult because of certain attributes of the object itself. An example such as (15) allows a speaker to do two things simultaneously: (a) to say that the whole process of solving the crossword is difficult and (b) to focus simultaneously on the role of that particular crossword (as opposed to some other imaginable crossword) in making it difficult.

A prediction that follows from this account is that in situations where the role of the patient is not particularly relevant to the characteristics of the process, then the raising structure should be less appropriate than the non-raising structure. For example, if I wish to express the idea that playing the violin quietly is a pleasant thing to do, I am much more likely to say *Playing the violin quietly is nice* than *The violin is nice to play quietly*, since the characteristics of a particular violin are irrelevant to the question of whether it is pleasant to play it quietly. Similarly, if I wish to say that the process of chatting to friends in a pub is an enjoyable way to pass the time (without wishing to focus on the question of whether chatting with friends is more enjoyable than chatting with other people), I am more likely to say *Chatting with friends in the pub is nice* rather than *Friends are nice to chat to in the pub*. On the other hand, if the particular properties of a violin make it a particularly good instrument to play, then it becomes more natural to profile it with the raising construction (*This violin is nice to play*); for similar reasons, *Those people were nice to chat to* is an entirely natural thing to say.

If this analysis of the raising structure is correct, it would not be surprising to find other structures in the language that involved a similar foregrounding of the patient with concomitant backgrounding of the process. The following are cases in point.

(16) *This crossword is difficult.*

(17) *This book is difficult.*

(18) *This operation is difficult.*

In these examples the process of backgrounding is taken one step further than in (15), with elimination of explicit reference to the process altogether. This is possible in (16) because there is a particular activity that is closely associated with crosswords—namely, solving them—so that this process need not be mentioned explicitly. The same applies *mutatis mutandis* to (17) and (18). One would normally use (17) to mean that the book is difficult to read (or possibly difficult to write) rather than that it is difficult to find or difficult to hold (unless there is something about the context that makes these processes salient) and one would normally expect (18) to mean that the operation is difficult to perform. In other words, the statement that attributes such as 'easy' or 'difficult' are not normally predicated of NPs (?*This chair is difficult*) has to be qualified by the observation that this is indeed possible in those cases where the referent strongly evokes a particular process or where the context of utterance does so—it would be quite natural to say *This chair is difficult* in a context in which I am trying to paint it, for example.

Nevertheless, it is important to make the point that these sentences are interpreted in precisely the same way as the raising structure illustrated in (15). That is, the predicate is deemed to apply to a process rather than to an entity, in spite of the fact that the subject is a noun phrase.

This argument is also supported by the existence of such NPs as *a difficult problem, a difficult period, a difficult request, an easy child, an impossible task,* and many others, in which the attribute applies to an understood process rather than to the noun referent as such. And yet another piece of supporting evidence for the analysis has to do with the so-called 'middle' construction in English, illustrated by an example such as (19), the meaning of which can be represented by (20).

(19) *This timber polishes easily.*

(20) *[X polishes the timber] is easy.*

In both the raising and middle constructions an attribute is assigned to a process carried out by an indefinite agent X. The difference between them is that, whereas in the object-raising construction the attribute is mapped onto a predicative structure with downgrading of the verb, in the middle construction the process is coded straightforwardly by the verb, as in the corresponding transitive structure. In both, the landmark is foregrounded and mapped onto the subject function.

5.7.2 Subject-raising

Alongside the so-called 'object-raising' construction illustrated above, there is also a 'subject-raising' construction that provides additional support for the analysis. This construction is illustrated by (21), which is to be contrasted with (22).

(21) *John is likely to win.*

(22) *That John will win is likely.*

Sentence (22) is interpretable with respect to the normal rules of English grammar, given that the attribute 'likely' is normally predicated of situations. This condition is met in (22) since the subject of the sentence is an expression that denotes a situation (the clause *That John will win*). Example (21), on the other hand, is problematic, since in this case the subject of the sentence (*John*) refers to an entity. Entities, however, cannot in themselves be deemed to be 'likely', so that a special rule of interpretation is required here to produce the appropriate reading, namely that it is John's winning that is likely.

There is a clear parallel here with the object-raising construction and a similar solution suggests itself. The components of meaning shared by both (21) and (22) are represented in figure 5.8, with the contrast between them involving a difference of focal prominence (figures 5.9 and 5.10).

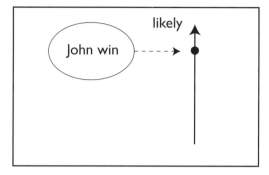

Figure 5.8 *That John will win is likely/John is likely to win*

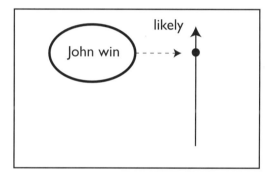

Figure 5.9 *That John will win is likely*

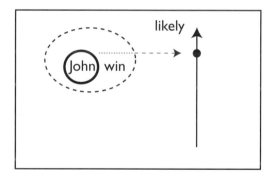

Figure 5.10 *John is likely to win*

Again, we see supporting evidence in the form of NPs such as the following.

(23) *A likely prime minister.*

(24) *A likely candidate.*

If I characterise someone as *a likely prime minister*, the epithet *likely* is not applied to the concept of 'prime minister' in the way that an epithet such as 'tall' might be. A tall prime minister is a prime minister who is tall but a likely prime minister is not a prime minister who is likely. Rather, *likely* is applied to the process of someone **becoming** prime minister. Similarly, if I refer to John as *a likely candidate*, I may mean that he is likely to become a candidate or, if he is already a candidate, that he is likely to win. In both cases, it is a process that is deemed to be likely, but only the LM of the process is coded, since the nature of the NP supplies sufficient information for the expression to receive a full interpretation. Here again we see the importance of frame knowledge in allowing certain interpretations.

Other adjectives that behave in a similar way are *possible* (*a possible prime minister*), *probable* (*a probable participant*), *certain* (*a certain winner*), *definite* (*a definite starter*), and *obvious* (*an obvious choice*).

5.8 The caused-motion construction

5.8.1 Distributional patterns

The cognitive analysis of the ditransitive and raising constructions leads us to the rather striking conclusion that constructions themselves have meaning, quite apart from the meanings of the words that occur in them. This contrasts with the generative view that constructions are formal structures that simply provide slots into which words and phrases are inserted according to their syntactic properties. In this section I consider a particular structure in some detail in order to develop the cognitive view. (The argument is based on Goldberg 1995.)

I will focus on a construction known as the caused-motion construction, illustrated by such examples as (25) and (26).

(25) *We ordered them out of the house.*

(26) *We forced them out of the house.*

The caused-motion construction has the form [$NP^1 - V - NP^2 - PP$], such that the verb denotes an action performed by the referent of NP^1, which causes the entity denoted by NP^2 to follow a path denoted by the preposition phrase. The issue of interest is the question of which verbs can appear in the construction.

In cases such as (25) and (26) there is a close relationship between the caused-motion construction and a related infinitival construction illustrated by (27) and (28).

(27) *We ordered them to go out of the house.*

(28) *We forced them to go out of the house.*

I will therefore consider these two constructions together. As the above examples show, some verbs appear in both constructions. This set includes not only *order* and *force* but also *coax, ask, invite, beckon, urge, allow,* and *let*.

(29) We *coaxed/asked/invited/beckoned/urged/allowed/him* to go out of the house.

(30) We *coaxed/asked/invited/beckoned/urged/allowed/him* out of the house.

However, verbs such as *instruct, tell, advise, beg, convince,* and *persuade* occur only in the infinitival construction.

(31) We *instructed/told/advised/begged/convinced/persuaded him* to go out of the house.

(32) *We *instructed/told/advised/begged/convinced/persuaded him* out of the house.

Conversely, *lure* occurs only in the caused-motion construction.

(33) *She lured him to go out of the house.

(34) She lured him out of the house.

At first sight, the apparently random nature of these patterns seems to suggest that the phenomenon is a matter of grammar. Verbs such as *instruct* might be deemed to be 'infinitival', the verb *lure* might be deemed to be 'prepositional', and verbs such as *order* might be deemed to be both 'infinitival' and 'prepositional'. Speakers of English would be assumed to have learnt these as arbitrary properties of specific verbs.

However, this approach begins to encounter problems when we look at some cases in more detail. For example, whereas *let* normally occurs quite happily in the caused-motion construction, the addition of an adjunct can sometimes cause the example to become less natural.

(35) She let Bill into the room.

(36) ?She let Bill into the room by leaving the door open.

Similar problems arise with the following pairs.

(37) (a) They laughed the poor guy off the stage.
      (b) ?They laughed the poor guy into the car.

(38) (a) He nudged the ball into the hole.
      (b) ?He nudged the ball down the hill.

(39) (a) John broke the eggs into the dish.
      (b) ?John broke the eggs onto the floor.

There is no obvious explanation for the fact that the first member of each pair here is natural, whereas the second is odd (on the assumption that there was a single nudge in (38b) and that in (39b) John did not intend to break the eggs). Problems also emerge with respect to verbs such as *sneeze* and *laugh*. Both of these are normally classified as intransitive verbs, to account for the unacceptability of such examples as *Sue sneezed the napkin* and *Sue laughed the poor guy*. This would in effect debar them from appearing in the caused-motion construction, which contains a direct object. But in fact, as Goldberg (1995: 54–5) has noted, such examples cannot be ruled out.

(40) *Sue sneezed the napkin off the table.*

(41) *They laughed the poor guy out of the room.*

Similarly, it seems surprising that (42) is natural, whereas (43) is pragmatically odd.

(42) *He washed the soap out of his eyes.*

(43) *?He washed the soap.*

These observations suggest that there is a subtle meaning difference associated with the contrast between the caused-motion construction and the infinitival construction. The obvious hypothesis to explore is that it is the meaning of the caused-motion construction itself that determines which verbs can appear in the structure and under what circumstances.

5.8.2 Conditions of use

As noted above, the caused-motion construction involves an 'Agent' (or Causer) causing a 'Patient' to move along a path. The basic condition governing the choice of verb is that it must refer to a process that has the potential to cause such movement to happen. However, this general constraint on the choice of verb is subject to more specific conditions.

Condition (A)

The path of motion must be completely determined by the causal force.

This is perhaps the most basic condition (for reasons to be outlined directly). It explains why a verb such as *nudge*, for example, can be used in (44) but not in (45) (unless the situation involves repeated nudges).

(44) *He nudged the ball into the hole.*

(45) *?He nudged the ball down the hill.*

In (44) the nudge is sufficient to cause the ball to drop into the hole (assuming that the ball is located close to the hole when the nudge is administered). But if someone nudges a ball and it then rolls down a hill, we are unlikely to describe this situation with (45). This is because the nudge causes the force of gravity to come into operation and it is this latter force that is perceived to be the most significant factor in the resulting situation.

Objectively speaking, gravity also plays a role in (44), of course. However, as we have noted many times before, the process of construal is not determined by objective factors. For practical human concerns, it is the nudge in (44) that plays the salient role in the process and this seems to be sufficient to justify the use of the caused-motion construction in this case.

Condition (B)

No cognitive decision on Y's part can mediate (saliently) between the causing event and the entailed motion.

This condition explains why verbs such as *order, force, invite, lure,* and *frighten* appear in the construction, whereas verbs such as *instruct, tell, advise, convince, persuade, plead,* and *beg* do not. Again, the condition needs to be interpreted with respect to the notion of construal. The receiver of an order clearly performs some cognitive activity in carrying it out; if this were not the case, it would be impossible to disobey an order. Nevertheless, it is natural in most cases to construe the order itself as the direct cause of the resulting movement. The verb *instruct,* on the other hand, has a weaker meaning than *order.* The prototypical frame for an order is a military context, in which orders are supposed to be obeyed without question. Instructions are associated with contexts in which the receiver of an instruction normally enjoys greater discretion. The greater involvement of the addressee in the relevant process is particularly obvious in the case of verbs such as *tell, advise, convince, persuade, plead, beg,* which do not occur in the caused-motion construction.

Conditions A and B are related to each other. They could in fact be subsumed under a more general condition to the effect that the process denoted by the verb must be construable as the **immediate cause** of the movement. Together they explain the contrast between the following pair.

(46) *They laughed the poor guy off the stage.*

(47) ?*They laughed the poor guy into the car.*

In (46) the path of motion is construable as fully determined by the process denoted by the verb. In (47), however, it is difficult to conceive of a situation in which the aim of ridiculing someone is specifically to get them into a car (as opposed to simply getting them to move away). For similar reasons, *She frightened him away* seems more natural than ?*She frightened him under the bed.*

Condition (C)

The causer must be an animate agent or natural force but not an instrument.

It is not unusual to find an instrument in the subject position in a normal transitive sentence.

(48) *The hammer broke the vase.*

(49) *His cane helped him to move around.*

However, an instrument does not normally occur in the subject position in the caused-motion construction.

(50) **The hammer broke the vase into pieces* (compare *John broke the vase into pieces*).

(51) **His cane helped him into the car* (compare *Sue helped him into the car*).

This condition too can be seen as a reflex of the more general requirement that the subject be construable as the immediate causer of the movement. Since instruments imply a controlling agent, they are difficult to construe as direct causers.

Condition (D)

The construction can be used if the verb denotes a change of state (or effect) that involves motion, provided that the activity is performed in the conventional way and is performed with the intention of causing the motion.

This subtle condition accounts for examples such as those in (52), and differentiates between (53) and (54) (assuming that John did not intend the eggs to land on the floor in the latter).

(52) *The butcher sliced the salami onto the wax paper/grated the cheese onto a serving plate/shredded the papers into the bin.*

(53) *John broke the eggs into the dish.*

(54) **John broke the eggs onto the floor.*

The criterion of conventionality explains the difference between the following pair.

(55) *The company flew me to London for an interview.*

(56) *?Mum flew me to London for a holiday.*

It is a conventional scenario (or 'script') for companies to buy plane tickets to bring people to an interview. There is no such conventional scenario for mothers to buy tickets to send their offspring on holiday.[4]

Condition (E)
The action denoted by the verb cannot imply an effect other than motion.

This condition accounts for the fact that, if Sam shoots Pam and she is flung across the room, it would be unnatural to use the caused-motion construction to describe this event.

(57) ?*Sam shot Pam across the room.*

This is because effects other than motion are strongly implied by the action of shooting. However, (57) would be quite natural if Pam were in a wheelchair and the verb *shoot* meant 'push quickly'.

This condition also offers an explanation for the rather odd fact that verbs such as *hit*, *strike*, and *clobber* occur quite happily in the caused-motion construction if the patient is inanimate, but less naturally if it is animate.

(58) *He hit/struck/clobbered/the ball to the boundary.*

(59) ?*He hit/struck/clobbered/me to the ground.*

The fact that pain as well as movement is an effect of these processes— if they are inflicted on human beings—seems to make examples such as (59) less natural than those in (58). The verb *knock*, however, does occur in the construction with an animate object (*He knocked me to the ground*), presumably because the milder nature of this process does not necessarily involve inflicting pain.

The range of conditions on the use of the caused-motion construction outlined above demonstrates the crucial role of semantic and pragmatic factors in what have traditionally been thought to be processes governed purely by grammar. There are powerful indications here that the construction of expressions is a process that draws on the full resources of our knowledge frame rather than on some subcomponent of the mind concerned purely with 'linguistic' knowledge in some narrow sense.

5.8.3 Radial network of the caused-motion construction

It is a significant finding of cognitive linguistics that constructions resemble other linguistic units (specifically, words and phrases) in that they are associated with a set of meanings comprising a radial network. The range of meanings expressed by the caused-motion construction include:

- X causes Y to move to Z by direct action.
    Harry pushed it into the box/sneezed it off the table.
- X causes Y to move to Z through the performance of a communicative act.
    Joe ordered him out of the house/asked her into the room/invited him to his cabin/beckoned him into the house/urged her into the office.

- X enables Y to move to Z.
  Sam allowed Bob out of the house/let Bill into the room.
- X prevents Y from moving from Z.
  Joe locked Harry in the bathroom/kept me outside the house.
- X assists Y to move to Z.
  Joe helped him into the car/guided him through the tunnel/showed her into the living-room.

Moreover, constructions (like words) participate in effects of contextual modulation (1.4). For example, just as the meaning of *strong* varies in construction with such words as *horse, argument, smell,* and *wine,* so the interpretation of the semantic relationship between a verb and a direct object varies according to whether the transitive construction or the caused-motion construction is involved. Consider:

(60) (a) *Sam tore the bandage.*

   (b) *Sam tore the bandage off my leg.*

(61) (a) *Jane ripped the poster.*

   (b) *Jane ripped the poster off the wall.*

Only in the (a) examples here (the transitive construction) is the direct object referent 'torn' or 'ripped' in the normal sense. Similarly, there is a subtle difference in meaning between the following pair:

(62) (a) *Sue squeezed the ball so that it went through the hole.*

   (b) *Sue squeezed the ball through the hole.*

In (62a) the squeezing and the passage of the ball through the hole are separate operations, whereas in (62b) the squeezing is an intrinsic component of the movement (Aske 1989).

5.9 Constructional distribution of verbs of removal

The claim that different constructions express subtle meaning differences provides an explanation for the fact that certain verbs that appear to be closely related semantically nevertheless exhibit distributional differences with respect to the range of constructions in which they occur. As an illustration of this point, we will focus on some distributional differences between verbs that refer to the process of removal—verbs such as *clear, dislodge, draw, empty, erase, evict, extract, mop, pluck, remove, rub, scrape, wipe* (Levin & Rappaport Hovav 1991).

One construction in which all these verbs occur is illustrated by the following examples.

(63) *John cleared the dishes off the table.*

(64) *John wiped the marks off the counter.*

(65) *John removed the stains from the carpet.*

That is, all these verbs occur in a construction of the form [V –NP^1 – FROM – NP^2] involving a process in which the entity designated by NP^1 is moved away from the entity designated by NP^2. (The position identified by FROM in this construction can be filled either by *from* or by other source prepositions such as *off* and *out of*). We will refer to the referent of NP^1 as the 'Mover' and the referent of NP^2 as the 'Source'.

However, these verbs differ with respect to other constructions. For example, only *clear* and *empty* occur in the construction illustrated in the following examples.

(66) *John cleared the table of dishes.*

(67) *John emptied the tub of water.*

(68) **John wiped the counter of marks.*

(69) **John removed the carpet of stains.*

In this construction the semantics of the direct object NP and the complement of the preposition *of* manifest a semantic reversal of the situation illustrated in (63)–(65) in that the direct object NP refers to the Source (not the Mover) and the prepositional complement refers to the Mover (not the Source). A further constructional difference is that *clear* and *empty* can occur in the intransitive construction illustrated in (70) and (71), whereas none of the other verbs can.

(70) *The skies cleared.*

(71) *The tub emptied.*

Levin and Rapport Hovav (1991) have suggested that verbs of removal can be subdivided into a number of different subclasses on the basis of these distributional differences. *Clear* and *empty* are change-of-state verbs—they refer to a process that results in a particular state of affairs without specifying how that result was achieved. Both in the intransitive construction and the *of* construction illustrated in (66)–(69), there is a focus on the resultant state of the process. In this respect the *of* construction differs from the [V – NP – FROM – PP] construction, in which the focus is on the process of movement rather than on the end result. (This contrast is reminiscent of the contrast in the dative alternation pattern discussed at the beginning of this chapter and has a similarly iconic character.) As evidence for this claim, note that in certain cases only one of these constructions is natural.

(72) *The judge cleared the accused of guilt.*

(73) *?The judge cleared guilt from the accused.*

The relatively abstract nature of the process of clearing someone of guilt seems to make focus on the process of movement rather strange. Significantly, *clear* and *empty* are derived morphologically from adjectives, which explains why they are highly compatible with focus on a resultant state. When someone has cleared the table of dishes and emptied the tub of water, the outcome is that the table is clear and the tub empty.

By contrast, although the processes referred to by the other verbs in the above list (*dislodge, draw, erase, evict, extract, mop, pluck, remove, rub, scrape, wipe*) do involve a change of state, they are not change-of-state verbs. What this rather paradoxical statement means is that these verbs are deemed by native speakers to lack a semantic characteristic (or feature) that is possessed by *clear* and *empty*—a feature called 'change-of-state' that is relevant to the potential occurrence of verbs in the constructions of the target language. Underlying this claim is the idea that one of the tasks facing language learners is to identify those semantic features that are relevant to constructional distribution and to classify verbs accordingly. This is by no means a straightforward task. There are many verbs that refer to processes involving a change of state (in fact this is true of most verbs), but there are only a small number of 'change-of-state verbs' in this technical sense.

The non-change-of-state verbs can be further subdivided according to whether they occur naturally in the so-called 'conative' construction illustrated below.

(74) *She plucked at her eyebrows.*

(75) *The dog scratched at the door.*

(76) *Jo rubbed at the counter.*

(77) *?Jo wiped at the counter.*

(78) *?The cleaner mopped at the floor.*

This construction implies that the process had little or no effect on the relevant entity, in which respect it contrasts with the transitive construction. So whereas *She plucked her eyebrows* implies that some hairs were removed, (74) does not; and, unlike *The dog scratched the door*, (75) suggests that the dog's scratching left the door unscathed. As for the contrast between (76) and (77), this derives from a subtle difference between the process of rubbing and that of wiping. Since the point of wiping a surface is to remove marks that are easy to remove (or to apply a substance such as polish that is easily applied), it is virtually impossible to wipe a surface without having the intended effect. On the other hand, rubbing is a more vigorous activity designed to remove more stubborn marks, so that it is possible to apply this process without the desired end being achieved, thus accounting for its occurrence in the conative construction.

As well as illustrating the subtle semantic differences between related constructions, this contrast again demonstrates the involvement of experiential knowledge in phenomena that are sometimes thought to be syntactic.

5.10 Conclusion

The data discussed in this chapter demonstrate that the process of learning a language is a different kind of task than has traditionally been thought to be the case. Until recently the process of combining words into sentences has been seen as a process that primarily involves 'grammatical' processes, governed by rules involving word-class concepts and rules of combination that refer to those concepts (for example, phrase-structure rules). Although rules of this kind clearly play some role in the process, it is clear from the data discussed here that much more subtle knowledge (typically involving experiential knowledge) is involved in creating constructions.

But there are deeper problems with the grammar-oriented approach. The traditional claim is that native speakers find examples such as *He ordered me into the room* quite natural, but those such as *He instructed me into the room* odd because *order* is marked in their mental lexicon with the grammatical property 'prepositional', whereas *instruct* is not.

But the question arises: on what basis would speakers have arrived at this conclusion? Such a conclusion cannot be based on the fact that a speaker has never heard a sentence such as *He instructed me into the room*, since the fact that we have never heard this sentence is no guarantee that it is not perfectly acceptable. It is a well-established fact that a particular individual's linguistic experience is characterised by many accidental gaps.

This problem is usually called the problem of 'negative evidence'. The general question is: how do speakers know whether a particular gap in their discursive experience is accidental or significant (that is, a reflex of a linguistic principle)? The approach to this question adopted by generative grammarians is to postulate innate knowledge. The native speaker knows that a particular structure is ill-formed on the basis of his or her innate knowledge of universal principles of language design.

There may be cases where this is indeed a plausible explanation. But the observations made in this chapter suggest an alternative approach. The ability of native speakers to make the subtle distinctions illustrated here can be explained, if we assume that they are able to construct generalisations about form-meaning relationships, on the basis of limited exposure. In particular, exposure to sentences such as *He ordered me in, He lured me in, He coaxed me in* may be sufficient for learners to arrive at the hypothesis that the use of this construction is appropriate where the patient bears minimal responsibility for the movement. Such a hypothesis would be a natural one to make if learners expected a general notion such as 'immediate causation' to play an important role in linguistic encoding. Similar points could be made about the other phenomena discussed in this chapter.

To claim that language learners expect a notion such as 'immediate causation' to play a role in linguistic encoding is, of course, to attribute to them some kind of innate knowledge of general principles of language design. But this kind of knowledge is much less arcane than are the highly abstract formal principles that are often postulated in formal theories of language acquisition, based on the generative paradigm. The general issue, then, is whether the brain contains some kind of mental 'organ' that is specific to language (in much the same way that the body contains specialised organs such as the heart and liver, each with their own specific function), or whether the principles that govern language acquisition are part of more general principles of cognitive development. The evidence discussed in this chapter tends to support the latter view.

Exercises

1 Sometimes, adverbs such as *rather, quite, so* can modify a PP (*rather under the weather, quite out of character, so near the edge*) and sometimes they occur between a preposition and an NP in a PP (*in rather a hurry, in quite a mess*). But there are many NPs where neither of these possibilities exists (**rather in the house, *quite at the library*). What kind of factors determine the distribution of these adverbs in these constructions?

2 Why is ?*She let him into the room by leaving the door open* odd, whereas *She let him into the room* is quite natural?

3 Consider the following sentences.
   This butter is too soft to use.
   The movie is too exciting to miss.
   The box is light enough to lift.
In what way are they related to sentences such as *The crossword is difficult to solve*? Why could the raising analysis not be applied to sentences of this kind?

4 What is the difference in meaning between *John swam across the Channel* and *John swam the Channel*? How would you account for this semantic contrast?

5 If you saw a group of people marching with placards bearing the slogan *Guns don't kill people—people kill people!*, would you guess that they were marching in support of private gun ownership or against it? What is it about the slogan *Guns kill people* that they object to?

6 Why do the examples below show that the transitive construction in English is a radial category?

   John kicked Fred, I remembered the party, I received a parcel, He appealed the decision, The police are door-knocking the neighbourhood.

7 There are a number of possessive constructions in English. One is illustrated by *John's mother*, another by *The mother of John*. Which of these constructions has the more extensive radial network? Illustrate your answer with examples.

8 What is the difference in meaning between the following pairs?

(a)   *He loaded muck on the truck/He loaded the truck with muck.*

(b)   *Bees are swarming in the garden/The garden is swarming with bees.*

(c)   *She sprayed paint on the wall/She sprayed the wall with paint.*

Is there any iconic relationship between the structure of the sentence and its meaning or are these meaning differences unrelated to the syntactic structure?

9 Why is the first member of each of the pairs below more natural than the second?

(a)   *He covered the wall with paint/*He covered paint on the wall.*

(b)   *He coated the wall with paint/*He coated paint on the wall.*

10 The verbs *consider, find, discover, observe, know* all occur in the construction illustrated by the sentence *I considered him to be a genius* (*I found him to be a genius, I discovered him to be a genius, I observed him to be a genius, I knew him to be a genius*). However, only *consider* and *find* occur in the structure illustrated by the sentence *I considered him a genius* (**I found him a genius, *I discovered him a genius, *I observed him a genius, *I knew him a genius*). Can you think of any semantic difference between *consider* and *find* on the one hand, and *discover, observe,* and *know* on the other, that might explain this contrast?

11 What is the difference in meaning between *I'm afraid to cross the road* and *I'm afraid of crossing the road*? Note that (a) below is quite natural, whereas (b) is odd.

(a)   *I'm afraid of falling down.*

(b)   *?I'm afraid to fall down.*

12 Consider the sentence *He never managed to start the assignment, let alone finish it*. Think up some more examples illustrating this use of the expression *let alone* and then say what it means or how it is used. Is there another expression in English that can be used as an alternative to *let alone* here?

Further reading

Foolen, A. & van der Leek, F. 2000, *Constructions in Cognitive Linguistics: Selected Papers from the Fifth International Cognitive Linguistics Conference, Amsterdam 1997*, John Benjamins, Amsterdam.

Goldberg, A. 1992, 'The inherent semantics of argument structure: the case of the English ditransitive construction', *Cognitive Linguistics* 3: 37–44.

——1995, *A Construction Grammar Approach to Argument Structure*, University of Chicago Press, Chicago.

——1996, 'Making one's way through the data', in M. Shibatani & S. A. Thompson (eds), *Grammatical Constructions: Their Form and Meaning*, Clarendon Press, Oxford, pp. 29–53.

Langacker, R. W. 1995, 'Raising and transparency', *Language* 71: 1–62.

Levin, B. & Rappaport Hovav, M. 1991, 'Wiping the slate clean: a lexical semantic exploration', *Cognition* 41: 123–51.

Sweetser, E. 1996, 'Mental spaces and the grammar of conditional constructions', in G. Fauconnier & E. Sweetser (eds), *Spaces, Worlds and Grammar*, University of Chicago Press, Chicago, pp. 318–33.

Taylor, J. R. 1995, *Linguistic Categorization*, 2nd edn, chapter 11: 'Syntactic constructions as prototype categories', Clarendon Press, Oxford, pp. 197–221.

Construction Grammar website:
<http://www.icsi.berkeley.edu/~kay/bcg/ConGram.html>.

Notes

1   In fact, the traditional distinction between prepositions and subordinating conjunctions has been eliminated in more recent approaches. *After* would now be analysed by most linguists as a preposition in both (1) and (2) (Huddleston 1984: 340; Burton-Roberts 1992; Lee 1999). But this leaves open the question of why *after* and *under* have different combinatorial properties.

2   I owe these two examples to Eve Sweetser (pers. comm.). *Dolphin-safe tuna* is tuna that has been caught with nets that don't harm dolphins.

3   This distinction is preserved in modern German—cf. *Ich gab ihm* (DAT) *das Buch* (ACC).

4   It is relevant to note a point concerning the role of conventionality in some instances of the transitive construction. Although this construction normally requires direct causation (so that it is inappropriate to say *I buried the box* if I got someone else to bury it), it is possible (for some speakers) to say *She painted her house, She buried her husband, She cut her hair last week* in cases of indirect causation (that is, getting someone else to perform the task), provided that conventional scenarios apply.

6

MENTAL SPACES

6.1 Introduction

In this chapter I consider a theory that has come to play an important part in
the overall framework of Cognitive Linguistics: the theory of mental spaces
(Fauconnier 1994). The theory has proved attractive to cognitive linguists
because of the light it throws on a wide range of linguistic phenomena,
including reference, conditionality, metaphor, and compositionality.

Following Fauconnier (1994), I start with examples such as the following.

(1)   *Plato is on the top shelf.*

(2)   *Van Gogh is fetching enormous prices these days.*

(3)   *Canberra has announced new initiatives.*

(4)   *This Bordeaux is superb.*

The curious characteristic of each of these examples is that the subject NP has
unusual referential properties. For example, *Plato* in (1) does not refer to the
Greek philosopher called Plato (as it usually does) but to a book written by
him; in (2) *van Gogh* refers not to the Dutch artist van Gogh but to his
paintings; in (3) *Canberra* refers to the Australian government rather than to
the place called Canberra; and in (4) *this Bordeaux* refers to a wine rather
than to the region of Bordeaux. In each case, then, the subject NP does not
refer to the entity to which it normally refers but to one that is conceptually
linked to it in some way.

It will be useful to distinguish terminologically between the two entities
involved in cases of this kind. Following Fauconnier I will refer to the object
that is the normal referent of the expression in question as the 'trigger' and
the entity to which the predicate applies as the 'target'. For example, in (1)
the person called Plato is the trigger and Plato's book is the target.

The sentences cited above are traditionally said to be examples of
'metonymy'—a process that exploits the fact that there is some kind of
pragmatic link between one entity and another. Metonymy is in fact another
example of the relevance of frame knowledge to linguistic usage, in that an

example such as (3) would be difficult to interpret for anyone who did not know that Canberra was the seat of the Australian government.

But why do we sometimes have recourse to this curiously indirect mode of reference? Part of the answer to this question probably has to do with economy. It is easier to say *Plato* or *Canberra* than it is to say *Plato's books* or *The Australian government*. But there are probably also deeper reasons. Examples (1) and (2) are particular manifestations of a very general conventional practice, whereby writers' and artists' names are used to refer to their creations. This practice is strongly motivated by the fact that we generally think of works of art as containing the spirit of the creator in some sense. In reading Plato's books, we come to know something of Plato the man. In other words, there is a sense in which Plato the person is indeed on the top shelf, if one of his books is there. Similarly, the quality and character of a wine is, to a large extent, a function of the place in which it was produced, which helps to motivate the usage illustrated in (4). The concept of focal prominence is relevant here too. Although the primary (focused) referent in these examples is clearly the book, the painting, or the wine, the producer or place is also present in some subdued, backgrounded form.

The modes of reference illustrated above rely on conceptual associations between objects of different kinds—connections that human beings construct 'for psychological, cultural or locally pragmatic reasons' (Fauconnier 1994:3). Following Nunberg (1979: 156), Fauconnier refers to such connections as 'pragmatic functions'. Linked with the concept of mental spaces, pragmatic functions provide an elegant and economical explanation for a wide range of linguistic phenomena.

6.2   Apparent semantic anomalies

Consider first the following example.

(5)   *In this painting the girl with blue eyes has green eyes.*

Sentences such as (5) pose considerable difficulties for formal models of semantics, since they seem to involve a contradiction. The fact that (5) is not anomalous can be explained by the distinction between trigger and target in the mental-spaces model. In this case, the target is the figure in the painting, since it is this entity to which the predicate 'has green eyes' applies. The trigger is a girl in the real world to whom the descriptor 'with blue eyes' applies. The reason why the phrase *the girl with blue eyes* can be used to refer (indirectly) to the target (the figure in the painting) is that there is a pragmatic function linking that figure to a real person—namely, the fact that the figure in the painting is a representation of the girl with blue eyes in the real world. In other words, the relevant function in this case relies on an understanding common to all human beings of the concept of 'representation', as it applies to the relationship between images and 'reality'.

The trigger and target exist in two distinct 'mental spaces', one space being (the speaker's) current reality, which contains the trigger, the other being the painting, which contains the target (see figure 6.1). An expression such as *in this painting* can therefore be considered to be a 'space builder'.

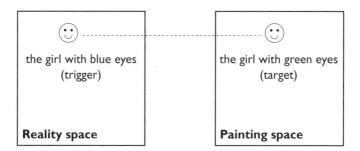

Figure 6.1 *In this painting the girl with blue eyes has green eyes*

As Fauconnier (1994) observes, unlike sentences (1)–(4), those such as (5) are not traditionally regarded as examples of metonymy. Yet in essence all these examples involve the same process—the exploitation of a relationship between a trigger and a target.

As another example involving an apparent contradiction, consider (6) in relation to (7).

(6)   *I'm taller than I am.*

(7)   *John thinks I'm taller than I am.*

Since (6) is semantically anomalous, it seems odd at first sight that (7) is well formed. This difficulty disappears in the mental spaces model. The problem with (6) is that it involves just one mental space (current reality). Since there is only one point on the tallness scale in a single mental space corresponding to the height of a given individual, and since the process of comparison involves two points, the sentence is anomalous. In (7), however, the expression *John thinks* is a space builder, creating a new mental space distinct from current reality space. Each of these spaces contains a point on a scale corresponding to John's height. When these two points are compared, the relevant point in John's 'think space' is found to be higher than the relevant point in current reality space. Such a comparison involves the construction of correspondences between various elements in the two spaces, represented by the dotted lines in figure 6.2. For example, there is a correspondence between the scale of tallness in each space: S^1 in reality space and S^2 in John's think space. There is also a correspondence between the point on the scale corresponding to my height in reality space (T^1) and the 'same' point in John's think space (T^2). What the sentence means is that T^2 is lower on the scale than the point that represents my height in John's think space (T^3).

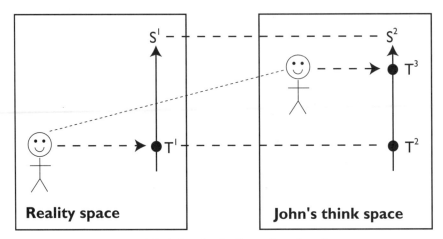

Figure 6.2 *John thinks I'm taller than I am*

Alternatively, the meaning of this sentence could be represented as a conceptual blend, as illustrated in figure 6.3. The process of blending involves merging the speaker's assessment of my height and that of John onto a single scale of tallness, enabling the relevant comparison to be made. In some respects this process is akin to the conceptual blends discussed in the previous chapter, where conceptual frames sharing common elements blend into a single conceptual structure.

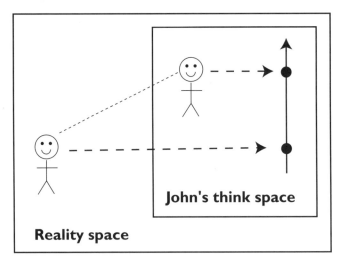

Figure 6.3 *John thinks I'm taller than I am* (blend)

In our everyday lives such conceptual blends are commonplace. As a small illustration of this point consider the following example. My office at the University of Queensland is located on the fifth floor of the Michie Building and the English Department office is located on the fourth floor. Occasionally, a student will knock at my door and ask where the departmental office is. I normally reply, 'It's on the next floor down—there!', pointing to a blank wall on the left. This instruction relies on the hearer's ability to construct a hypothetical floor based on the floor on which she is currently situated but differing from it in that the position occupied by the blank wall in her current reality is occupied by the departmental office. This in effect is a conceptual blend of elements drawn from two different mental spaces. Nobody has the slightest difficulty in interpreting this instruction, because the process of blending that it involves is unremarkable.

6.3 Referential ambiguities

One advantage of the mental spaces model is that it provides an elegant account of certain referential ambiguities. Consider (8).

(8) *The prime minister was ten years old in 1949.*

On its most natural reading this sentence means that the person who is currently prime minister was ten years old in 1949. In order to construct this interpretation, the hearer has to establish a correspondence between a person who is currently prime minister (the trigger) and a person who was ten years old in 1949 but not prime minister at that time (the target). In this case, the relevant function is the understanding that the entities in question are different manifestations of the same person. There is, however, another (pragmatically implausible) reading for (8)—namely, that the person who was prime minister in 1949 was ten years old at that time. In this case only one temporal space is involved.

As a further example of referential ambiguity, consider the following pair:

(9) *Ed thinks he's a hero.*

(10) *In that movie Ed thinks he's a hero.*

Whereas (9) has only one meaning (assuming that *he* does not refer to someone other than Ed), (10) is ambiguous. It can mean either that (real world) Ed thinks the character he plays in the movie is a hero or that the character Ed plays in the movie thinks that he is a hero (compare figures 6.4 and 6.5).[1] On the latter reading the sentence is like examples (1)–(4) in that the entity to whom the subject NP normally refers (real world Ed) is not the entity to whom that expression refers in this instance.

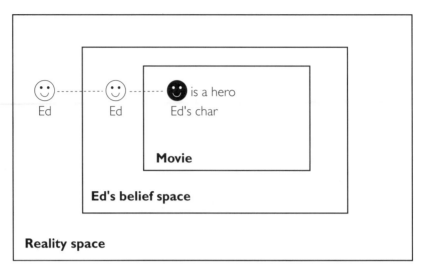

Figure 6.4 *In that movie Ed thinks he's a hero* (real world Ed's belief)

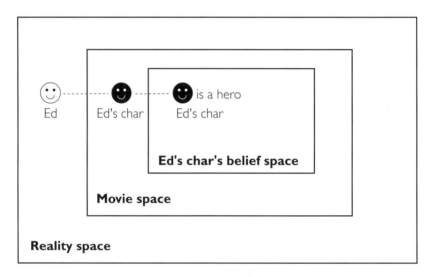

Figure 6.5 *In that movie Ed thinks he's a hero*
(Ed's character's belief)

The ambiguity of the following example can be accounted for in a similar way.

(11) *Jean wants to marry a Norwegian.*

On one reading (represented in figure 6.6) there is a person who is a Norwegian in the speaker's current reality space and who is also the person who Jean marries in her 'want space'. (Jean may or may not know that he is a Norwegian.) There is, however, another reading such that Jean wants the person she marries to be a Norwegian. This meaning is represented in figure 6.7, where there is no person in the speaker's reality space corresponding to the (hypothetical) Norwegian in Jean's want space. Traditional accounts of this ambiguity appeal to a contrast between the feature values 'specific' and 'non-specific' applicable to indefinite NPs, but this fails to capture the relationship with the other cases discussed here.

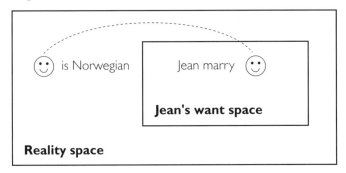

Figure 6.6 *Jean wants to marry a Norwegian* (specific reading)

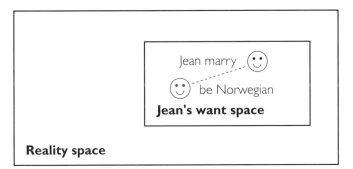

Figure 6.7 *Jean wants to marry a Norwegian* (non-specific reading)

Since linguistic forms such as *if, want, think,* and so on, are space builders that can introduce clauses containing other space builders (*If John wants X, John thinks that Mary wants X,* and so on), it follows that spaces can be embedded within other spaces. Consider:

(12) *Jean thinks she wants to marry a Norwegian.*

This structure is associated with at least three readings. The first reading corresponds roughly to the first reading of (11), involving a correspondence between a person who is a Norwegian in the speaker's current reality and the person whom Jean thinks she wants to marry. The only difference here is that she is unsure whether she wants to marry him—a meaning that derives from the placement of her 'want' space within her 'belief' space (figure 6.8).

The second reading corresponds roughly to the second reading of (11), where there is no relevant Norwegian in the speaker's reality space, so that the sentence means 'Jean thinks that she wants the person she marries to be Norwegian' (implying that she is not sure) (figure 6.9).

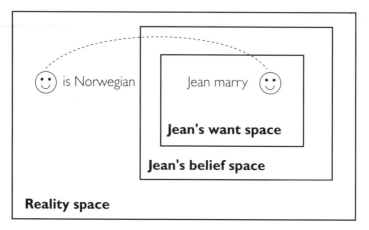

Figure 6.8 *Jean thinks she wants to marry a Norwegian (specific reading)*

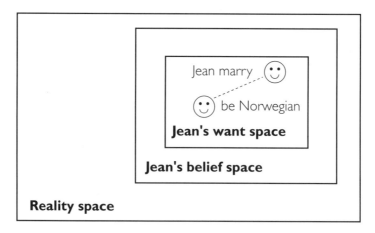

Figure 6.9 *Jean thinks she wants to marry a Norwegian (non-specific reading)*

However, a third reading of (12) emerges from the fact that *Jean thinks* creates a space of its own. On this reading the person she marries in her want space corresponds to a person who is a Norwegian in her belief space. But this person may not be a Norwegian in the speaker's current reality space (*Jean wants to marry Sven—she thinks he's Norwegian but in fact he's*

Danish). This meaning is represented in figure 6.10, where the fact that Jean definitely wants to marry the person in question is captured by the fact that her want space and her belief space are independent of each other.

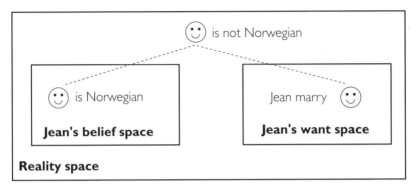

Figure 6.10 *Jean thinks she wants to marry a Norwegian*
(in fact he is not Norwegian)

6.4 Tense and mood

In some languages, semantic contrasts of the kind illustrated above are signalled by differences of tense or mood. Consider the following examples from French.

(13) *Jeanne veut épouser quelqu'un qui **est** Norvégien.*

Jean wants to marry someone who is [indicative form] Norwegian.

(14) *Jeanne veut épouser quelqu'un qui **soit** Norvégien.*

Jean wants to marry someone who is [subjunctive form] Norwegian.

Example (13) means that there is a Norwegian whom Jeanne wants to marry, whereas (14) means that she wants the person she marries to be Norwegian. The fact that there is a 'real' Norwegian in (13) is marked by the indicative form *est* whereas the fact that there is no such person in the speaker's reality space in (14) is signalled by the subjunctive form *soit*.

Contrasts of this kind can show up in English. Consider:

(15) *I hope Jean has green eyes.*

(16) *I wish Jean had green eyes.*

One of the ways in which the meaning of *hope* differs from that of *wish* has to do with the nature of the space constructed by each verb. Whereas the space constructed by *hope* is distinct from reality space, it is not necessarily incompatible with it. If one hopes that something is the case, then this allows for the possibility that it is indeed so. We can therefore characterise the relevant space as 'real hypothetical' (or 'real condition', to adopt the terminology of 4.3.1). By contrast, if one wishes that something were true, then this means that it is not; the relevant space is 'unreal hypothetical' ('unreal condition'). This explains the contrast between the present-tense form in (15) and the past-tense form in (16)—and also explains the ungrammaticality of the converse patterns:

> (17) *I hope Jean had green eyes (reference to present situation).

> (18) *I wish Jean has green eyes.

A similar explanation can be provided for the semantic contrast between (19) and (20).

> (19) If Jean has green eyes ...

> (20) If Jean had green eyes ... (reference to present situation).

The space constructed by if may be either 'real hypothetical' (if one does not know whether the relevant situation is true or not) or 'unreal hypothetical' (if one knows that it is not). Situations of the first type (for example, (19)) are marked by present tense, whereas those of the second type (for example, (20)) are marked by past tense.

6.5 Change predicates

A special type of referential ambiguity is associated with so-called 'change predicates' such as get bigger, get taller, go faster, and so on (Sweetser 1996). For example, consider (21).

> (21) Sue's house keeps getting bigger.

The most obvious reading of this sentence involves a situation in which the size of Sue's house keeps increasing (perhaps because she is constantly having extra rooms built on). But (21) can also mean that every time Sue moves to a new house, it is bigger than the last one. On the first reading, the noun phrase Sue's house has a 'normal' interpretation in that, like most noun phrases, it refers to a specific entity in the world. On the second reading, it has a 'variable' reading. It stands for a range of different entities, each of which counts at a particular time as 'Sue's house'. Each of these entities will be referred to as a 'value' for the variable 'Sue's house'.[2]

The mental spaces model provides a natural way of accounting for examples of this kind. The verb keep, which occurs in (21), is a space builder; its normal function is to set up a series of chronologically ordered mental spaces. The conceptualiser scans these spaces, noting that the size of the entity that counts as 'Sue's house' in any given space is larger than the corresponding entity in the chronologically preceding space (figure 6.11). Again, this meaning can be represented as a conceptual blend (figure 6.12).

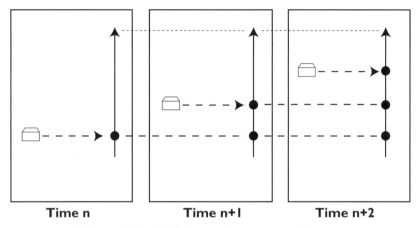

| Time n | Time n+1 | Time n+2 |

Figure 6.11 *Sue's house keeps getting bigger*

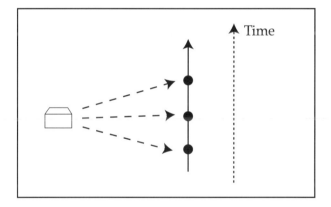

Figure 6.12 *Sue's house keeps getting bigger* (blend)

The fact that examples of this kind involve a scanning process is particularly clear in such examples as (22).

(22) *The paint gets darker as you move along the fence.*

In this case the different values of the variable 'the paint on the fence' are not objectively discrete in the way that the values of the variable 'Sue's house' are. The elements that are compared here are parts of a whole, yet they must have autonomous status in order for the relevant comparisons to be possible. They are in fact created by the scanning process defined by the expression *as you move along the fence*, which constructs a series of mental spaces each containing a different manifestation of 'the paint on the fence', such that each succeeding section is perceived as darker than the previous one.

In both (21) and (22) the subject of the change predicate is a singular NP; however, the most characteristic examples of NPs with a variable interpretation are plural (examples from Sweetser 1996).

(23) *The trees get smaller as you go up the mountain.*

(24) *The telephone poles get taller as you go along the road.*

(25) *The cars get three feet longer when you enter Pacific Heights.*[3]

Here again we are dealing with comparisons between parts of a whole, the parts being defined by the series of spaces created by a mental scan. In (23), for example, the set of 'trees on the mountain' is divided into a series of subsets located at gradually increasing altitudes, with the average height of each subset being lower than that of preceding subsets. The scanning sequence is determined by the path defined by the *as*-phrase. For example, it would be possible to describe the situation to which (23) refers by saying *The trees get taller as you go down the mountain.*

Similarly, in (24) the same situation can be expressed with a sentence that involves no change other than the substitution of *shorter* for *taller*, provided that the scanning process operates in the opposite direction (*The telephone poles get shorter as you go along the road*). And (25) also allows an alternative coding (*The cars get three feet shorter when you leave Pacific Heights*). As in cases discussed earlier (for example, the apparently paradoxical fact that *The land rises from the river* and *The land falls to the river* can both describe the same situation), the role of perspective is crucial.

In some cases, the scanning sequence is determined not by an explicit clause but by implicit pragmatic factors. For example, I might use (26) in a situation in which I am contemplating my three teenage children and commenting on the fact that the youngest child is taller than the next youngest, who in turn is taller than the eldest.

(26) *My children are getting taller.*

In this case, the situation could not normally be coded as *My children are getting smaller* because the scanning sequence is determined here by the chronological sequence inherent in the pragmatics of the relevant frame— namely, the fact that the eldest child was born before the youngest. However, this sequence could be reversed in certain contexts—for example, if the children entered the room one after the other with the youngest (and tallest) coming in first, it would not be inappropriate to code the situation as *My children are getting smaller.*

Sweetser (1996) has made the interesting observation that some predicates allow only the 'normal' or individual interpretation as opposed to the variable interpretation. Consider the following pairs of examples.

(27) (a) *The trees get taller as you move up the mountain.*

(b) *?The trees grow as you move up the mountain.*

(28) (a) *The cars get three feet longer when you enter Pacific Heights.*

    (b) *?The cars lengthen by three feet when you enter Pacific Heights.*

(29) (a) *Every time he buys a new car, it goes faster.*

    (b) *?Every time he buys a new car it accelerates.*

(30) (a) *Ramsbottom's Christmas speech gets shorter every year.*

    (b) *?Ramsbottom's Christmas speech shrinks every year.*

The striking fact about these examples is that the second member of each pair is odd, because it does not have a variable~value reading. The relevant meanings are:

(27b) 'A particular set of trees all grow in the short time that it takes for you to move up the mountain.'

(28b) 'A particular set of cars become longer.'

(29b) 'Every time he buys a new car, it accelerates.'

(30b) 'Ramsbottom gives the same speech every Christmas and it grows shorter.'

All of these meanings are pragmatically implausible. By contrast, the (a) members of each pair have a natural variable~value reading. For example, the reading for (30a) is that Ramsbottom gives a different speech every Christmas and that each successive speech is shorter than the last.

The formal difference between the members of these pairs is that the (a) examples contain a periphrastic predicate (for example, a verb–adjective or verb–adverb combination such as *get longer, get taller, went faster, and so on*), whereas the (b) examples contain a predicate consisting of a single word (*lengthen, grow, accelerate, shrink,* and so on). So the question arises: why do periphrastic predicates allow either the individual or the variable~variant interpretation, whereas monolexemic predicates allow only the individual interpretation?

Sweetser (1996) argues that this contrast has to do with iconicity. It is well known that that there is a general tendency for monolexemic predicates to refer to situations that are construed as unitary events, and for periphrastic predicates to refer to situations construed as non-unitary events—that is, as less tightly knit sequences of events. This contrast is a familiar one with respect to the contrast between *kill* and *cause to die*, for example, in that only the latter can be used to refer to actions that accidentally or inadvertently lead to someone's death. Now a sentence such as *The trees grow* is construed as a single event in that it refers to a straightforward (objective) change of state affecting a particular set of trees. On the other hand, the situation described by *The trees get smaller as you move up the mountain* is not an event of this kind. In fact, it is not even a change of state in the normal sense (none of the trees in question undergoes any change). The processes that underlie this sentence occur solely in the mind of conceptualisers as they make the relevant comparisons. In this sense, these examples provide a further illustration of some of the subtleties associated with the question of the degree to which linguistic forms are arbitrary or iconic, and they illustrate (once again) the crucial role of construal in language.

6.6 Reflexives

The mental spaces model also helps to solve a number of problems involving pronominal reference. Consider, for example, the case of reflexive pronouns. The normal situation is that, if a direct object is coreferential with the subject of the same clause, then it is realised as a reflexive pronoun.

(31) *I kicked myself.*

(32) *You kicked yourself.*

(33) *We kicked ourselves.*

An accusative pronoun form can occur in this position only if it is not coreferential with the subject (*He kicked me, You kicked us, We kicked them*). So *John kicked him* can only mean that John kicked someone other than John.

However, problems arise for this 'rule' in examples such as the following.

(34) *If I were you, I'd hate myself.*

(35) *If I were you, I'd hate me.*

One problem is that (35) ought to be ungrammatical, since there is no obvious reason why **I would hate me* is ungrammatical as an independent sentence but acceptable in a construction such as (35). A second problem is that it is far from obvious how to account for the difference in meaning between (34) and (35).

The mental spaces model offers an elegant solution to these problems. In its role as a space builder, the *if* of *If I were you* constructs a mental space containing a person who is essentially the addressee but whose 'mind' is that of the speaker.[4] Following Talmy (1988: 69) and Lakoff (1996), I assume that our conception of the human mind involves a distinction between two components—the Subject and the Self. The Subject is essentially the seat of our rational and moral judgments, whereas the Self is that part of our personality that interacts directly with the world. In the ideal situation, the Subject and Self are in harmony (compare *She's a very together person*), with the Self acting in accordance with the directions of the Subject. However, the Self can escape such control and perform acts under its own agency (compare *I couldn't stop myself, I got carried away*).

Given this split between Subject and Self, we can now refine the analysis given above. Sentences such as (34) and (35) set up a mental space (or hypothetical world) in which there is a counterpart of both 'I' and 'you' but that differs from current reality in that the counterpart of you contains my Subject instead of yours. This situation is represented in figure 6.13, in which my Subject is represented by the rectangle with diagonal lines and your Self is represented by the face drawn with the broken line. In reality space, my Subject is located in my Self (the upper face drawn with the thin line) and your Subject (the rectangle with the horizontal lines) is located in your Self. In the *if* space, on the other hand, the counterpart of you is occupied by my Subject.

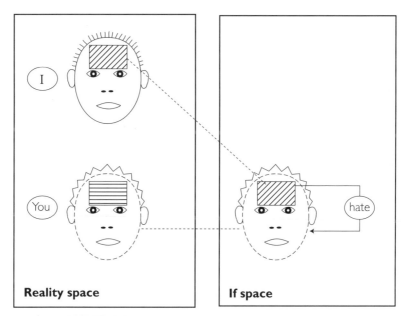

Figure 6.13 *If I were you I'd hate myself*

Now, the situation in which (34) would be uttered is one in which I strongly disapprove of the way you behave. This means that, in the mental space constructed by the *if*-clause, the fact that you behave badly (in my terms) would cause you to experience self-hatred, because your judgments and feelings would be driven by my moral judgments. And since the hatred is self-directed (it is experienced by the constructed 'you' against your Self), it is appropriate to use a reflexive pronoun, following the normal rule.

By contrast, (35) is used when I disapprove of my own actions (whereas you seem not to) or when I have harmed you in some way, so that the constructed 'you' has grounds for hating 'me' (the speaker). In this case, then, the hatred is not self-directed, and once again the normal rule applies. That is, the lack of coreference makes it appropriate to use an accusative pronoun form (figure 6.14). (As in the examples discussed at the beginning of this chapter, the form that fills the Subject position in these examples does not have its normal referential properties.)

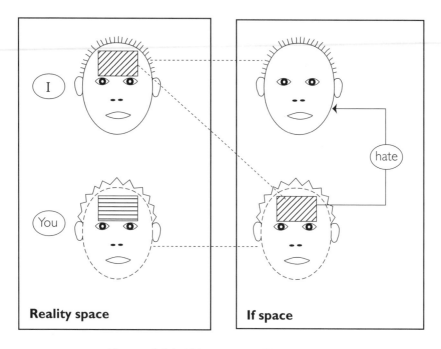

Figure 6.14 *If I were you, I'd hate me*

Lakoff's analysis constitutes an imaginative application of the mental spaces model here to the task of finding a solution to a specific formal problem in language. The problem arises from the fact that, if we assume the existence of only one world (Objective Reality), then the pronouns *I* and *me* must always be coreferential, since they both refer to the speaker. The contribution of the mental spaces model is to show that, in producing and interpreting sentences of this kind, conceptualisers use pronoun forms to enact reference in different spaces.[5]

Although the distinction between Subject and Self is essentially a philosophical construct, it is not arrived at in this case through abstract theorising. Rather, it is based on the observation of everyday ways of using English and on formal processes such as the selection of pronominal forms. In acquiring these ways of talking and these rules of grammar, speakers of English have come to acquire a particular way of thinking about the human personality.

6.7 Conclusion

The mental spaces model is a powerful theoretical tool in that it provides a unitary explanation for a varied range of observations involving both formal phenomena (for example, the contrast between subjunctive and indicative forms, between reflexive and accusative forms of pronouns, between periphrastic and monolexemic predicates) and semantic phenomena (metonymy, referential ambiguity, variable interpretations of noun phrases). It meshes closely with a range of concepts that have been introduced in previous chapters on independent grounds, including perspective, mental scanning, and construal. This model will be invoked at various points in subsequent chapters.

Exercises

1 Draw mental space diagrams to capture the ambiguity of the sentence *Max hopes to meet a minister* and explain how your diagrams capture this ambiguity.

2 Why do we use the past-tense forms *were* and *had* in an example such as the following?

> *Imagine a society in which children were brought up with other children and had no contact with their parents.*

What connection does this use have with 'normal' uses of the past tense?

3 Why do we use a modal construction in such examples as the following?

> *If it should turn out that John has no money …*
>
> *Should a suitable donor be found …*

What connection does this use have with other uses of *should*?

4 In French, certain constructions involving a superlative expression contain a subjunctive form. For example, the sentence *Cette langue est la plus belle que j'aie jamais entendue* means 'This language is the most beautiful I have ever heard', but the form *aie* is the subjunctive form of the verb *avoir* ('have') rather than the 'normal' indicative form *ai*. Why is the subjunctive form used in this case?

5 Identify ambiguities in the following sentences and say how the mental spaces model would account for them.

(a) *If Jack were older, his grey hair would inspire confidence.*

(b) *In the other room, the chandelier looks fine.*

(c) *In* Uneasy Rider *Jane Fonda's brother takes a cross-country motorcycle trip with his sister.*

(d)   *The president has been commander in chief since 1776.*

(e)   *If Sue is offered a new job, her boss will offer to give her a secretary.*

6 Why is the sentence *Policemen are getting younger every year* pragmatically more plausible than *Dogs are getting younger every year*? Draw some diagrams illustrating how the following sentences might be represented in the mental spaces model.

(a)   *Athletes are getting fitter every year.*

(b)   *The trees get smaller as you climb the mountain.*

7 John has had a sex-change operation and is now called Joanna. Would you refer to this event as 'his sex-change operation' or 'her sex-change operation'? What factors might come into play in making this choice? How is the mental spaces model relevant?

8 Comment on each of the following pairs.

(a)   *Don't offer me chocolates—I know myself.*
Don't offer me chocolates—I know me.

(b)   *Last night I dreamt I was Kim and I kissed myself.*
Last night I dreamt I was Kim and I kissed me.

9 Give some examples other than those cited in the text illustrating the claim that we conceptualise the human mind as divided into two parts.

Further reading

Fauconnier, G. 1994, *Mental Spaces*, Cambridge University Press, Cambridge.
——1999, 'Methods and generalizations', in T. Janssen & G. Redeker (eds), *Cognitive Linguistics: Foundations, Scope and Methodology*, Mouton, Berlin, pp. 95–127.
——& Turner, M. 1996, 'Blending as a central process of grammar', in A. Goldberg (ed.), *Conceptual Structure, Discourse and Language*, CSLI Publications, Stanford, pp. 113–30.
Lakoff, G. 1996, 'Sorry, I'm not myself today: the metaphor system for conceptualizing the self', in G. Fauconnier & E. Sweetser (eds), *Spaces, Worlds and Grammar*, University of Chicago Press, Chicago, pp. 91–123.
Sweetser, E. 1988, 'Grammaticalization and semantic bleaching', *Proceedings of the Berkeley Linguistic Society*, 14: 389–405.
——1996, 'Role and individual interpretations of change predicates', in J. Nuyts & E. Pederson (eds), *Language and Conceptualization*, Cambridge University Press, Cambridge, pp. 116–36.
——1996, 'Mental spaces and the grammar of conditional constructions', in G. Fauconnier & E. Sweetser (eds) 1996, *Spaces, Worlds and Grammar*, University of Chicago Press, Chicago, pp. 318–22.

——1999, 'Compositionality and blending: semantic composition in a cognitively realistic framework', in T. Janssen & G. Redeker (eds), *Cognitive Linguistics: Foundations, Scope and Methodology*, Mouton, Berlin, pp. 129–62.

——& G. Fauconnier 1996, 'Cognitive links and domains: basic aspects of mental space theory', in G. Fauconnier & E. Sweetser (eds), *Spaces, Worlds and Grammar*, University of Chicago Press, Chicago, pp. 1–28.

Notes

1   The first reading would be somewhat more salient with the ordering: *Ed thinks that in that movie he's a hero*. Incidentally, there are other possible interpretations for (10), including the reading that the character played by Ed in the movie thinks that the counterpart of real world Ed in the movie is a hero.

2   The contrast between 'variable' and 'value' is also relevant to sentences such as *The prime minister was appointed by the Queen*. On the variable reading this sentence means that every prime minister was appointed by the Queen. On the value reading, it means that the particular person who is prime minister at the moment was appointed by the Queen. The first reading is sometimes called the 'role' reading (Fauconnier 1994; Sweetser 1996) and the second the 'individual' reading.

3   This example was recorded by Claudia Brugman (Sweetser 1996: 135).

4   Since this hypothetical 'you' acts in accordance with the mental apparatus (attitudes, judgments, moral principles) of the speaker, this formula is an ideal vehicle for giving advice (for example, *If I were you, I'd go and see John*).

5   A rather separate issue is why we use *I* rather than *you* to refer to the constructed 'you'. In other words, why do we say *If I were you, I'd go and see the boss* rather than **If I were you, **you'd** go and see the boss*? If the latter were in fact the general pattern, we would presumably say *If I were you, you'd hate yourself* instead of (34) and *If I were you, you'd hate me* instead of (35). The distribution of reflexive and accusative forms would be the same but the nature of the problem would be rather different, since neither of the main clauses here would constitute an apparent violation of the normal rules (see Lakoff 1996 for discussion).

7

LANGUAGE CHANGE

7.1 Introduction

The central concepts in cognitive linguistics have obvious implications for language change. For example, the notion of radial networks raises obvious questions about how such networks grow over time. Do they grow outwards from the core? Does the core of the network shift over time? How and why do some nodes come to be added and others deleted?

There are also obvious implications for change in the concepts of frame, foregrounding, and backgrounding. Given that any semantic unit (morpheme, word, construction) involves profiling a particular area of conceptual space, the possibility arises that certain examples of semantic change are the result of changes affecting the degree of salience of the various elements of the relevant frame—for example, the emergence into the foregrounded area of components that were part of the background at an earlier time and the converse. Linguistic changes can also be expected to be triggered by frame shifts involving, for example, cultural or technological developments.

The human capacity to perceive and construct conceptual relationships across different areas of experience—the capacity that underlies metaphor—must also be an important factor in language change. If such a capacity did not exist, then every experience would be unique, requiring a distinct linguistic unit to refer to it. Languages could change only by adding new items daily in order to cope with new experiences.

There will be space in this chapter to consider only a relatively small range of illustrative examples. The focus will be on a number of cases in which change in meaning has involved extension from a relatively concrete domain to more abstract meanings.

7.2 Example: *soon*

In Modern English, the word *soon* can be used to express two different types of meaning. Its basic meaning is 'shortly after a temporal reference point'. For example, in (1) the relevant reference point is midday, whereas in (2) it is the moment of speaking.

(1) *John arrived soon after midday.*

(2) *John will arrive soon.*

In some utterances, however, the comparative form of *soon* has acquired a specialised meaning.

(3) *I'd sooner wash the dishes than dry them.*

Here, the meaning of *sooner* has nothing to do with time. (3) does not mean that I will wash the dishes before drying them; rather, it expresses the notion of preference. The question, then, is how this non-temporal meaning has come to be grafted onto a form that is essentially temporal. The fact that the word corresponding to *sooner* in other languages can also express the notion of preference suggests that this is not an arbitrary relationship.[1]

In Old and Middle English, the meaning of *soon* was slightly different from its modern meaning. For example, in (4) (from the Middle English period) it meant 'immediately after' rather than 'shortly after'.

(4) *He sayd þis word ful soyn.* (fourteenth century, *OED*)[2]

'He said this word immediately.'

The shift to the modern temporal meaning shows up in the Early Modern English period.

(5) *How came ye so soone to daie?* (1535, *OED*)

(6) *What, all so soone asleep?* (1610, *OED*)

With this development we begin to see the emergence of concepts other than those involving time alone. Consider:

(7) *Which way came I Through so immense a space so soon?* (1664, *OED*)

(8) *Too large a work to be compleated so soon.* (1772, *OED*)

Although both of these examples are concerned primarily with time, there is a suggestion in each case that the event or task was accomplished with less difficulty than had been expected. This non-temporal notion of relative ease or difficulty is more prominent in examples such as the following.

(9) *Thou wouldst as soone goe kindle fire with snow as seeke to quench the fire of Loue with words.* (1591, *OED*)

(10) *Where so soon As in our native Language can I find That solace?* (1671, *OED*)

The point of saying (9) is not to compare the time it takes to kindle fire with snow with the time taken to quench the fires of love with words, but to compare the difficulty of each task. Indeed, in Modern English we would use the non-temporal word *easily* rather than the temporal *soon* in this case: *You could just as easily kindle fire with snow as try to quench the fires of love with words, Where can I find that solace (comfort) as easily as in our native language?* The emergence of this type of meaning presumably follows from the fact that it takes longer to perform difficult tasks than easy tasks, so that time can function as an indicator of relative difficulty. In the context of the mental spaces model, we can think of the link between time and degree of difficulty as a constructed correspondence across mental spaces.

In the following examples we see a rather different semantic modulation emerging.

(11) *He thought the Sunne would soner haue fallen from his circle, then that kyng Lewes .. would haue dissimuled.* (1548, OED)

(12) *For he'll abuse a stranger just as soon as his best friend.* (1777, OED)

In these cases it is the (non-temporal) notion of likelihood or probability that is expressed by *soon* rather than the notion of ease or difficulty. In Modern English we would normally say *He thought it more likely that the Sun would have fallen* for (11) and *He is just as likely to abuse a stranger as his best friend* for (12). This development is somewhat less easy to account for, since there is no necessary correlation, objectively speaking, between the degree of likelihood of an event and its relative imminence.

Two central theoretical concepts in Cognitive Linguistics offer an explanation for this development. One is the notion of 'force dynamics', introduced by Talmy (1988). Talmy notes that there are many expressions in English that involve the conceptualisation of events in terms of opposing forces. The domain of time provides many examples. There are countless expressions in English showing that we conceive of our passage through time as analogous to physical movement along a path. Moreover, since we have no option but to move forward into the future, it is natural to think of ourselves as being projected into the future by some abstract force that carries us along. Essentially, this force is the nature of current reality, which contains certain potentialities for future events. An event that we deem to be likely is one for which current reality contains a strong potentiality, by definition. This makes it natural to think of ourselves as being projected more strongly towards likely events than towards unlikely ones, which in turn makes it natural to think that our 'arrival' at such events will happen 'sooner' than our arrival at less likely events.

A second concept that sheds light on this semantic extension from time to probability is Langacker's (1990: 315) notion of 'subjectification' (3.7.6). Since the potential for future events resides in current reality, the assessment of the degree of likelihood of a given event must be based on a conceptual scan performed by a speaker (conceptualiser) leading from the present into the relevant conceptual space (future or hypothetical). For example, in producing a sentence such as (12), the speaker must perform two mental scans that relate current reality to each potential event (in this case abusing a stranger and abusing his own best friend). Let us suppose that such a scan is facilitated, if current reality contains a strong predisposition towards the relevant event. Translated into spatiotemporal terms, this would mean that such events would be perceived as closer to current reality than unlikely events. In the case of events of equal probability (as in (12)), the scan from current reality to each event would be experienced as taking the same amount of time, which is essentially what (12) says.

Thus, the *soon* of examples such as (11) and (12) refers not to real time (the time from a reference point to an actual event) but to the time it takes a conceptualiser to perform a given mental scan. Of course, such a mental scan is applicable to all cases in which *soon* is used, including examples such as (5) and (6), which involve 'real time'. But the significant point is that it is the gradual highlighting of the processing time dimension (at the expense of the real time dimension) that facilitates the emergence of extended meanings. (For discussion of conceived time and processing time, see Langacker 1990: 78.)

These explanations, based on force dynamics and subjectification, do not have to be seen as alternatives. Since the assessment of the forces relevant to the evolution of current reality inevitably involves some kind of processing or scanning operation, the two hypotheses work together to provide a coherent explanation for the extension from the temporal to non-temporal domains illustrated in these examples.

The meanings expressed by *soon* in examples (7)–(11), which emerged in Middle English, have since disappeared. However, as was noted at the outset, there is one non-temporal meaning that has survived—namely, the one we find in examples such as *I'd sooner wash the dishes than dry them*. The preceding discussion provides a ready explanation for this usage. In force dynamic terms, the situation here is that if a speaker's mental state is conceptualised as a force projecting her into the future, then her preference projects her more strongly towards one task than the other. This means that the task of scanning that leads from the present to the preferred event is accomplished more easily than the scan that leads to the dispreferred event, so that again it becomes natural to code the relevant experience in temporal terms.

7.3 Example: *still*

In Modern English, the meanings expressed by *still* constitute a radial category. Consider:

(13) *John still lives in London.*

(14) *It was pouring with rain but he still went out.*

(15) *You must try still harder.*

(16) *Keep still!*

In (13) *still* expresses a temporal meaning, signalling the continuing existence in the present of a state of affairs that began in the past. In (14) it expresses a (non-temporal) 'adversative' meaning, signalling that a particular event happened or that a particular state exists, in spite of expectations to the contrary. In (15) it intensifies the meaning of the adverb it modifies. In (16) it means 'motionless'.

The original meaning of *still* is the last of these. In Old English and early Middle English we find numerous examples of *still* meaning 'motionless', but no examples of the temporal and adversative meanings.

(17) *Se widfloʒa wundum stille hreas on hrusan.* (OED, *Beowulf*)

'The dragon from wounds still fell to ground.'

(18) *He astereth thone rodor and tha tunglu and that eorðan gedeð stille.* (c.888, OED)

'He moves the sky and the stars and the earth makes still.'

(19) *Mars .. ne rested neuer stille But throng now here now þere.* (c.1374, OED)

'Mars (not) rests never still but thrusts now here now there.'

(20) *Hold you still.* (1590, OED)

By early Modern English the word had acquired a temporal meaning (though one that is slightly different from the meaning we find in later Modern English). The following examples contain tokens of *still* with the meaning 'always' or 'constantly'.

(21) *They learne to liue as if they were still at the point to dye.* (1581, OED)

'They learn to live as if they were always about to die.'

(22) *Thus haue I prov'd Tobacco good or ill; Good, if rare taken; Bad, if taken still.* (1617, OED)

'Thus have I proved tobacco good or bad; good if taken rarely, bad if taken constantly.'

The conceptual basis for this development is clear: the notion of the spatial stability of a physical entity has extended to encompass that of the temporal stability of a process, either in the sense of the continuation of a stable situation (as in (21)) or the repeated occurrence of the same event (as in (22)).

It seems plausible to suggest that this development paves the way for the emergence of the adversative meaning, since the situation in which a speaker draws attention to the temporal stability of a given state of affairs or process is often one in which one might have expected things to be otherwise. This imbrication of the two types of meaning is seen in the following examples.

(23) *While they pant after Shade and Covert, they still affect to appear in the most glittering Scenes of Life.* (1711, OED)

(24) *For e'en though vanquished, he could argue still.* (1770, OED)

(25) *Nothing can make such a room healthy. Ventilation would improve it, but still it would be unhealthy.* (1861, OED)

In each of these cases the temporal and adversative meanings are both in play. In (23) the proposition 'They affect to appear in the most glittering scenes of life' refers to a situation that continues to exist in the present time contrary to an expectation derived from the context. Similarly, in (24) and (25) the propositions 'He could argue still' and 'Still it would be unhealthy' describe situations whose continued existence runs counter to expectations derived from the previous clause. In other words, in a significant range of examples, we see the emergence of an association between a temporal and an adversative meaning that makes these uses indistinguishable from modern uses. The extension from the basic meaning of 'motionless' thus involves a chain:

- Motionless (spatial domain) ⟶
- Continuing event or state (temporal domain) ⟶
- Counter to expectation (extension from temporal domain)

As we move towards Modern English, a number of other non-temporal meanings begin to emerge. The first is concerned with the heightened or increased manifestation of a condition (for example, *John must try still harder*) and is illustrated by the following example.

(26) *Sir Arthegall renewed His strength still more, but she still more decrewed.* (1596, OED)

In this case, it is useful to be able to invoke the mental spaces model for an explanation for the development. A sentence such as *John still lives in London* (containing temporal *still*) involves three mental spaces:

- a reference space
- a default expectation space
- a focal space.

The reference space is a past-time situation in which John lived in London (since the sentence entails that John lived in London at some time in the past); the default expectation space is a present-time (unreal) situation in which John no longer lives in London; and the focal space is the present-time (real) situation in which he continues to live in London. *Still* highlights the contrast between the default space and the focal space—that is, between the expectation and the reality (figure 7.1).

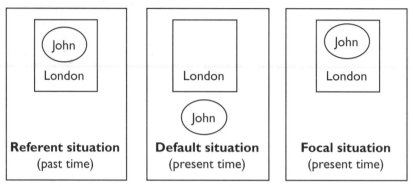

Figure 7.1 *John still lives in London*

In a sentence such as *John must try still harder* (where *still* has an intensifying meaning), there are three corresponding mental spaces. The reference space is a past period of time extending up to the present, in which John devoted a certain degree of effort to the relevant task (so that this mental space contains a measurement scale as well as a process). The default expectation space is a future situation in which John continues to perform the same task, expending the same amount of effort. The focal space is a desired future situation in which John performs the same task with increased effort. The focus here is on the scalar contrast (rather than on the polarity contrast) between the default space and the focal space (figure 7.2).

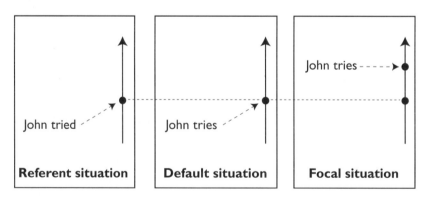

Figure 7.2 *John must try still harder*

It could be argued that we have moved here into the realms of the fanciful in attempting to construct a cognitive relationship (of a very abstract kind) between meanings that are in fact unrelated. However, it is relevant to note that the same relationship between temporal continuation and heightened manifestation of a condition is also found in other languages. The forms *encore* in French and *noch* in German, for example, can express both meanings.

(27) (a) *Il est encore ici.* (He is still here.)

     (b) *Cela est encore plus intéressant.* (That is still more interesting.)

(28) (a) *Er ist noch hier.* (He is still here.)

     (b) *Das ist noch interessanter.* (That is still more interesting.)

This indicates that there is indeed a real cognitive association to be captured here.

7.4 Examples: *may, can*

7.4.1 *may* and *can* in Modern English

The modal verbs in English provide another good illustration of the role of abstract cognitive processes in language change. In this section, we will focus on the modal verbs *can* and *may*.

Each of the modals constitutes a radial category in modern English. For *may* we can identify three distinct types of meaning: root, epistemic, and deontic. Consider:

(29) *I tell you this so that you may make other arrangements.*[3]

(30) *John may be right.*

(31) *You may leave immediately.*

In (29) the meaning of *may* has to do with your capacity to 'make other arrangements'. This is the root meaning of *may*. It can be paraphrased as 'be able to' and the process referred to in the complement typically involves an action. The term 'root' points to the fact that the notion of capability associated with *may* in (29) is conceptually (and historically) basic.

Example (30) illustrates the epistemic meaning, paraphrasable as 'It is possibly true that'. In these cases the complement of *may* refers not to an action but to a proposition (for example, 'John is right'). The type of meaning expressed by *may* in (30) is concerned with the degree of the speaker's commitment to the truth of the relevant proposition and is therefore concerned with what the speaker knows.

In (31) *may* means 'It is permitted that'. This type of meaning (deontic), like the root meaning, typically involves an action. The term 'deontic', which is derived from a Greek word meaning 'binding', is most appropriately applied to the notion of 'requirement'. For example, the meaning of *must* in *You must go now* is deontic, in that the subject is 'bound' (constrained) by a requirement to perform a particular action; however, it is also applied to the concept of permission because of the close semantic connection between the concepts of permission and requirement. (To say that someone is permitted to do X is equivalent to saying that they are not required not to do X.)

These three types of meaning are also found in other modals. For example, *can* expresses a root meaning in (32) (where it refers to physical ability), an epistemic meaning in (33) (where it refers to the epistemic status of the proposition 'John is right'), and a deontic meaning in (34) (permission).

(32) *I can lift it easily.*

(33) *John can't be right.*

(34) *You can leave whenever you like.*

The same range of meanings is also found in *could* (that is, the past-tense form of *can*).

(35) *I could lift it easily yesterday.*   [root: capability]

(36) *John could be right.*   [epistemic: truth value]

(37) *He said we could do whatever we wanted.* [deontic: permission]

The modals *must* and *will* provide further examples.

(38) *John must be right.*   [epistemic: truth value]

(39) *You must leave immediately.*   [deontic: requirement]

(40) *He will be there by now.*   [epistemic: truth value]

(41) *John just won't help.*   [root: willingness]

Will can, of course, also be used to refer to events in future time, a use that is probably best subsumed under the epistemic category (Huddleston 1984: 173).

7.4.2 Historical development of *may* and *can*

The situation in Modern English, then, is that the modal verbs manifest a considerable degree of semantic overlap. This was not always the case. The root meanings associated with each modal were originally distinct. So, whereas *can* and *may* are often interchangeable in Modern English (for example, *You can/may leave now if you wish*), in Old English there was a significant semantic difference, with *cann* meaning 'know' or 'know how to' and *magan* meaning 'have the power to'.

cann

(42) *þætt I shall **cunnenn** cwemenn Godd.* (c.1180, Denison 310)[4]

That I shall **know how to** please God.

(43) *Leofre ys us beon beswungen for lare þænne hit ne **cunnan.*** (Denison 309)

Dearer is to-us be flogged for learning than it not to **know.**

We would rather be flogged for learning than not know it.

(44) *But it sufficeþ too hem to **kunne** her Pater Noster and to beleeue wel.* (c.1425, Denison 310)

But it suffices to them to know their Paternoster and to believe well.

magan

(45) *He naefre hine ofersuiðan **meahte**.* (Denison 303)

He never him overcome *was able*.

He *was never able* to overcome him.

(46) *Ne **magon** hie ond ne moton ... þinne lichoman deate gedælan.* (Denison 303)

Not be-able they and not are-permitted your body death to deal.

They *are not able* nor are they allowed to kill you bodily.

(47) *And wiþ her feyned disputacions and false exposicions scleen it in hemself and in opere as miche as þei **may**.* (c.1425, Denison 304)

And with their feigned disputations and false expositions destroy it in themselves and in others as much as they *are able*.

(48) *Make we mery quyl we **may** and mynne vpon joye.* (*Gawain*, line 1681)[5]

Make we merry while we *are able* and think upon joy.

Vestiges of *may* expressing a root meaning of this kind can be found in more recent texts.

(49) *But I daresay he **might** come if he would.* (1816, Austen, *Emma*)

But I daresay he *would be able* to come if he wished.

(50) *Under this proposal, what would happen is that where the NCSC was concerned about some conduct it would—and it **may** under its existing powers—investigate.* (ACE, A02: 270)

(51) *Then be happy with what you are and confident about what you **may** be and don't be deterred.* (ACE, A09: 1812)

(52) *I am afraid this is the bank's final word. I tell you this so that you **may** make arrangements elsewhere.* (Coates 1983: 132)

Examples of the root meanings of *must* and *will* are also found in these examples—note the use of *moton* (Modern English *must*) in (46) meaning 'be allowed to', and *would* in (49) meaning 'be willing to'.

Given these marked differences between the root meanings of each of the modals, the question is: how has the present complex situation come about? What exactly are the conceptual connections between the various types of meaning: root, epistemic, and deontic?

Let us consider first the way in which the root meaning of *cann* has extended from that of 'know' or 'know how to' to the more general meaning of 'be able to', which is a prerequisite for further extension to epistemic and deontic meanings. Consider the following example from Middle English.

(53) ... *that ho so euer schuld dwelle at Paston schulde have nede to conne defende hymselfe.* (1445, Denison 310)

... that whosoever should dwell at Paston should have need to **know how** to defend himself.

Here I have glossed *conne* as 'know how to', in accordance with its general Old English meaning. However, the fact that the ability to defend oneself requires physical attributes as well as mental ones would make a more general interpretation of *conne* ('be able to') entirely plausible. In other words, it is possible for the speaker or writer of such a sentence to have mental attributes foremost in mind in using *conne* but for a hearer or reader to interpret it as referring to ability in a more general sense.

We can generalise from this example. In most situations, to say that someone knows how to do something is to imply that they also have the physical ability to do it. This allows the hearer some degree of interpretive latitude—that is, to activate such inferences more strongly than the speaker. Given that an interpreter is also a speaker of the language, such interpretations can become established over time, leading to a semantic change. In cognitive linguistics terms, this process can be described as one in which the relationship between foregrounded and backgrounded elements shifts, so that components of meaning that were earlier foregrounded (for example, mental abilities) are backgrounded, or even eliminated. It is still possible to use *can* with mental abilities in mind (for example, *John can understand French*), but they are no longer an obligatory component (for example, *John can lift really heavy weights*).

One feature of the semantic shift in *cann* that seems rather puzzling at first sight is the fact that the relevant semantic space was already occupied by *magan*—that is, since *magan* meant 'have the power/ability to do X', one might have expected the semantic extension of *cann* from the domain of mental ability to that of physical ability to be inhibited. However, at a very early stage *magan* itself began to undergo semantic extension from the physical to the epistemic domain and this may well have created space for the expansion of *cann*. The following examples illustrate this point.

(54) *And hi ða ealle sæton, swa swa **mihte** beon fif ðusend wera.* (Denison 298)

And they then all sat as as **might** be five thousand men.

(55) *Wel þaet swa **mæg**.* (Denison 298)

Well that so **may**.

That may well be so.

(56) *Swiþe eaþe þaet **mæg** beon þaet sume men þencan ...* (Denison 299)

Very easily that *may* be that some men think ...

It may very well be that some men think ...

(57) *Eastewerd hit **maeg** bion syxtig mila brade oþþe hwene braedre.*
(Denison 299)

Eastward it *may* be sixty miles broad or a-little broader.

(58) *Ic axige hwæðer hit **mihte** gedafenian abrahame þam halgan were.*
(Denison 300)

I ask whether it *might* befit Abraham the holy man.

Here, *magan* does not express the notion of physical ability, as in examples (45)–(52), but that of epistemic possibility.

This change presumably came about because there is a strong conceptual link between the root meaning of physical ability and the epistemic meaning of possibility in that both are concerned with the nature of evolving reality. Consider:

(59) *We are able to overcome them.*

(60) *He may leave tomorrow.* (It is possible that he will leave.)

In both (59) and (60) the speaker says that the nature of reality at a given point in time is such that it contains the potentiality for a specific future event. The difference is that in (59) the potential for reality to evolve in a particular way is located in a specific property (or set of properties) of the subject referent, whereas in (60) it is located in more general properties of the current situation, though these may be connected to specific properties of the subject (if he has plans to leave, for example).

Epistemic uses are not confined to the possibility of future actions or events. In (54)–(58), the complement of *mihte* expresses a proposition relating to current reality. These examples are therefore further removed from the root meaning than is (60). In other words, we find a continuum of gradually increasing abstraction from propensities of specific entities towards a future event ((59)) to a more general propensity of current reality to a future event ((60)), and then to a general potential in current reality for a certain proposition to prove to be true ((54)–(58)) (Sweetser 1988; Langacker 1990: 333–7). In all these cases, there are two semantic components: the attributes of reality at a given time (the 'potential') and a situation or proposition causally linked to those attributes (the 'effect'). In the root meaning, the potential is located in a relatively concrete domain (typically, the physical attributes of human beings), whereas in the epistemic use it consists in the possibilities inherent in current reality. But even some of the epistemic uses remain closely tied to the concrete. In (57), for example, the question of the truth of the proposition 'The lake is sixty miles wide' is linked to the observed properties of a physical entity.

The shift from the root meaning to the epistemic plane had a number of grammatical consequences in the Old English and Middle English periods.

One salient feature of the examples in (54)–(58) is that the subject of the epistemic modal is often the impersonal pronoun *it* or *that,* contrasting with the pronouns or full noun phrases (NPs) in the root examples. Some linguists consider the impersonal pronoun to be a purely 'grammatical' (that is, meaningless) element, meeting the need for English sentences to have a grammatical subject. Cognitive linguists, however, take the view that the impersonal pronoun has semantic content—specifically, that it refers to current reality. This clearly fits well with the argument that there is a cognitive connection between the root and epistemic meanings, and it also provides some explanation for the fact that in some Old English examples such as (54) the subject is missing entirely. Since current reality is in effect the context of utterance, it can be taken as a given, as part of what Langacker (1990: 318) calls the 'ground'.

This view of the relationship between the root and the epistemic meaning relates this example of language change to the general process of subjectification (3.7.6). As we have seen, one factor involved in the change has to do with the source of the 'potential'. In the root usage it is an 'on-stage' entity in the relevant situation. In the epistemic usage it shifts to current reality, as conceptualised by the speaker. This is precisely what is involved in the process of subjectification, so that the example provides a striking illustration of Langacker's (1990: 334) claim that subjectification is a significant process in language change.

7.4.3 Deontic meanings

The above argument not only provides an explanation for the connection between root and epistemic meanings found in many languages but also explains how these relate to deontic meanings involving obligation and permission. The notion of permission that is associated with some uses of *can* and *may* in Modern English is closely related to the meaning of ability—if one is able to do something, this means that the nature of reality allows you to do it. Example (48) provides a clear illustration of this connection. Although I have glossed *while we may* as 'while we are able', it could equally well be glossed as 'while we are permitted'. Another Middle English example in which the distinction between ability and permission is somewhat blurred is (61).

> (61) *ʒe may lach quen yow lyst* ... (Gawain, line 1502)
>
>   You may take (a kiss) when you please ...

The same applies to examples (50) and (51). Here we have another example of the way in which elements of the frame can move from the background into the foreground in the process of semantic change.

7.5 Examples: *will* and *be going to*

The verb *go* is primarily a verb that encodes movement in physical space, but it is also used in many languages to refer to events in future time. For example, if I say *This decision is going to affect everyone*, I am clearly not referring to movement in physical space. Again there is a question to be answered here. How is it that the same verb is used in expressions such as *John is going to the shop* and *This decision is going to affect everyone*?

At one level the explanation is not difficult to find. The use of 'go-futures' is clearly another manifestation of a transfer from the domain of space to that of time—a transfer that occurs in many other facets of language use, as we have seen. To explain the details of the process, however, we need to invoke once again the concepts of frame, foregrounding, and subjectification.

There are many uses of *go* in which the speaker is concerned exclusively with the movement of an entity in space. If the semantic range of the verb did not extend beyond this, there would be little motivation for the use of *go* for future time reference. What strengthens this motivation is the fact that movement is typically associated with intentionality (and result). In other words, intentionality is often part of the frame in situations where there is movement on the part of a (typically human) entity. Such intentionality can be explicitly encoded.

(62) *John went to Sydney to see Mary.*

(63) *John is going into the kitchen to make a cup of coffee.*

In such cases there are two main components in the situation:
(a) physical movement of an entity from place X (Source) to place Y (Goal)
(b) intention to perform a future event at Y.
The main feature of the development to *go* futures is a foregrounding of (b) at the expense of (a). This is facilitated in cases where the goal is not encoded. For example, the *go* of (63) can only be interpreted as a verb of motion. The sentence foregrounds both the movement of John and his intention to perform an action. However, encoding of the goal is not obligatory. If a speaker chooses to say *I'm going to make a cup of coffee*, for example, he may still have in mind both the movement and the intention to perform an action, but the fact that the goal is not encoded has the potential to background the movement, so that an interpreter could quite naturally focus on the intention. Here are the seeds of a shift from the locative to the temporal domain.

This development is only part of the process. Since sentences such as *The decision is going to affect everyone* do not involve movement or intentionality, something else is needed to explain the use of *go* in cases of this kind. This need is met once again by the concept of subjectification.

An example such as (63) is strongly objective. It involves an observed entity following a physical path to a physical location, where an observable action will be performed. In *John is going to make a cup of coffee* the degree of 'objectivity' (in the sense in which this term is used here) is essentially the same as that in (62), providing that the process of movement in physical space is strongly foregrounded.

If a hearer produces a rather different interpretation, foregrounding intentionality at the expense of movement, then this interpretation takes on a more subjective (or abstract) character. In this case, the path is located in time rather than in physical space and involves mental scanning rather than a physical path. This kind of shift is reminiscent of the contrast between *Vanessa walked across the road* (physical path followed by an observable entity) and *Vanessa is sitting across the table from John* (virtual path traced by a conceptualiser performing a mental scan), as discussed in 3.7.6. There is one difference, however. In *John is going to make a cup of coffee* (with foregrounding of the notion of intentionality), both John and the conceptualiser follow the relevant path, whereas in *Vanessa is sitting across the table from John*, only the conceptualiser does so. To this extent the degree of subjectification is slightly lower in the *go* example.

These observations provide an explanation for the final shift from examples such as (64) (with intentionality) to (65) (non-intentionality).

(64) *John is going to make a cup of coffee.*

(65) *The decision is going to affect everyone.*

Since (64) involves a conceptualisation in which both the subject referent and the conceptualiser follow a virtual path (through time), it is a short step from there to cases such as (65), where the only movement is that of the conceptualiser (as in *Vanessa is sitting across the table from John*). In other words, here, as in other cases discussed, the conceptual shift from one type of meaning to another involves intermediate cases in which both the old and the new meanings are active (see Wilkins 1996: 269 for an explicit statement of this principle).

Evidence for the plausibility of this account of *go*-futures can be found in the fact that in languages where a *go*-future coexists with another type of future, there seems to be a subtle difference in meaning that can be traced back to the historical source. Consider, for example, the difference between (66) and (67).

(66) *Smith will beat Jones tomorrow.*

(67) *Smith is going to beat Jones tomorrow.*

For most speakers (67) has a slightly more confident ring than (66). This would follow from the claim that (67) suggests that the conceptualiser is already on a path leading to Smith's future victory.[6]

7.6 Conclusion

In this chapter a number of ways have been noted in which concepts from Cognitive Linguistics can throw light on semantic change. In particular, the discussion explains why the meanings of words tend to have the character of radial networks. Meanings that are implicit in the use of particular forms at earlier times can become more prominent over time, to the extent that they come to form new elements in the network (and in some cases supplant entirely the earlier meaning). The concept of frame is crucial in this process. If the meaning of a given linguistic form were tightly circumscribed, there would be no opportunity for elements that belong to the frame or background to become more strongly activated over time. Also, the fact that no two speakers of a language bring precisely the same frame to the interpretation of utterances builds flexibility and variability into the communicative situation, and this undoubtedly plays a not insignificant part in the process of change. We will return to this point in chapters 11 and 12.

Exercises

1 Which two kinds of meaning can be expressed by (a) the word *while* and (b) the word *since*? For each word, which do you think is the older meaning? How do you think the second meaning has developed out of the first in each case?

2 The role of metaphor in linguistic change can be illustrated by the polysemy of words for body parts. For example, the word *arm* can be applied to a chair, a tree, a river, and the sea (among other things). What range of phenomena can the following words be applied to: *eye*, *foot*, *head*, *mouth*, *neck*?

3 The utterance *Cheers!* used to function purely as a toast—that is, it was uttered only when the speaker was about to take a drink. However, in recent years it has come to be used in a much wider range of situations. Give some examples of the range of situations in which it is now used and say how these extensions may have come about.

4 The contrast in older forms of English between *thou* and *you* once marked differences of power, with high-status people using *thou* to low-status people and low-status people using *you* to high-status people. Later the contrast came to mark differences of solidarity rather than power, with people who were on intimate terms using *thou* to each other and people who were not on intimate terms using *you* to each other. What might have caused this shift?

5   The English perfect construction did not begin to emerge until late in the Old English period and was still rare up till 1400. What light does the following example from *Beowulf* throw on its origins?

> *hefde sē gōda cempan gecorene*
>
> had the good one warriors chosen
>
> 'The good one had warriors chosen/had chosen warriors.'

6   Consider the following quotations from the *Oxford English Dictionary* (second edition, 1989) for the word *even*.

(a)   c. 1300 *Hi wende **evene** south.*

(b)   c. 1470 *Neuer were there foure knyghtes **euener** matched.*

(c)   1550   *In the west he turnit him **ewin** about.*

(d)   1458   *Now God geve us grace to folowe treuthe **even**.*

(e)   1480   *The wind was **euen** contrary vnto him.*

(f)   1577   *Be well assured that you bye them [draught oxen] **even** matched.*

(g)   1594   ***Even** thus the warlike god embraced me.*

(h)   1611   ***Euen** so haue I sent them into the world.*

(i)   1728   *That Poet of ours makes his Verses run as **even** as a Carpenter can draw his Line.*

(j)   1808   *It was **even** as Saxo Grammaticus relates.*

These examples show that *even* has expressed the following meanings at various stages in the history of English:
*   'directly', 'due' (as in *due east* and so on) (compare (a), (c), (e))
*   'equally' (compare (b), (f))
*   'precisely' (compare (g), (h))
*   'steadily' (compare (d))

Below are some citations for the words *gay, pretty, rude*. Describe the range of meanings associated with each of these words over the centuries.

gay

(a)   1717   *The perpetual spring makes everything **gay** and flourishing.*

(b)   1812   *Smiles wander o'er thy placid face As if thy dreams were **gay**.*

(c)   1826   *As spruce a cavalier as ever pricked **gay** steed on the pliant grass.*

(d) 1834 *They were now in that quarter which was filled with the **gayest** shops.*

(e) 1843 *Edward was the handsomest, the **gayest**, and the bravest prince in Christendom.*

(f) 1847 *For some years he lived a cheerful, and even **gay**, though never a dissipated life, in Paris.*

(g) 1860 *The Collinsia verna, a **gay**, dark purple flower.*

(h) 1870 *Their costumes were **gay** with ribbons.*

(i) 1880 *I knew he was **gay** and careless.*

(j) 1891 *This elder Narcissa had led a **gay** and wild life while beauty lasted.*

(k) 1897 *My patient was a married man, who admitted having been very **gay** in married life.*

(l) 1899 *The Copper, perceiving that he had come very near getting **Gay** with our First Families, apologized for Cutting in.*

(m) 1900 *Oh! that first kiss! how proud of it we are, what **gay** dogs we feel!*

(n) 1901 *He got **gay** one day. I warned him once, and then I threw him off the distributing floor.*

(o) 1911 *And I wouldn't get **gay** round her.*

(p) 1915 *The flush on the little man's face deepened. 'Are you trying to get **gay** with me?' he demanded dangerously.*

pretty

(a) 1486 *Holde vp yowre hande a **praty** way of from the Malarde.*

(b) 1577 *Andrew White a good humanician, a **pretie** philosopher.*

(c) 1579 *A place of some **pretty** heighth.*

(d) 1599 *Their bowes be short, and of a **pretie** strength.*

(e) 1656 *Swine also they have in **pretty** number.*

(f) 1671 *The King at last thought of a very **pretty** way to suppress him, and this was by a stratagem.*

(g) 1703 *With a **pretty** strength press the middle of one end of your Work.*

(h) 1707 *They have in Kent a **pretty** way of saving of Labour in the digging of Chalk.*

(i) 1712 *There goes the **prettiest** fellow in the world for managing a jury.*

(j) 1852 *The transfer of his commission, which brought a **pretty** sum into his pocket.*

rude

(a) 1483 *He coude not conuerte the euyll, **rude** and wylde peple.*

(b) 1489 *What nedeth me for to extoll his fame With my **rude** pen?*

(c) 1529 *At the Loge with the **rude** hand and hevy hert of hym that ys assurydly yours with herte and prayer.*

(d) 1536 *They shall leave their cure not to a **rude** and unlerned person but to a good, lerned and experte curate.*

(e) 1555 *I my selfe sawe a masse of **rude** goulde (that is to say, such as was neuer molten).*

(f) 1568 *They spake shamefully of them, like to **rude** people without all humanitie.*

(g) 1586 *The **rude** people he framed to a civilitie, and their maners he reformed and brought to the English order.*

(h) 1609 *Even to him, that is covered with **rude** linen.*

(i) 1609 *Some obey whilest they are **rude** or in a low state, but having got a little knowledge or advancement disdaine their advancers.*

(j) 1621 *Let him suffer no **rude** matter vnwrought as Tinne, Iron, to bee transported out of his country.*

(k) 1651 *The **rude** people taking pleasure in singing, or reciting them.*

(l) 1691 *He confesses he has been but a **rude** observer of them.*

(m) 1697 *Skins of Beasts, the **rude** Barbarians wear.*

(n) 1746 *Here the **rude** chisel's rougher strokes I traced.*

(o) 1776 *Either the **rude** or manufactured produce.*

(p) 1788 *It was the design of Otho the third to abandon the **ruder** countries of the north.*

(q) 1812 *The production of metals from **rude** ores.*

(r) 1831 *The blessed Pasuntius fled to far-distant monasteries, dissembling his name, that there, as if a **rude** and new monk, he might discharge the lowest offices.*

(s)   1844   *The cotton in its **rude** state.*

(t)   1849   *The London clergy set an example which was bravely followed by their **ruder** brethren all over the country.*

(u)   1854   *A **rude** metaphorical or analogical approximation to exact expression.*

(v)   1865   *We must now revert to still earlier times and **ruder** races of men.*

(w)   1865   *The new religion was first promulgated by **rude** men unacquainted with learning and rhetoric.*

(x)   1882   *Fig. 27 shows in a **rude** way the absorption by cobalt glass cut in wedge form, and corrected by an equal prism of clear glass.*

7 Describe some of the factors that motivate the range of meanings associated with each of the above words.

Further reading

Aijmer, K. 1985, 'The semantic development of *will*', in J. Fisiak (ed.), *Historical Semantics: Historical Word Formation*, Mouton, Berlin, pp. 11–22.

Blank, A. & Koch, P. (eds) 1999, *Historical Semantics and Cognition*, Mouton, Berlin.

Györi, G. 1996, 'Historical aspects of categorization', in E. H. Casad (ed.), *Cognitive Linguistics in the Redwoods: The Expansion of a New Paradigm in Linguistics*, Mouton, Berlin, pp. 175–206.

Johnson, M. 1987, *The Body in the Mind: The Bodily Basis of Meaning, Imagination and Reason*, chapter 3: 'Gestalt Structure as a Constraint on Meaning', University of Chicago Press, Chicago, pp. 41–64.

Langacker, R. W. 1990, *Concept, Image and Symbol*, chapter 12: 'Subjectification', Mouton, Berlin, pp. 315–44.

Michaelis, L. A. 1996, 'Cross-world continuity and the polysemy of adverbial *still*', in G. Fauconnier & E. Sweetser (eds), *Spaces, Worlds and Grammar*, University of Chicago Press, Chicago, pp. 179–226.

Sweetser, E. 1988, 'Grammaticalization and semantic bleaching', *Proceedings of the Berkeley Linguistics Society* 14: 389–405.

Traugott, E. C. 1982, 'From propositional to textual and expressive meanings', in W. P. Lehmann & Y. Malkiel (eds), *Perspectives on Historical Linguistics*, John Benjamins, Amsterdam, pp. 245–72.

——1988, 'Pragmatic strengthening and grammaticalization', *Proceedings of the Berkeley Linguistics Society* 14: 406–16.

——1989, 'On the rise of epistemic meanings in English', *Language* 65: 31–55.

——1993, 'The conflict promises/threatens to escalate into war', *Proceedings of the Berkeley Linguistics Society* 19: 348–58.

Wilkins, D. 1996, 'Natural tendencies of semantic change and the search for cognates', in M. Durie & M. Ross (eds), *The Comparative Method Reviewed:*

Regularity and Irregularity in Language Change, Oxford University Press, New York, pp. 264–305.

Winters, M. E. 1992, 'Diachrony within synchrony: the challenge of cognitive grammar', in M. Pütz (ed.), *Thirty Years of Linguistic Evolution*, John Benjamins, Amsterdam, pp. 503–12.

Notes

1 In German *eher* can mean either 'sooner' or 'rather', and in French there is an obvious connection between *plus tôt* ('sooner') and *plutôt* ('rather').

2 Examples marked 'OED' are from the *Oxford English Dictionary*, 1st edn, 1933.

3 This item is based on an example of Coates (1983: 132).

4 Examples marked 'Denison' are taken from Denison (1993).

5 Examples marked '*Gawain*' are from *Sir Gawain and the Green Knight* (Moorman, 1977).

6 Note that *It's unlikely that Smith will beat Jones tomorrow* is more natural than *?It's unlikely that Smith is going to beat Jones tomorrow*.

8

COUNT AND MASS NOUNS

8.1 Introduction

It was noted in earlier chapters that one of the defining features of Cognitive Linguistics is its view of the nature of the relationship between form and meaning. The traditional view, firmly asserted by Saussure ([1915] 1974) is that this relationship is characterised by arbitrariness—the forms of language bear no direct relationship to their meaning.

This view is undoubtedly correct in certain respects. For example, there is nothing about the form of words in a particular language that bears any relationship to their meaning—with the minor exception of onomatopoeic words such as *crack*, *crunch*, *creak*, and so on.[1] This does not mean that the form–meaning relationship is always totally arbitrary. In general, the cognitive claim is that grammatical structure is more strongly motivated than has traditionally been thought to be the case. In this chapter, we explore this issue with respect to various types of noun in English.

Nouns can be divided into a number of different subclasses with respect to their inflectional properties.

- Class A These are prototypical nouns, having both a singular form and a plural form: *cat ~ cats*.
- Class B These nouns have only a singular form: *equipment ~ *equipments*; *furniture ~ *furnitures*; *crockery ~ *crockeries*.
- Class C These nouns have only a plural form: **scissor ~ scissors*; **trouser ~ trousers*; **clothe ~ clothes*.[2]
- Class D These nouns have both a singular and a plural form but they are identical: *sheep ~ sheep*; *deer ~ deer*; *salmon ~ salmon*.

The distinction between class A nouns and class B nouns has a number of other grammatical reflexes.

- The singular form of class B nouns occurs without a determiner in positions typically occupied by noun phrases (*Furniture is useful*, *I bought furniture*, *I'm looking for furniture*), but this is not generally true of class A nouns (**Cat is useful*, **I bought cat*, **I'm looking for cat*).

- The indefinite determiner a occurs with class A nouns (*a cat*) but not with class B nouns (*a furniture).
- The determiner *much* occurs with class B nouns (*much furniture*) but not with class A nouns (*much cat).
- Expressions such as *a lot of* occur with the singular form of class B nouns (*a lot of furniture*) but not with the singular form of class A nouns (*a lot of cat).

These observations have led linguists to make a terminological distinction between 'count' nouns (class A) and 'mass' nouns (class B). The question on which I will focus in this chapter is whether this distinction is motivated or arbitrary.

Certain examples seem to support the view that it is arbitrary. For example, there seems to be no obvious reason why *vegetable* is a count noun but *fruit* is (normally) a mass noun. Ware (1979: 22) makes this point in the following terms:

> Turning now to why it is that words sometimes have count occurrences and sometimes mass occurrences, we are immediately faced with the problem of a tremendous amount of variation that appears unnecessary and inexplicable (...) There is a count–mass difference between *fruit* and *vegetable* but they apply to things that for all accounts and purposes seem to be alike. Nor can I see anything that would explain the count–mass difference between *footwear* and *shoe*, *clothing* and *clothes*, *shit* and *turd* or *fuzz* and *cop*.

Other contrasts that could be taken to support the arbitrariness view involve examples such as *noodle* (count) and *rice* (mass), *bean* (count) and *spaghetti* (mass). For example, why do we refer to lots of noodles in a bowl as *these noodles* (using the plural form of a count noun) but to lots of grains of rice in a bowl as *this rice* (using the singular form of a mass noun)?

In many cases, however, there is an obvious basis for the distinction between count nouns and mass nouns. There is a strong tendency for count nouns to refer to 'objects' and for mass nouns to refer to 'substances'. For example, the fact that *cup*, *cat*, and *table* are count nouns whereas *custard*, *water*, and *sand* are mass nouns seems far from arbitrary. What then is the distinction between 'objects' and 'substances', and can it be used to motivate the count/mass distinction in general?

8.2 Count and mass phenomena

Let us take as the starting point the fact that solid physical objects such as bicycles and cats are typically designated by count nouns, whereas liquids such as water and oil are typically designated by mass nouns. One salient difference between solid objects such as bicycles and cats on the one hand and liquids such as water and oil on the other is that the former have a characteristic shape and well-defined boundaries, whereas the latter lack such a characteristic profile, moulding themselves to the shape of their container. And whereas solid objects have an internal structure typically consisting of discrete components (a bicycle has a frame, wheels, handlebars, pedals, and so on), liquids tend to be internally homogeneous. One consequence of this is that any particular 'segment' of a liquid counts as equivalent to any other segment. For example, if I dip a cup into a pond and remove some water, then this particular segment of 'water' is, for all practical purposes, identical to any other segment of water that I might have scooped up. But most parts of a bicycle are different from the other parts.

Consider now such phenomena as slime, mud, and silt. In terms of their texture, these are intermediate between solids and liquids but they resemble liquids more than solids with respect to their external boundaries (they lack a characteristic shape) and internal structure (they tend to be homogeneous). It is therefore not surprising that the corresponding nouns belong to the mass category (*several slimes, *these muds).[3]

The same applies to internally homogeneous solids such as earth, clay, and cement. Chemically speaking, of course, all these substances consist of particles (as indeed does water), so that in this sense they are made up of large numbers of elements. But this is irrelevant to practical human concerns—and therefore to language.

When we come to consider phenomena such as sand, sugar, rice, soot, dust, and so on, we begin to approach the point where there is a potential motivation for construal in terms of a collection of individuated objects rather than a substance. The particles of which sugar and sand are composed are at least discernible to the human eye. In principle, therefore, there is no intrinsic reason why English should not have a word that refers to a single grain of sugar (for example, *flig*), in which case I might point to a pile of sugar and say *Here are some fligs*. But there are obvious reasons why there is no such word. Whenever sugar manifests itself to us, it always does so in the form of a conglomerate of thousands of 'fligs', tightly packed together, so that the word *flig* would serve little practical purpose. Moreover, sugar in this form behaves just like water. It moulds itself to the shape of a container and is internally homogeneous.

Some of these points also apply to noodles, but grammatically speaking we have now crossed the mass/count frontier, since *noodle* is a count noun. Individual noodles are bigger than individual grains of rice, which provides some motivation for the grammatical distinction. (It is easier to eat a single noodle than a single grain of rice.) It has to be said, however, that a single noodle is unlikely to be of great interest to anyone. To take a similar example, there is very little difference between the size of the particles that make up a pile of gravel and those that make up a pile of pebbles, but *gravel* is a mass noun, whereas *pebble* is a count noun.[4]

Although there is undoubtedly a certain degree of arbitrariness in these cases, located as they are at the boundary between objects and substances, this does not mean that there is no semantic motivation for the count/mass distinction in general. In fact, the indeterminacy that we find in cases such as *gravel* and *pebbles* is precisely what one would expect in a theory in which the objective properties of entities are subject to processes of perception and construal. Time and again in language, we come across situations where the distinction between two categories is semantically motivated, but where the behaviour of phenomena located at or near the boundary is not wholly predictable. Just as a pile of gravel is not a prototypical mass phenomenon (since it is composed of a number of perceptually distinguishable particles), so pebbles and noodles are not prototypical count phenomena, given that individual pebbles and noodles are generally not as perceptually salient as individual cats and bicycles and are of much less interest to human beings.

One strong argument for the claim that there is a semantic basis for the count/mass distinction is the fact that some nouns have both count and mass uses, associated with a clear difference in meaning. Consider:

(1) (a) *Could I have a potato?* (count)

(b) *Could I have some potato?* (mass)

(2) (a) *I'll have an egg.* (count)

(b) *I'll have some egg.* (mass)

(3) (a) *I'd like a pumpkin.* (count)

(b) *I'd like some pumpkin.* (mass)

(4) (a) *There were a lot of newspapers in the box.* (count)

(b) *There was a lot of newspaper in the box.* (mass)

(5) (a) *There's a glass on the table.* (count)

(b) *It's made of glass.* (mass)

Potatoes, eggs, and pumpkins normally manifest themselves as unitary, individuated, countable objects and they may retain this character in cooking and serving. However, if a potato or pumpkin is mashed or an egg scrambled, its character changes. It becomes a homogeneous substance from which portions can be removed or further portions added without changing its character. These examples show that, strictly speaking, the terms 'count' and 'mass' do not refer to types of noun but to particular uses of nouns, though it is true that many nouns normally appear only in one or the other use-type, given the nature of the entity that they designate.

It would be a mistake, however, to attempt to motivate the count/mass distinction purely in terms of the physical properties of phenomena. Consider, for example, the case of liquid substances. I began this discussion by observing that liquids are typically designated by mass nouns (*I'll have some water*, *There's beer in the fridge*, *He drank a glass of wine*). However, count uses of these nouns are by no means unusual.

(6)   *There were several wines on show.*

(7)   *He drank a few beers.*

(8)   *The waters were rising.*

These uses have a variety of motivations. As far as wine is concerned, human beings find it highly relevant to their everyday concerns to divide the phenomenon into various subtypes. Since each such subtype is an individuated entity, it is designated by a count noun, as in (6). Example (7) can also be interpreted in this way (that is, as meaning that he drank a few types of beer), but it is more likely to be used to refer to a rather different kind of countable phenomenon such as the contents of a container (*He drank several wines, Two sugars please*). In (8) floods are typically fed by water from different sources (for example, different rivers), so that even after they have merged, they can still be conceptualised as different entities.[5] (This usage may also be motivated by the fact that flood water manifests itself in different places.) In objective terms the nature of the phenomenon in (8) is of course no different from any other manifestation of water as a mass. If the claim were that objective criteria determined linguistic form, then this usage would constitute a powerful counterexample. But if language reflects conceptualisation, it is not difficult to identify a cognitive basis for the example.

So far, it has been argued that mass phenomena are characterised by internal homogeneity. Let me now consider nouns such as *cutlery, furniture,* and *crockery*. These phenomena seem to constitute a counterexample to the argument, since they refer to collections of discrete, countable entities. The motivation for their assimilation to the mass category has to do with the level at which the concept applies. A set of knives, forks, and spoons can either be construed as a collection of separate objects performing different functions (cutting food, picking up food, stirring liquids) or as a collection of objects which manifest themselves contiguously and which all perform the same function (facilitating the consumption of food). At this level, any part of the phenomenon counts as equivalent to any other part. Similarly, a collection of chairs, tables, and cupboards is subject to alternative construals. We can think of them either as a group of separate objects or as a unitary entity with a single function—that is, as 'furniture'.

Note, however, that more general levels of categorisation do not always produce a mass noun in English. The concept 'tool', for example, constitutes a superordinate category with respect to hammers, screwdrivers, drills, and so on, but *tool* is nevertheless a count noun. As in the case of 'cutlery', we are dealing here with an experientially related set of entities that perform different functions at one level and a single function at a more abstract level. But the grammatical character of the form *tools* continues to foreground the essentially plural nature of the phenomenon. On the other hand, the same set of entities could be designated by the mass noun *equipment*, which foregrounds their functional unity.

This observation helps to explain the contrast between *fruit* and *vegetables*. Like *cutlery*, *furniture*, *crockery*, and *equipment* the word *fruit* is a manifestation of a general pattern in the language, such that the grammatical character of the word foregrounds the pragmatic contiguity and functional similarity of the entities that constitute the category. *Vegetables* is a manifestation of a different pattern, whereby the abstraction to a superordinate level is realised lexically but where the grammatical character of the word continues to highlight the essentially plural and diverse nature of the phenomenon, as in the case of the word *tools*. Again, there is nothing in reality that **requires** the language to work in this way (that is, nothing that requires a grammatical distinction between *fruit* and *vegetables*), but there is no difficulty in identifying characteristics of the phenomenon that **motivate** the distinction.

The contrast between *clothing* and *clothes* constitutes a similar case. Whereas the unitary nature of the phenomenon is captured by the fact that the word *clothing* has only a singular form, the diverse nature of the objects that constitute the category and the fact that different items normally occur together are reflected in the fact that *clothes* has only a plural form.

8.3 Nouns lacking a singular form

So far, we have focused on the distinction between class A nouns (count) and class B nouns (mass). However, it was noted at the beginning of the chapter that there is also a subcategory of nouns (class C) that lacks a singular form, *clothes* being a member thereof. Nouns of this type can be further divided into a number of subclasses according to the nature of the motivation.

As far as ailments such as measles, mumps, shingles, hives, and haemorrhoids are concerned, the motivation for the inherently plural character of the corresponding nouns is obvious. This is also true of words such as *pants*, *braces*, *scissors*, *shears*, *binoculars*, *tweezers*, *clippers*, *tongs*, *goggles*, *spectacles*, *glasses*, and so on, though the motivation for the inherent plurality of these forms has not always been recognised. Gleason (1961: 224), for example, writes:

> ... by a convention of English, *pants* is plural. Interestingly enough, this
> is not an isolated case; compare *trousers*, *breeches*, *shorts*, *slacks*, etc.
> This whole group of words are grammatically plural with no evident
> semantic justification.

It is interesting to speculate about the factors that led Gleason to make this surprising observation, since it cannot have escaped his notice that a prominent feature of these objects is that they consist of two identical parts. Gleason's comment presumably derives from the fact that a pair of trousers is a unitary object, so that in one sense there is no obvious reason why the language should treat such a garment differently from any other unitary object, particularly when other items of clothing such as coats and shirts, which also possess two identical parts, are designated by count nouns. Certainly there are many languages that use ordinary count nouns to refer to a pair of trousers (*pantalon* in French, *Hose* in German). Again, however, this clearly does not mean that the use of a plural noun is unmotivated, nor that the distinction between *trousers* on the one hand and *coat* or *shirt* on the other is arbitrary. After all, the sleeves of coats and shirts do not constitute as great a proportion of the whole garment as do the legs of a pair of trousers. What is missing, then, from Gleason's way of thinking about these examples are the notions of foregrounding, construal, and motivation.

8.4 Nouns with identical singular and plural forms

The class D words identified at the beginning of this chapter (*salmon, cod, sheep, pheasant, mackerel,* and so on) differ from other noun classes in that they have identical singular and plural forms (compare *this salmon ~ these salmon, one cod ~ several cod,* and so on). The fact that most of the phenomena in question belong to the same conceptual domain suggests that there is some underlying rationale here—that the class of nouns with this unusual grammatical property do not constitute an arbitrary set.

The semantic property shared by most of these nouns is that they traditionally belong to the domain of hunting and fishing. In other words, the phenomena in question constitute a food resource. When someone catches a fish, it is both an individual entity and a representative of the species to which it belongs. This latter property is salient in this context because it involves characteristics that are crucial to the general fishing scenario—whether the catch is edible, how it will taste, how many will be needed to make it a viable meal, and so on. To put it slightly differently, when you are fishing for 'salmon' (or indeed simply buying 'salmon' at the fishmonger's), it is relatively immaterial which particular individual you acquire. What is important is that it is 'salmon' rather than 'cod' or 'mackerel'. This property relates entities of this kind to mass phenomena. Just as any arbitrary portion of water is equivalent to any other portion, so any individual salmon is as good a representative of its species as any other from the point of view of the consumer. The grammatical character of these nouns, therefore, seems to be a reflex of a general ambivalence concerning the individuated and mass aspects of the phenomenon. Their individuated character is often highly salient (the difference between catching one salmon and several can be important), so that it is useful to have a singular ~ plural contrast, but the absence of explicit plural marking seems to be a reflex of the fact that the individual is an arbitrary manifestation of a general resource.

This particular set of words was cited by the American linguist Benjamin Lee Whorf as an example of what he called a 'cryptotype' (Whorf 1971: 92). Whorf's argument was that there are many examples across the languages of the world where an unusual grammatical property is associated with what appears at first sight to be a rather random collection of words but where, on closer analysis, such examples provide subtle insights into the culture of the native speakers of the language in question (see Dixon 1972: 306–11 for another example involving the Australian Aboriginal language Dyirbal). Whorf cited a number of such cryptotypes from Native American languages as part of an argument that the structure of one's first language plays a crucial role in determining the way in which an individual comes to view the world.

As far as the class D words are concerned, it is doubtful whether they have any great significance with respect to this argument, since it seems plausible to surmise that there are many human societies whose members have the same view of phenomena such as salmon, cod, mackerel, and so on, as speakers of English, whether or not the words that refer to those phenomena have similar grammatical characteristics to their English counterparts. However, it does not seem unreasonable to accept part of Whorf's argument—namely, the claim that there is some underlying motivation or rationale for this particular grammatical feature located in the sociocultural history of speakers of English.

8.5 Conclusion

The discussion in this chapter supports the general claim of cognitive linguists that grammar is a much less arbitrary phenomenon than has traditionally been thought to be the case. It is important not to overstate this claim. Cognitivists do not argue that grammatical properties are invariably explicable in terms of underlying cognitive or pragmatic factors—that is, that grammar is wholly determined by such factors. As has been noted, the fact that *vegetable* is a count noun whereas *fruit* is normally used as a mass noun is an arbitrary fact **to some extent**. Given that both terms involve a generalisation across a somewhat disparate set of phenomena, the option is available for the concept to be treated either as a collection of individuated entities or as a mass. This does not mean, however, that the grammatical count/mass distinction is entirely arbitrary. The crucial concept that allows a degree of arbitrariness to be reconciled with the notion of motivation is construal. Since this concept specifically allows for alternative ways of conceptualising a situation, it allows for phenomena that are perceptually similar to be treated either as grammatically similar or as grammatically different.

Certainly we sacrifice here some of the determinacy that linguists have often hankered after in their search for linguistic generalisations, but given the fact that language is a social phenomenon subject to the constraints of convention and cultural variability, total determinacy may prove to be an unrealistic goal in linguistic description and theory. In the next chapter we pursue this theme with respect to certain grammatical characteristics of verbs, taking up the count/mass distinction in a more abstract form.

Exercises

1 Which of the following words can be used either as a count noun or as a mass noun? For those that can be used in either way, say under what circumstances they would be used in one way or the other.

   beauty, drama, grass, onion, paper, red, theatre

2 Why is *garlic* a mass noun, whereas *olive* and *radish* are count nouns, even though a clove of garlic is sometimes as big as an olive or a radish?

3 Why is it possible to say *The house was pervaded by the smell of cat*, when *cat* is normally used as a count noun?

4 Construct pairs of sentences and corresponding contexts with the following nouns used as (a) count nouns and (b) mass nouns.

   bread, beer, coal, dog, oil, room, sausage, space, spider

5 The nouns *socks* and *trousers* both occur quite naturally in construction with the expression *a pair of* (*a pair of socks, a pair of trousers*). However, they differ in that *sock* has both a singular and a plural form, whereas *trousers* has only a plural form. Why? Construct two list of nouns that naturally occur in the construction *a pair of* X, such that one set behaves like *sock*, the other like *trousers*.

6 Although individual seeds are usually not much bigger than grains of sand or particles of rice, *seed* is used as a count noun (*I have four seeds in my hand*) whereas *sand* and *rice* are not (**I have four sands/rices in my hand*). Is there any reason for this? Why do you think *hair* can be used as a count noun, even though individual hairs rarely impinge on our attention?

7 In Polish the words for 'garden fork', 'rake', 'musical organ', 'mouth organ' are plural. This is also true of the word for 'violin', but the word for 'cello' is a normal count noun with both a singular and a plural form. What might be the reason for this?

8 Consider the sentences *We trapped a bear in the woods* and *We went bear-trapping in the woods*. In the first sentence the word *bear* is a

prototypical count noun but in the second it is not in that (a) it occurs without a determiner and (b) it cannot take a plural inflection (*Bears-trapping*). In the first sentence *bear* is also prototypical semantically in that it refers to a specific, individual member of the class of bears. In what way is *bear* in the second sentence semantically non-prototypical?

9 The contrasts referred to in the previous question also apply to the verb *trap*. In what sense is *trapped* in the first sentence prototypical in both syntactic and semantic terms, whereas *trapping* in the second sentence is not?

Further reading

Langacker, R. W. 1987, *Foundations of Cognitive Grammar*, vol. 1, *Theoretical, Prerequisites*, chapter 1: 'Nouns', Stanford University Press, Stanford.
——1990, *Concept, Image and Symbol*, chapter 3: 'Nouns and verbs', Mouton, Berlin, pp. 60–100.
Pelletier, F. J. (ed.) 1979, *Mass Terms: Some Philosophical Problems*, D. Reidel, Dordrecht.
Wierzbicka, A. 1985, 'Oats and wheat: the fallacy of arbitrariness', in J. Haiman (ed.), *Iconicity in Syntax*, John Benjamins, Amsterdam, pp. 311–42.

Notes

1   Even onomatopoeic words are not straightforward imitations of the sounds they refer to in that they conform to the phonological patterns of the language.
2   The claim that there are no singular forms *scissor* and *trouser* is based on the fact that examples such as *This scissor is sharp*, *That trouser is small* are ungrammatical. There is in fact one context in which singular forms are found: noun compounds such as *a scissor movement, a trouser press.*
3   Nouns such as *slime* and *mud* can have count uses with the meanings 'type of slime', 'type of mud'.
4   On the other hand, pebbles have a more individuated character than particles of gravel.
5   Similarly the expression *the snows of yesteryear* is motivated by the fact that different snowfalls are involved.

9

PERFECTIVE AND IMPERFECTIVE USES OF VERBS

9.1 Introduction

An important insight of recent work in Cognitive Linguistics is that the semantic basis for the distinction between count and mass uses of nouns discussed in the previous chapter also applies (at a more abstract level) to verbs (Langacker 1987: 258–62, 1990: 87). And just as the semantic distinction explains many aspects of the grammatical behaviour of nouns, so the same distinction explains many aspects of the grammatical and semantic behaviour of verbs.

Consider the contrast between the types of situation described by the following sentences.

(1) *John kicked the horse.*

(2) *John liked the horse.*

The event designated by (1) is similar in certain ways to the kind of entities typically referred to by count nouns—physical objects. Just as a physical object has clearly defined boundaries in space, so the event of kicking a horse has well-defined boundaries in time. The process can be said to have a beginning (the moment at which John begins to move his leg) and an end (the moment at which the leg makes impact). This means that, just as physical objects can be placed next to each other in space, so events of this kind can be placed next to each other sequentially in time—that is, they can be chained together in a narrative, with one event finishing before another begins (*Max stopped the horse and John kicked it*). By contrast, situations such as the one described by (2) do not have clearly defined temporal boundaries.

Another property of the situation designated by (1) that it shares with physical objects is internal heterogeneity. The process begins with John balancing himself on one leg, then pulling the other leg back, and then propelling it forward to make contact with the horse. Thus the configuration changes from one moment to the next. This characteristic corresponds to the internal heterogeneity of most physical objects. Just as the process of kicking something is made up of a number of different configurations, so an object such as a bicycle is made up of a number of different components (frame, wheels, handlebars, pedals, and so on). One consequence of this is that a particular part of the process of kicking something is not equivalent to any other part in much the same way that the parts of a bicycle are different from one another.

The situation described by (2) differs from kicking a horse in all these respects. The process of John's liking the horse has neither a clear onset nor a clear termination. One consequence of this is that the past tense in (1) places the event entirely in the past, whereas in (2) it simply means that the situation obtained at the relevant past time, leaving open the possibility that it still obtains. (It is not contradictory to say *John liked the horse when he first bought it and for all I know he still does.*) Moreover, stative situations such as (2) are internally homogeneous in contrast with dynamic situations such as (1). In this respect they are like the phenomena referred to by mass nouns. Just as a handful of sand is much like any other handful of sand, so any temporal segment of the process of John's liking the horse is identical to (and therefore counts as equivalent to) any other temporal segment.

We will therefore distinguish between 'perfective' situations such as (1), involving an event that is bounded and internally heterogeneous, and 'imperfective' situations such as (2), involving a state of affairs that is unbounded and internally homogeneous. Up to a point this distinction can also be applied to verbs, since a verb such as *kick* is typically used perfectively, whereas a verb such as *know* is typically used imperfectively. However, just as many nouns can be used to refer either to count or to mass phenomena, so many verbs can be used to refer either to perfective or to imperfective situations. For example, the contrast between *The soldiers quickly surrounded the castle* and *A moat surrounded the castle* involves a contrast between a perfective situation (event) and an imperfective situation (state). Strictly speaking, then, the terms 'perfective' and 'imperfective' apply to particular uses of verbs rather than to verbs themselves. Nevertheless the terms 'perfective verb' and 'imperfective verb' will be used in the following discussion as a convenient shorthand, except in cases where there is a possibility of confusion.

There are a number of grammatical differences between perfective and imperfective verbs. One is that perfective verbs occur naturally with progressive aspect, whereas imperfective verbs do not.

(3)   *John was kicking the horse.*

(4)   ?*John was liking the horse.*

A second difference is that perfective verbs are not used in the simple present tense to refer to a currently ongoing event. For example, it would be odd to refer to an event that the speaker is currently observing by saying *Look, John kicks the horse!*, whereas it would be quite normal to refer to a currently observed state of affairs by saying *Look, John likes the horse!* These observations require explanation. We will deal with each of them in turn.

9.2 Progressive aspect

Consider the following contrasts.

(5)   *John was kicking the horse.*

(6)   *John was building a canoe.*

(7)   **John was liking the horse.*

(8)   **Harry was resembling his father.*

The reason why the verbs *kick* and *build* naturally occur in the progressive form, whereas *like* and *resemble* do not, can best be explained by a photographic analogy. A single still photograph cannot track a perfective situation as it evolves through time. Although one can photograph 'John was kicking the horse' or 'John was building a canoe', one cannot photograph 'John kicked the horse' or 'John built a canoe'; these temporally extended events can only be captured by series of photographs or by a film.

There is in fact a paradox here. If one cannot capture 'John kicked the horse' in a photograph, how can we say that a particular image is a photograph of 'John was kicking the horse'. In other words, how can we extrapolate from a frozen moment in time to the event as a whole, given that the event is internally heterogeneous? In one sense, we cannot. The fact that the photograph shows John balanced on one leg, with the other pulled back and the horse in front of him, does not necessarily mean that he is in the process of kicking it. He may be dancing near it or tripping over it or jumping around next to it. In another sense, though, we do (and indeed must) make such an extrapolation. The only way in which we can make sense of such an image is to 'see' it as part of a larger holistic (bounded) event.

What this means is that progressive aspect involves two distinct conceptual levels: the subpart of the event that is in focus at a particular reference point, and the event as a whole. Just as we see a photograph as both a moment frozen in time as well as part of a larger bounded event, so in interpreting a progressive form such as *John was kicking the horse* we focus on a particular moment but also construe it as part of a larger whole. This freezing function of the progressive explains why it typically co-occurs with expressions that refer to a particular moment in time such as *at eight o'clock, when I walked in* (*At eight o'clock I was working in the library*, *When I walked in, Mary was smoking a cigarette*, and so on), even though the temporal period occupied by the event as a whole ('work in the library', 'smoke a cigarette') does not coincide with the reference point.

This also explains why the progressive normally does not co-occur with imperfective verbs. Since the progressive requires that the event be conceptualised not only as a moment in time but also (at a higher level) as an individuated, bounded situation, it is normally incompatible with an imperfective situation, given that this is inherently unbounded.

There are some cases where a progressive does indeed occur on an imperfective verb, and the special reading produced by such a combination provides support for the analysis given above. Consider the following contrasts.

(9) (a) *A statue of Chomsky stands in Great Court.*

    (b) *A statue of Chomsky is standing in Great Court.*

(10) (a) *This machine lacks a control lever.*

    (b) *This machine is lacking a control lever.*

(11) (a) *This road winds through the mountains.*

    (b) *This road is winding through the mountains.*

In each of the (b) cases the progressive conveys a suggestion of temporariness. For example, (9a) represents a state of affairs that is permanent (for all practical purposes), whereas (9b) implies that the statue has only recently been placed there and may not be staying. Similarly, (10a) would normally be taken to be a comment on the machine's design, whereas in (10b) there is a strong suggestion that the situation is temporary—that the machine ought to have a control lever. And whereas I would say (11a) if I were looking at a map, I would tend to say (11b) while I was in the process of driving along the road (while the situation was in flux). The reasons why these examples support the above analysis is that this suggestion of temporariness clearly derives from the fact that the progressive imposes a temporally bounded interpretation on the relevant situation.

The suggestion of temporariness can even be imposed on sentences referring to habitual events. Consider:

(12) (a) *Thelma dyes her hair these days.*

    (b) *Thelma is dyeing her hair these days.*

Both of these have a habitual reading, but (12b) suggests that this is either a recent development or one that is unlikely to last. The habitual reading in this case is imposed by the adjunct *these days*, but the normally stative-like reading associated with habituality is coloured by the fact that the progressive imposes a bounded reading on the situation construed in its entirety.

9.3 Simple present tense on perfective verbs

We turn now to another feature of the behaviour of perfective and imperfective verbs that is normally deemed to be grammatical but that can be explained with reference to meaning.

It is a peculiarity of English that a simple present tense form cannot normally be used to refer to an ongoing action in present time. In French, for example, one says *Marie rit* to mean 'Mary is laughing'; in German one says *Maria lacht*. But in English one does not say *Mary laughs* to express this meaning, nor does one say *She sleeps, She runs, She cries*, to mean 'She's sleeping', 'She's running', 'She's crying'. This constraint applies only to perfective verbs. There is nothing strange about such forms as *She knows the answer, She likes ice-cream* to refer to present states of affairs. How, then, does the meaning of the present tense in English differ from the meaning of the corresponding form in other languages, such as French and German?

The answer to this question can be derived from a number of exceptions to the above observation—that is, from examples where the present-tense form is used on a perfective verb to denote a currently ongoing action. I will argue (following Langacker 1990: 90) that the function of the present tense with perfective verbs in English is to impose a holistic (perfective) construal on the action, such that the time period occupied by the action (from start to finish) is conceived as coinciding with the period occupied by the utterance, within a small margin of tolerance. So, the reason why we cannot say *Look there, John kicks the horse!* is that the time period occupied by the event does not coincide with the time taken to produce the utterance. Evidence for this claim comes from a number of special cases involving demonstrations, commentaries, present-tense narratives, and performatives.

One situation where the simple present-tense form of an action verb is used to refer to an ongoing situation is in 'demonstrations'. For example, television cooks typically say such things as *I pour the milk into the mixture* just as they carry out the action. A striking feature of these utterances is that the speaker is in a position to control the timing of the action so that it coincides closely with the timing of the utterance. The utterance starts more or less as the action to which it refers starts, and finishes as the action finishes.

A second piece of evidence comes from sports commentaries. In radio and television commentaries, we often hear such utterances as *Smith gets the ball, Smith passes to Jones, Jones shoots*, referring to ongoing events in the game. These are also cases where the beginning and end of the relevant events coincide closely with the beginning and end of the utterances that describe them.

The analysis also provides an explanation for the narrative present use (*So this guy comes up to me and he says …*) In most cases the temporal period occupied by the kind of event reported in an oral narrative is significantly longer than the utterance that describes it. But in a narrative, the event does not take place in the context in which the utterance is produced. Instead, each event in the sequence is conceptualised by both speaker and hearer as the narrative unfolds and there is no reason why the period of conceptualisation cannot coincide with the timing of the utterance. In fact, it is required to do so, since otherwise the hearer would be unable to follow the story. Moreover, the fact that the present tense ties the timing of the action sequence directly to the timing of the utterance sequence provides an explanation for the 'immediacy effect' that has often been noted as a property of this particular usage. To reinvoke the photographic analogy, it is as if one were watching a speeded-up film, in which the events happen in synchronicity with the narrative.[1]

Performative utterances such as *I apologise, I sentence you to death, I pronounce you man and wife* constitute another class of sentences containing a perfective verb inflected with a simple present tense. They provide particularly strong evidence for the claim that the simple present tense construes the timing of the event as congruent with the timing of the utterance, since in these cases there is total congruity between the utterance and the relevant action. The point about performatives is that they are in fact actions. To say *I apologise* is to perform the act of apology, so that the beginning and end of the action coincide precisely with the beginning and end of the utterance. Similarly to say *I sentence you to death* is to perform the act of sentencing.

9.4 Simple present tense on imperfective verbs

The claim that the simple present tense imposes a constraint on the relevant situation, such that there must be congruence between the temporal duration of the relevant situation and that of the utterance, seems at first sight to be inconsistent with the fact that this form occurs quite naturally on imperfective verbs. In the case of an utterance such as *John lives in London*, for example, it is clearly not the case that the temporal duration of the situation coincides with that of the utterance. In order to explain this observation, we need to adopt the view that the conceptualisation of a situation involves a process of scanning and sampling, a view that was implied by the above discussion of progressive aspect. In claiming that the progressive 'freezes' an ongoing action at a particular moment in time, we are in effect suggesting that hearers sample a particular segment of the evolving situation as they perform an overall mental scan.

The same claim can now be applied to examples such as *John lives in London*. The occurrence of the simple present-tense form causes the hearer to sample a segment of the situation of John's living in London that is temporally congruent with the duration of the utterance. But, as has been noted, the crucial difference between imperfective and perfective situations (or more generally between mass and count phenomena) is that any segment of an imperfective situation is equivalent to any other segment because of its internal homogeneity. In this sense a segment of an imperfective situation can be deemed to 'stand for' the situation as a whole, in much the same way that a handful of sand and the beach of which it forms a part both count unproblematically as 'sand'.

This observation connects with the fact that, although the simple present-tense form does not normally occur on perfective verbs in reference to current ongoing actions (with the exceptions noted above), it does occur on such verbs in reference to habitual actions that began in the past and are expected to continue into the future. For example, a sentence such as *John goes to work by bus* forces a habitual reading (whereas the sentence *John went to work by bus* can refer either to a single event in the past or to a series).[2]

The reason why a simple present tense forces this reading should now be clear. A series of events is, in effect, an imperfective situation. Unlike a single event of John's going to work by bus, a series of such events is unbounded in time (it has no clear beginning or end) and is internally homogeneous, since the individual events of which it is constituted are identical to each other. In other words, a simple present tense normally forces a habitual reading on a perfective verb because only in this way is the meaning of the present tense (in English) compatible with such a verb. The only way that congruence can be achieved between the temporal duration of the event and the time taken to produce the utterance is by treating the relevant portion of the event as equivalent to the whole. Since this is a characteristic of imperfective situations and since habitual situations are imperfective, the habitual reading imposes itself.

There are one or two other imperfective uses of perfective verbs that fit with this point. One such use involves sentences expressing so-called 'timeless truths' such as *Oil floats on water* or *The sun rises in the east*. These examples are similar to those discussed in the previous paragraph, in that they could be said to refer not to a single perfective event occurring at a specific moment in time but to an imperfective situation that is temporally unbounded and internally homogeneous.

A second case involves examples such as *Smith meets Jones in the Wimbledon final tomorrow*, which seems to refer to a punctive event in future time and therefore appears at first sight to be problematic for the analysis given above. The occurrence of a simple present-tense form in cases of this kind follows from the fact that the primary reference is not in fact to a future event but to a present plan or schedule to which that event belongs. In other words, the primary reference is to a current imperfective situation. If the nature of a future event is such that it cannot be part of such a plan or schedule, then the simple present cannot be used in this way (**Smith beats Jones in the Wimbledon Final tomorrow*).

9.5 Conclusion

The theoretical apparatus of Cognitive Linguistics makes it possible to provide an economical explanation for a wide range of apparently unrelated phenomena here, involving two basic features of grammar: tense and aspect. The notion of construal is once again crucial to the analysis. It would be impossible to account for these phenomena without invoking the claim that language does not reflect objective properties of situations but mediates conceptualisation. Of particular interest is the relationship between count phenomena and perfective situations on the one hand and that between mass phenomena and imperfective situations on the other. Concepts such as internal structure and bounding apply in strikingly similar ways to both, suggesting that 'count' and 'mass' are overarching phenomena deeply rooted in human cognition. These relationships are at the root of the construction of time as space that is pervasive in so many areas of English and other languages.

Exercises

1 Consider *I see a light on the mountain, I see a flash on the mountain, I see a flashing light on the mountain.* Which of these sentences is odd? Why?

2 For each of the sentences below say whether it has (a) only a perfective reading, (b) only an imperfective reading, or (c) both a perfective and an imperfective reading.

   (a)   *Sally went from Phoenix to Arizona.*

   (b)   *The road went from Phoenix to Arizona.*

   (c)   *The crowd divided into two groups.*

   (d)   *The artery divided into two main branches.*

3 Consider the following (edited) observations from Langacker (1982: 275).

   (a)   'The only way this trajector can occupy all the points on the trajectory is by occupying them successively through time; the specifications of the trajectory are not satisfied at any single point in time but only by summarising over a bounded time span.'

   (b)   'In these cases the subject is such that it can occupy all of the points on the path simultaneously; for any point in time … it describes a configuration constant through time and fully instantiated at every point in time.'

   To which of the examples in the previous question does comment (a) apply and to which does comment (b) apply?

4 Give example sentences illustrating (a) a perfective use, and (b) an imperfective use of each of the following verbs:

   stretch, lie, rise, have, look.

5 Consider:

(a) *He is stupid*

(b) *He is tall*

(c) *He is being stupid*

(d) **He is being tall.*

Why is (d) ill formed when (c) is well formed?

6 Normally, a perfective verb cannot occur in the simple present tense in English without producing a habitual reading. For example, *John catches the 8.15* cannot mean that he is catching the 8.15 at this moment; it can only mean that he catches it habitually. Why then can sentences such as *I name this ship 'Bounty', I bet you $5 he'll win, I advise you to stay away* have a non-habitual reading, even though the verbs in question are perfective?

7 Under what circumstances could *John catches the 8.15* have a non-habitual reading?

8 The text claims that the use of a progressive form with a stative verb tends to produce a temporary reading. Give some examples of your own to illustrate this point involving the verbs *enjoy, hope, like, live, remain, seem*.

Further reading

Ikegami, Y. 1993, 'Noun–verb homology and its typological implication', in R. A. Geiger & B. Rudzka-Ostyn (eds), *Conceptualizations in Mental Processing in Language*, Mouton, Berlin, pp. 801–14.

Jackendoff, R. 1992, 'Parts and boundaries', in B. Levin & S. Pinker (eds), *Lexical and Conceptual Semantics*, Blackwell, Oxford, pp. 9–45.

Langacker, R. W. 1982, 'Remarks on English aspect', in P. J. Hopper (ed.), *Tense-Aspect: Between Semantics and Pragmatics*, John Benjamins, Amsterdam, pp. 265–304.

——1987, *Foundations of Cognitive Grammar*, vol. 1, chapter 7: 'Processes', Stanford University Press, Stanford, pp. 244–74.

——1990, *Concept, Image and Symbol*, chapter 3: 'Nouns and verbs', Mouton, Berlin, pp. 60–100.

Mourelatos, A. P. D. 1981, 'Events, processes and states', in P. Tedeschi & A. Zaenen, *Syntax and Semantics: Tense and Aspect*, vol. 14, Academic Press, New York, pp. 191–212.

Notes

1 Langacker's (1990: 78) distinction between conceived time and processing time is relevant to this point.
2 There is a certain symmetry in this analysis of progressive aspect and the simple present-tense form in English. Just as progressive aspect produces a temporary (perfective) reading on a verb whose normal use is imperfective (for example, *A statue of Chomsky is standing in Great Court*), so the simple present-tense form produces a habitual (imperfective) reading on a verb that is normally used perfectively (*John goes to work by bus*).

10

CAUSATION AND AGENCY

10.1 Introduction

This chapter is concerned with the coding of causation, a topic that raises a number of issues central to Cognitive Linguistics: the nature of categories, the relationship between cognition and language, and the role of cultural norms in the construction of agency.

Causation plays a central role in everyday human experience. When we turn on the tap, we know that water will flow. We flick the light switch to put the light on, and turn a door handle to open the door. If one of these anticipated events fails to happen, we are momentarily baffled. But we do not assume that the laws of cause and effect have suddenly ceased to operate. If the light fails to come on, we assume that the globe has blown, or that there has been a power cut, or that the switch is faulty.

Because of the multiple causative factors involved in any situation, causation is particularly subject to the process of construal. Consider, for example, the following sequence of events.

- Bill's wife, Sue, tells him she intends to leave him.
- Bill is not concentrating on his driving on his way to work.
- Bill crashes into Fred's car.
- Fred gets out of his car and yells insults at Bill.
- Bill hits Fred.
- Fred has a heart attack.
- Fred dies.

Although one might report this scenario as *Bill killed Fred*, one could hardly report it as *Sue killed Fred*, even though Sue can be said to have instigated the chain of events. One would be even less likely to report it as *Fred killed himself*, although Fred played a causative role in the scenario too. In other words, the use of language often involves constructing some entity (typically, a person) as the primary causative factor in some situation. We will refer to this entity as the 'Causer'. In this sense language abstracts away from the details of the complex causative factors that may have produced a particular situation.

How does a speaker select a Causer? The above scenario suggests that a number of factors are involved. One is the directness of the relationship between the various components of the situation and the final result. It is Bill's assault on Fred that is the 'immediate cause' of Fred's death rather than Sue's conversation with Bill, so this makes Bill a much better candidate for the role of Causer than Sue. But there are constraints on the choice of 'immediate cause'. It is inconceivable that we would report the above incident as *Bill's fist killed Fred*, for example. The problem with this is that it suggests that Bill's fist functioned independently of Bill's mind and this runs counter to the fact that we normally hold people responsible for what their body parts do.

10.2 Causation in English

One of the first studies in modern linguistics that raised key issues involving causation was Fillmore (1968). In his groundbreaking study, Fillmore argued that there were certain universal conceptual categories in terms of which we perceive and understand the circumstances surrounding states and events. Examples of these categories (which he called 'cases') were as follows.

Agent	the typically animate perceived instigator of the action identified by the verb
Instrument	the inanimate force or object causally involved in the action or state identified by the verb
Dative	the animate being affected by the state or action identified by the verb
Locative	the location of the state or action identified by the verb.
Objective	the semantically most neutral case

The argument was that these concepts could be applied directly in the semantic analysis of sentences. Consider:

(1) *John opened the door.*
(2) *The key opened the door.*
(3) *Sue heard a noise.*
(4) *This room is hot.*
(5) *The ice melted.*

Fillmore argued that in (1) 'John' is an Agent, in (2) 'the key' is an Instrument, in (3) 'Sue' is a Dative, in (4) 'this room' is a Locative, and in (5) 'the ice' is an Objective. As well as promising some revealing insights into human cognition, this approach seemed to provide an elegant explanation for a number of linguistic facts. For example, Fillmore suggested that only those verbs that designate a process involving an Agent can occur in the imperative, which would explain the apparent ungrammaticality of *Hear a noise!*, assuming the subject of *hear* to be a Dative. The theory also explains neatly the apparent synonymy of *This room is hot* and *It's hot in this room*, given that the subject of the former and the prepositional phrase in the latter are both tokens of Locative. And it would explain why the set of noun phrases (NPs) that occur as the subject of intransitive verbs such as *melt* is identical to the set of NPs that occur as the object of their transitive counterparts (compare *The ice melted, John melted the ice*), if both positions are occupied by Objectives.

Fillmore's argument was based on an assumption characteristic of the linguistics of the time that situations can be characterised in terms of a certain set of objectively defined component features. This view is of course in direct opposition to the argument developed here that language is subjective in that it codes human conceptualisation and construal. Fillmore has in fact played a prominent part in the development of cognitive theory, partly as a result of the emergence of major problems with case grammar. (The following discussion is based on Nishimura (1993)).

One problem for the theory emerges from pairs such as the following.

(6) (a) *Bill broke the window with a stone.*

     (b) *A stone broke the window.*

(7) (a) *Bill killed Jane with poison.*

     (b) *Poison killed Jane.*

(8) (a) *John calculated the cost with a computer.*

     (b) *A computer calculated the cost.*

Given the definitions of the various cases, it is clear that the subject referent in each of the (a) examples here must be an Agent (since they are all animate) and that the subject referent in each of the (b) examples must be an Instrument (since they are all inanimate). But there is a difficulty with this analysis having to do with the fact that sentences such as (9), (10), and (11) are odd.

(9)   ?*A screwdriver opened the tin.*

(10) ?*An abacus calculated the cost.*

(11) ?*A stick attacked John.*

Since Instruments such as 'a stone', 'poison', and 'a computer' can fill the subject function in (6b), (7b), and (8b), there is no obvious reason why NPs such as *a screwdriver, an abacus*, and *a stick* should not have the same capability.

Furthermore, consider the following examples.

(12) *John was killed with poison.*

(13) *Poison killed John.*

Example (12) involves a process in which the participants are an unspecified Agent, a Dative (John), and an Instrument (poison). Now, if Instruments can function as subjects, then (13) ought to be synonymous with (12), since it too contains an Instrument (implying an unspecified Agent) and a Dative. But there is an important difference between (12) and (13) in that (13) could be used if John drank the poison accidentally, whereas (12) could not (Nishimura 1993). In fact (13) is much closer in meaning to (14)—which could also be used to describe an accidental death—than it is to (12).

(14) *John was killed by poison.*

However, (14) is problematic in the case grammar model. The semantically based definitions of the cases suggests that here too 'poison' should be analysed as an Instrument, but this would fail to account for the evident semantic contrast between (12) and (14).

The obvious solution to these problems is to analyse 'poison' as an Instrument in (12) but as an Agent in both (13) and (14). But this is not possible in the case grammar framework, given that the distinction between an Agent and an Instrument is based on the contrast between animates and inanimates. Moreover, we still have no explanation for the difference between the (b) examples in (6)–(8), which are natural, and examples (9)–(11), which are odd.

A further difficulty for case grammar has to do with sentences such as (15).

(15) *The car broke the window with its fender.*

As Fillmore himself noted, sentences of this kind pose a problem, since they apparently involve two Instruments—'the car' and 'its fender'. However, the theory allows only one instance of a particular case per clause (in order to exclude such examples as **I hit the roof with a stick with a whip*). In any event, the idea of one instrument using another is inconsistent with the idea that an instrument is an entity that is manipulated but is not itself a manipulator.

Fillmore (1968: 23) suggested that this problem could perhaps be solved by deriving (15) from the semantic structure for the sentence *My car's fender broke the window* by means of a transformation that he called 'Possessor Raising'. This transformation would apply to any subject NP containing a possessor phrase, raising an NP out of the possessor phrase into the subject position. In this case it would move the NP *the car* out of the possessor phrase *the car's* into the subject position, converting the remainder of the subject NP into a preposition phrase headed by *with*, positioned at the end of the clause, giving *The car broke the window with its fender* (figure 10.1).

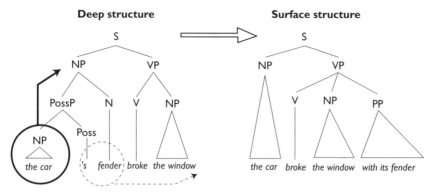

Figure10.1 *The car broke the window with its fender*
(raising analysis)

However, while Possessor-Raising seems to solve one problem, it gives rise to a new set of difficulties. For example, it claims that a sentence such as *Caruso broke the window with his voice* ought to be ambiguous. On one reading it would be a straightforward example of a sentence comprising an Agent ('Caruso'), a process ('break'), an Objective ('the window') and an Instrument ('his voice'), analogous to *John hit the ball with a stick*. On the other reading it would derive from the semantic structure for *Caruso's voice broke the window* via Possessor-Raising, with the NP *Caruso* promoted into the subject position from the possessor phrase *Caruso's* in the NP *Caruso's voice*. On this reading, Caruso would not be interpreted as an Agent. However, the claim that the sentence is ambiguous is at best problematic. Furthermore, in the case of a sentence such as *The book's cover inhibited sales*, the Possessor-Raising rule would generate the highly unnatural sentence *?The book inhibited sales with its cover*.

The cognitive approach provides a relatively straightforward solution to these problems, since it does not assume that situations in the real world are characterised by objectively defined properties. As was noted above, the causative factors leading to a particular state or event are usually complex. This means that there is often a certain amount of scope for competing construals. In a situation where John threw a stone that broke a window, we have a choice between construing the event in any of the following ways.

(16) *John broke the window.*

(17) *John broke the window with a stone.*

(18) *A stone broke the window.*

The choice between these depends on whether we wish to give prominence to John's role in the process or to that of the stone. (If we decide to foreground John's role, we have a further choice as to whether we wish to mention the stone at all.) The reason why this choice is available is that either John or the stone can be construed as the Causer. In one sense, the stone has a more immediate causative role than John, since it is the entity that makes physical contact with the window. But we know that the trajectories of objects such as stones are normally (though not always) the direct result of actions consciously performed by human beings, which places stone-throwers firmly in the immediate causative arena.

The cognitive approach claims that there is a significant contrast between the semantic role of the stone in *A stone broke the window* and its role in *John broke the window with a stone*. In this model, the subject of a verb denoting an action is consistently interpreted as the entity immediately and primarily responsible for the action (that is, as an Agent), whereas a preposition phrase headed by *with* identifies an entity that participates in the causative chain only under the control of another entity. This accounts for the semantic contrast between (12) (*John was killed with poison*) and (13) (*Poison killed John*).

The degree to which there is a choice of Causer is dependent on the pragmatics of the situation in question and our general understanding of causation. Consider, for example, the contrast between (8b) (*A computer calculated the cost*) and (10) (?*An abacus calculated the cost*). It is, of course, relatively easy to conceptualise the computer as an autonomous agent, since it carries out complex calculations using algorithmic processes invisible to its human operator. Once the appropriate key has been pressed, the operator sits back and waits till the computer obligingly presents the results of its internal, inscrutable operations. By contrast, an abacus does not operate independently in this way. At every step of the calculation the role of the operator is crucial and salient, so that it is not easily construable as primarily responsible for the relevant calculations.

Similarly, we find relatively subtle contrasts between examples such as (19) and (20).

(19) *This key opened that door.*

(20) ?*The key opened that door.*

Arguably, (19) is rather more natural than (20) because it draws attention to the properties of a particular key. In this case it is natural to see the relevant entity as having a primary causative role in the process, even though in objective terms it is a manipulated entity. The absence of this contrastive element in (20) makes it more difficult to envisage a context in which it might naturally be used (unless there is some suggestion that it was a key rather than some other instrument that was used to open the door).

Again we see in these examples the degree to which the naturalness or unnaturalness of a particular example is dependent on pragmatic factors and how relatively minor lexical or grammatical changes can affect acceptability. Observations of this kind are difficult to account for in a model that focuses on the formal properties of sentences in isolation from the situations to which they refer.

10.3 Causation in Japanese

Although all languages have ways of expressing causation, there are differences across languages with respect to the question of how far and in what ways linguistic markers associated with causation (such as the grammatical subject in English) can be used to refer to non-prototypical Causers. We will consider some differences between English and Japanese in this respect (again following Nishimura 1993).

In the previous section, I argued that the entity to which the subject of an action verb refers is interpreted as the immediate and primary Causer (Agent) in the chain leading to the event. Potential counterexamples to this claim in English are sentences such as *Sue broke her leg when she fell over, John sprained his ankle while playing soccer, John cut his finger while slicing the salami*, where it seems more appropriate to interpret the situation as one in which something happens to the subject referent rather than one that he or she caused. In other words, it seems that the subject referent should be interpreted as a Patient rather than as an Agent in such cases.

Nishimura (1993: 510) points out that there are a number of sentence types in Japanese that pose a similar problem. A particularly interesting pair are the following:

(21) *Hahaoya-wa   kotsujiko-de   kodomo-o   shinaseta.*
Mother-topic   traffic-accident by child-object   die-causative-past.
'The mother had her child die in a traffic accident.'

(22) *Hahaoya-wa   kodomo-ni   kaze-o   hikasete   shimatta.*
Mother-topic child-dative   cold-object   catch-causative perfect.
'The mother had her child catch cold.'

Each of these examples contains a causative verb, the subject of which is the word *hahaoya* ('mother'). But it seems odd to interpret the mother as a primary and immediate Causer in a situation where her child is killed in a traffic accident or catches a cold. It has been suggested by some linguists that in these sentences too the subject referent is a Patient (or Experiencer) rather than an Agent.

Nishimura argues that the subject referents are indeed Agents here, albeit non-prototypical ones. Part of the evidence for this claim is the fact that, whereas (21) is quite natural, (23) is not.

(23) *?Sono kodomo-wa   kotsujiko-de   hahaoya-o   shinaseta.*
The child-topic   accident-by   mother-object   die-causative-past.
'The child had his mother die in a (traffic) accident.'

If a Patient can function as the subject of the verb *shinaseta*, there is no reason why (23) should not be as natural as (21).

The obvious explanation for the contrast between (21) and (23) is that, whereas mothers are held to be responsible for looking after their children, children are not held to be responsible for their mothers. Therefore, if a child is killed in a traffic accident in circumstances where the mother was not exercising due care and attention, then she can be deemed to have had a role in the causative chain that led to the accident. Nishimura suggests that in Japanese ways of speaking (and thinking), this causative link between the mother's behaviour and the outcome is sufficiently direct for her to be construable as an Agent. For similar reasons, a sentence such as *Taro burned his school in a fire that broke out the other day* cannot be used to refer to an accidental event if Taro was a pupil, but it would be appropriate if he were the Principal and therefore bore some responsibility for the school. The fact that the corresponding English sentences are not natural ways of coding the relevant situations suggests that the notion of moral responsibility in Japanese carries greater weight in assessing the degree of directness of causation than is the case in English.

This observation brings us back to examples such as *Sue broke her leg when she fell over, John sprained his ankle playing soccer, John cut his finger while slicing the salami*. Nishimura's observations regarding the relevance of the notion of moral responsibility in examples such as (21) and (22) may have some bearing on these examples in English. Note, for example, that it would hardly be appropriate to use these structures in circumstances when someone other than the subject referent was clearly to blame (?*Sue broke her leg when Fred tortured her on the rack*, ?*John cut his finger when his wife stabbed it with a knife*). Even in a case such as *John broke his leg when his wife pushed him over*, there is a suggestion that his wife did not intend to cause the injury, so that she cannot be deemed to be entirely responsible. In other words, in *Sue broke her leg when she fell over*, Sue can be interpreted to be the immediate Causer of the event (and therefore an Agent) simply by virtue of the fact that she failed to exercise due care and attention. Thus, a general conclusion can be drawn to the effect that, although there are circumstances where conventions in the two languages differ, situations involving bodily injury are dealt with similarly in each. The notion of moral responsibility here is sufficiently strong in both cultures for non-prototypical Agents to be conventionally coded in agentive terms.

There may also be a connection here with another oddity of English usage. In some parts of the English-speaking world, speakers are sometimes heard to say such things as *Mrs Jones buried her husband last week* to refer to Mr Jones's funeral. The example seems odd, given that Mrs Jones can hardly be deemed to be a prototypical Agent in these circumstances. The explanation for the convention may again have to do with the notion of responsibility. Local cultural norms make Mrs Jones primarily responsible for arranging her husband's funeral, so that the event can be construed as one in which she (agentively) discharges that responsibility.

One important difference between Japanese and English is that, whereas examples such as *Poison killed John*, *Tetanus killed John*, *Excessive drinking killed John* are natural in English, they are not so in Japanese. In general, the concept of agency cannot be extended to include inanimate entities in Japanese as easily as it can in English.

Nishimura argues that the reason for this has to do with differences between the two languages with respect to foregrounding and backgrounding. The claim is that the processes expressed by agentive verbs are conceptually complex in that they contain both an action component and a result component. In cases of prototypical agency (for example, *Bill killed John*) both of these components are foregrounded, and there is no difference here between the two languages. However, in cases such as *Poison killed John*, the result component is foregrounded and the action component backgrounded. (Since poison is a non-prototypical Agent, it is not perceived as being 'active' in the sense in which an animate entity is.) Nishimura's claim is that the ill-formedness of sentences containing inanimate Agents in Japanese derives from the fact that the action component cannot be backgrounded in this way. On the other hand, Japanese—unlike English—can background the result component, so that it is possible to say in Japanese (but not in English) 'I burned it but it didn't burn' (Ikegami 1985).

There is a problem with one feature of this analysis—namely, the claim that Japanese does not allow downgrading of the action component. If this were so, we would not expect cases such as (21) and (22) to be natural (the same applies to the Japanese counterparts of examples such as *Sue broke her leg*), since in each of these cases, the action component is indeed backgrounded (in the sense that there is no intentional action). I therefore propose a slightly different characterisation of the similarities and differences between the two languages.

The prototypical agentive scenario involves a number of different semantic components, including intentional action, result, and moral responsibility. In Japanese, certain situations in which the action component is backgrounded but where the notion of responsibility remains salient can be assimilated to the Agent category. Extension from the prototypical scenario also applies when the result is backgrounded (as Nishimura argues) in cases such as *I burned it but it didn't burn*. Examples such as *Poison killed him* are unnatural in Japanese because of the absence of the notions of action **and** of moral responsibility.

In English, the significant factor in extension is the degree of directness of the causative connection to the result. Inanimate entities are construable as Agents, provided that they can be construed as having some degree of behavioural autonomy (*A computer calculated the cost*) or salient properties that are crucial to the process (*This key opens that door*). The notion of moral responsibility plays some part in extension from the prototype as it does in Japanese (*I cut my finger*) but this is more constrained than in Japanese. It certainly applies in cases involving bodily injury, but not to those cases such as the mother–child traffic accident scenario exemplified in (21).

10.4 Conclusion

The theory of case grammar developed by Fillmore in the late 1960s and early 1970s straddles the boundary between objectivist and cognitive approaches to language. It had an objectivist flavour in that it assumed (as did other linguistic theories of the time) that any given situation could be characterised in terms of a limited and autonomous set of components derived from intrinsic properties of participants in the situation (for example, animacy or inanimacy), which were mapped directly onto linguistic form. But it also had a cognitive dimension in that it postulated a universal set of cognitive categories that structure the way in which human beings perceive and interpret the world around them. Since these categories were thought to derive from properties of the human mind and to have direct reflexes in the grammars of specific languages, there was a sense in which Fillmore was already developing a theory based on the notion of a common basis for cognition and language.

There seems to be little doubt that the notions of agency and causation are indeed universals of human thought in something like the sense indicated by Fillmore. Such notions play a crucial role in all human languages, though the way in which they manifest themselves varies from one language to another. In English, one of the main reflexes of agentivity is the grammatical notion of subject; in other languages the notion is often marked inflectionally. But the fact that all languages mark the concept in one way or another is a strong argument for its universality.

One important respect in which our understanding of agency has progressed since the 1970s has to do with the notion that causation and agency are subject to prototypicality effects. The prototypical example of agency is a situation where a human actor intentionally performs an action that impinges on another entity, causing it to undergo a significant change of state, and there is a great deal of common ground in the way such prototypical situations are treated cross-linguistically. Where languages differ is in the way they deal with non-prototypical cases of agency—for example, situations involving an action that does not produce a change of state or one where a change is produced by an inanimate entity with only marginal human involvement. A language such as Japanese restricts the notion of agent to a narrower range of situations than English, though we have noted one or two cases to which Japanese extends the concept, whereas English does not.

The fact that agency manifests prototypicality effects also means that it is a frequent site of negotiation and contestation. Even as mundane an event as breaking a household object can be subject to different construals (*You've just smashed my best vase!*, *It just dropped out of my hands!*) involving different interpretations of agency and responsibility. This point also applies to large-scale social issues. For example, since the mid 1990s there has been an ongoing and unresolved debate in Australia concerning the question of whether the prime minister should apologise on behalf of the nation for the appalling colonial treatment of Aboriginal people. Underlying this issue are difficult questions concerning the identity of the Causers of past events, when these Causers involve problematic concepts such as 'the Australian government' and 'Australian society'. In the next two chapters we take up issues of this kind involving contrasting construals and competing notions of agency and responsibility at various levels of human interaction.

Exercises

1 A sentence such as *The suspect was questioned for four hours* is sometimes called a 'truncated' passive, since the agent of the action is not mentioned explicitly. In this respect it contrasts with a 'full' passive such as *The suspect was questioned by detectives for four hours*. There are many reasons for selecting a truncated passive construction rather than a full passive (or indeed an active construction) to code a particular event. What reasons might account for the selection of a truncated passive in each of the following?

(a) *Sue was arrested yesterday.*

(b) *Sue was mugged yesterday.*

(c) *Ten people were injured when police charged the demonstrators.*

(d) *James was knighted yesterday for services to industry.*

2 Can you think of any other types of construction in English that allow the agent of an action to be omitted?

3 If A says to B *Has the grass been cut this week?* what might A mean and why might A say it in this way?

4 Talmy (1988) has observed that there are many words and constructions in English that have to do with forces that entities exert on each other and on the environment. For example, *make* is associated with a situation in which a causative Agent (Agonist) exerts on a resistant entity (Antagonist) towards a particular action. On the other hand, *let* is associated with a situation in which a potentially powerful Agonist avoids imposing an obstacle on the inherent tendency towards an action on the part of an Antagonist. Using these concepts of Agonist, Antagonist, inherent tendency, and so on, describe the meaning of some of the following words and expressions.

> *agree to, bother to, bring oneself to, dare to, decline to, dissuade from, encourage to, fail to, finally* (as in *We finally opened the door*), *forbid, force oneself to, furthermore, get* (as in *He got the door open*), *get to* (as in *She got to go to the park*), *hinder, however, supposed to, keep* (as in *the ball kept rolling*), *let,*

manage, may, moreover, need, nevertheless, ought, preclude, push (as in *She pushed him into applying for promotion*), *refrain from, refuse, relent, reluctant, remain, require, resist, restrain, should, spare, stay, still, supposed to, threaten, urge to, wouldn't* (as in *The window wouldn't open*).

5   Taylor (1995: 206–7), following Lakoff (1977), and Hopper & Thompson (1980), suggests that the agent in a prototypical transitive construction is characterised by the following semantic properties.

- •   It is a highly individuated entity, distinct from the direct object referent (the Patient) and from the background environment.
- •   It is exclusively responsible for the event.
- •   It is the sentence topic—that is, it is what the sentence is about.
- •   It acts consciously and volitionally, and thus controls the event.
- •   It intends the action to affect the Patient.
- •   The Agent's action on the Patient is direct physical contact.
- •   The Agent and Patient stand in an adversative relationship.

For each of the sentences below, say whether the Agent is prototypical or non-prototypical. For each non-prototypical Agent, say which of the features in the above list does not apply.

(a)   *John washed himself.*

(b)   *The lightning destroyed the building.*

(c)   *Mary killed the spider.*

(d)   *Two thousand dollars will buy you a good used car.*

(e)   *It's trying to rain.*

(f)   *Hypocrisy annoys everyone.*

(g)   *Mary sprained her ankle.*

(h)   *I bought a new hat yesterday.*

(i)   *Mary helped John with the assignment.*

(j)   *John obeyed the instructions.*

(k)   *I've forgotten the address.*

6   Consider the following German sentences.

(a)   *Heidi schlug den Mann* ('Heidi hit the man').

(b)   *Heidi küsste den Mann* ('Heidi kissed the man').

(c)   *Heidi folgte dem Mann* ('Heidi followed the man').

(d)   *Heidi half dem Mann* ('Heidi helped the man').

In (a) and (b) the NP following the verb is in the accusative case (*den Mann*), whereas in (c) and (d) it is in the dative case (*dem Mann*). Can you suggest any explanation for this?

7 Consider the following Japanese sentences.

(a) *Taroo-ga*   *ziroo-o*   *ik-ase-ta.*

    Taro-NOM   Jiro-ACC   go-CAUS-PAST.

(b) *Taroo-ga*   *ziroo-ni*   *ik-ase-ta.*

    Taro-NOM   Jiro-DAT   go-CAUS-PAST.

Both sentences mean 'Taro caused Jiro to go', but there is a grammatical difference in that in (a) the direct object NP is marked with accusative case (*ziroo-o*), whereas in (b) it is marked with dative case (*ziroo-ni*). There is also a semantic contrast such that one sentence suggests that Jiro is willing to go, whereas the other does not carry this implication. Which meaning do you think is associated with which sentence and why?

8 How do ergative languages differ from nominative/accusative languages with respect to the notion of agency? (You may need to consult a dictionary of linguistics, such as Crystal 1997, for a definition of ergative languages.)

Further reading

Achard, M. 1993, 'Causative structures in French', *Proceedings of the Berkeley Linguistics Society* 19: 1–12.

Fillmore, C. J. 1977, 'The case for case reopened', in P. Cole & J. M. Sadock (eds), *Syntax and Semantics*, vol. 8, Academic Press, New York, pp. 59–81.

Hopper, P. J. & Thompson, S. A. 1980, 'Transitivity in grammar and discourse', *Language* 56: 251–99.

King, R. T. 1988, 'Spatial metaphor in German causative constructions', in B. Rudzka-Ostyn (ed.), *Topics in Cognitive Linguistics*, John Benjamins, Amsterdam, pp. 555–85.

Langacker, R. W. 1990, *Concept, Image and Symbol*, chapter 9: 'Transitivity, case and grammatical relations', Mouton, Berlin, pp. 209–60.

Nishimura, Y. 1993, 'Agentivity in cognitive grammar', in R. A. Geiger & B. Rudzka-Ostyn (eds), *Conceptualizations and Mental Processing in Language*, Mouton, Berlin, pp. 487–530.

Talmy, L. 1988, 'Force dynamics in language and thought', *Cognitive Science* 12: 49–100.

Turner, M. 1987, *Death is the Mother of Beauty*, chapter 4: 'Causation', University of Chicago Press, Chicago, pp. 139–83.

11

COGNITIVE LINGUISTICS AND DISCOURSE ANALYSIS

11.1 Introduction

We have observed in the previous chapters that Cognitive Linguistics assigns a crucial importance to the notion of construal in linguistic coding. The idea that everyday social talk involves an ongoing process of construal raises a number of questions for the analysis of discourse. It suggests, for example, that communication will be successful to the extent that participants succeed in aligning their construals—a process that may involve ongoing negotiation as the discourse unfolds. It also suggests that misunderstandings and arguments are likely to arise in situations where there are significant discrepancies in this regard. In other words, the process of construal should be a major focus of discourse analysis.

There has already been a considerable amount of work on some aspects of this issue. For example, researchers in the area of cross-cultural communication (Eades 1982; Gumperz 1982; Tannen 1982; Clyne 1994; Scollon & Wong Scollon 1995) have investigated the difficulties that can arise when participants in a given discursive interaction come from different cultural backgrounds with different assumptions and expectations about the communicative process. In the Critical Linguistics and Critical Discourse Analysis movements (Fowler & Kress 1979; Fairclough 1989, 1992a, 1992b, 2000; Chouliaraki & Fairclough 1999) a good deal of attention has been devoted to the relationship between language and perspective.

However, these research traditions have emerged from different theoretical backgrounds and have to a large extent worked independently of each other. Most studies in cross-cultural communication come from anthropology-based research traditions such as the ethnography of communication, whereas Critical Linguistics and Critical Discourse Analysis have emerged from theories of grammar, such as systemic functional grammar and generative grammar. With the advent of Cognitive Linguistics, we have for the first time a theory that is highly focused on grammatical theory but which also has the potential to provide a basis for a developing social theory of language.

I will use some data involving a family argument to illustrate this claim. The discussion focuses on some of the main constructs in Cognitive Linguistics: frames, radial categories, and profiling.

11.2 Frames

There is a difficulty associated with the application of the concept of 'frame' to discourse analysis that needs to be addressed at the outset. Most discussions of this concept in Cognitive Linguistics suggest that background knowledge relevant to a particular linguistic expression is shared by all members of the relevant speech community. Up to a point this is obviously true—if it were not so, mutual understanding would be impossible. However, since an individual's knowledge base is inevitably a function of his or her own personal experiences, it follows that there must be discrepancies across individuals with respect to at least some linguistic expressions.

Terms involving activities or areas of specialised knowledge are an obvious case in point. But the observation also applies to many everyday expressions. Consider, for example, the term *party* (in the sense of 'social gathering'). In one sense all native speakers of English know the meaning of the word *party*. Yet there are significant differences across individuals with respect to precisely how this term is understood—a young child has a different concept of 'party' from that of a teenager, and a teenager's interpretation of the term is often different from that of an adult (and there are no doubt differences across individuals within these groups.) The word *party* is one of the major triggers for an extended family argument to be discussed directly.

The data to be analysed here consist of material made available by the Australian Broadcasting Commission and the British Broadcasting Corporation in the form of a television series called *Sylvania Waters* (screened in both Australia and the UK). The series features a real Australian family, whom I will briefly describe below. The data for the series were collected over six months, during which time the family had given permission for the camera crew to appear at any time in the family home and film ongoing interactions between family members. The series of twelve programs was constructed out of extracts from these extensive periods of filming.

There are certainly some aspects of the series that make the data from it less than ideal for discourse analysis. The fact that the family members were aware that they were being filmed for a television series undoubtedly caused some element of 'acting' to enter into the behaviour of some of the participants from time to time, and for certain inhibitions to affect the behaviour of others. There are, however, some factors mitigating this problem. One has to do with the time over which the filming took place. A period of six months is long enough for participants to become accustomed to the presence of a camera in the home. Moreover, the interactional norms operating in groups where members know each other well often override the constraints of the recording situation (Blom & Gumperz 1986: 427; Labov 1972a: 188; Lee 1989: 56). In any event, as Milroy (1992: 66) points out, language is always observed within a social context of some kind, so that the notion of an unobserved, uncontaminated speech style is an idealisation.

Most of the data to be cited here are drawn from a protracted argument in which there are a number of 'channel cues' (Labov 1972b: 95) such as increased tempo, high volume, and marked pitch variation, which suggest that self-monitoring was at a minimum. Perhaps the crucial point is that the discourse was not in any sense scripted, so there are good reasons to suspect that the kind of frame conflicts and semantic shifts at work here also apply to conversational interactions generally and to argument in particular.

The central couple in the series are Noeline Baker (a New Zealander) and Laurie Donaher (an Australian). When the project started, they had known each other for thirteen years and, after living together for most of that time, were planning to get married. They had several children between them, but only one, Michael (Noeline's son by her first marriage and fifteen years old at the start of the series), lived with them at the time the series was made.

The following is a transcript of a dispute concerning the arrangements for Michael's sixteenth birthday party, to be held in their home. The argument starts with Michael's suggestion that he will have to get his older brother Paul to come over to keep out gatecrashers.

(1) **Michael** *I'm gonna have to get Paul to come over, too.*
   Noeline *Why?*
   Michael *So people don't crash the party.*
   Noeline *They won't crash the party, sweetheart, you can easily put them off.*
   Michael *Oh yeah yeah, maybe twenty years ago, Mum, you know. Today ... if ... there'd be easy another forty people if you didn't have a person at the gate.*
   Laurie *Bullshit.*
   Michael *Look, I don't want to be embarrassed, you know.*
   Noeline *But ... Don't you think it's a little bit dramatic saying you've gotta have a bouncer at a private person's party?*
   Michael *Okay ... Fine ... We'll leave the gate open. We'll leave the pontoon there, and you see you just see. You ... you think I'm so stupid. But if you ... you look around and open your eyes, you'll see. We'll wait till the night.*
   Noeline *I think we'll just have a nice orderly party, thank you. All right?*
   Michael *I'm just warning you, that's all. I'm just saying ... either ... either Laurie's at the gate or someone's gotta be there.*

Noeline	*Laurie can be at the gate then. (Pause) What's the password?*
	(Laughs)
Michael	(Looks down, picks at hairs on hand.) [14][1]

One difference here between Noeline and Laurie on the one hand and Michael on the other with respect to the word *party* has to do with whether a party is likely to attract gatecrashers. Clearly this has nothing to do with 'the meaning' of the word *party* in the narrow sense. One can predict with some confidence that no dictionary definition of the word *party* refers to gatecrashers. Nevertheless, gatecrashers do form a component of Michael's frame for this word, whereas this is not the case for Noeline and Laurie. This frame discrepancy is one of the major triggers for the ensuing argument and it has a number of consequences for the way in which the argument develops.

Interestingly, Michael's reference to gatecrashers does not change Noeline and Laurie's frames. Although he attempts to tell them that an event of this kind will inevitably attract gatecrashers, they refuse to accept this suggestion (which is why the argument continues). Their understanding of what a 'party' is (and what kind of events are typically associated with parties) seems to be strongly resistant to understandings based on the experiences of others. Frames are in some sense models of how the world ought to be rather than how it is (see Lakoff's (1987: 68–76) discussion of idealised cognitive models).

A further discrepancy between Noeline's and Laurie's frame for 'party' and that of Michael involves invitations to the event. The discrepancy shows up in the following extract.

(2)   **Noeline**   *Tell them not to bring friends.*
       Michael   *Oh, how'm I gonna do that?*
       Laurie   *Of course you are.*
       Noeline   *It's by invitation only.*   [91]

For Noeline and Laurie, invitations to parties are interpreted exclusively, whereas for Michael they are not. This gives rise to quite different expectations concerning how many people can be expected to turn up, which becomes the focus of much of the ensuing argument. Moreover, this frame misalignment produces a very specific misunderstanding here in that Laurie completely fails to process the *how* in Michael's question. In asking *How am I gonna do that?* Michael is signalling that asking people not to bring friends is not sanctioned by his frame. But since this is not part of Laurie's frame, he interprets Michael's question quite differently. The same misalignment shows up later in they way Michael responds to the following suggestion from Noeline.

(3)   **Noeline**   *But when they walk down the side and they're not meant to be*
                 here, can't you walk up and say, 'Listen mate you can't stay

> here'? Can't you do that? Isn't that what you normally do? If
> someone came to my front door to a party that weren't ...
> wasn't meant to be here, I'd go and say 'You can't come in'.
> Can't you do that?   [169]

This shows that Noeline's frame is more closely aligned to Laurie's than Michael's. Since invitations are (or should be) interpreted as exclusive, it is quite acceptable to ask people who weren't invited to leave. Michael's response to this suggestion is to shake his head in frustration.

One word that plays a crucial role in the argument is *bouncer*, used by Noeline in response to Michael's first suggestion that there should be someone at the gate. It is the use of this word that seems to give Noeline the idea that there is likely to be trouble at the party and much of the ensuing argument follows from this. Again, the concept of 'frame' explains this process. Noeline's choice of the word *bouncer* clearly creates in her mind images of violence, establishing a conceptual connection between the proposed party and rowdiness in nightclubs. This connection is so strong that it continues to feed into the subsequent development of the dispute. On several occasions Michael insistently and vehemently repeats that his suggestion is designed not to produce trouble but to avoid it (*All I said is that you got to have someone at the gate to stop people I don't want comin' in here coming in here ... That's all I said ... I never said anything about fights.* [151]). But for Noeline and Laurie the concept of 'bouncer' is so closely associated with violence that by the end of the argument they are constructing the situation in terms of Michael's having invited people who are likely to cause trouble (*If you're inviting these sort of people, I don't want them in my home*).

In some exchanges the frame conflict comes to the surface of consciousness for at least some of the participants. When Noeline says, *But we're not going to have fights* [149], echoing earlier remarks by Laurie (*We're certainly not going to start bloody having fights or bloody well trouble in this joint* [70]), Michael points out that the possibility of 'fights' was never part of his conceptualisation of the event.

(4) **Michael**   I said, I never said a fight. This is a figment of someone's
    imagination. Laurie's come up ... 'Oh yeah there's gonna be a
    brawl in my back yard'. All I said is that you got to have
    someone at the gate to stop people I don't want comin' in here
    coming in here. That's all I said. I never said anything about
    fights. [153]

Michael then explicitly identifies the issue as an intergenerational frame clash.

(5) **Noeline**   But when they walk down the side and they're not meant to be
    here, can't you walk up and say 'Listen mate you can't stay
    here'? Can't you do that? Isn't that what you normally do? If
    someone came to my front door to a party that weren't ...
    wasn't meant to be here, I'd go and say 'You can't come in'.
    Can't you do that?

Michael	(Pause, shakes head) *You guys are livin' in the past, I think.*
Laurie	*No we're not. No we're not.*
Noeline	*We're living in our home. We're living in our home.*
Laurie	*We're living in our time, right here and now.*
Noeline	*We're living in our home. We're living in our home, Michael.*
Laurie	*We're not living in the past.*
Michael	*Right, so we get out there and we do the twist and the bop and the shimmy shimmy and whatever, do we?*
Laurie	*Don't know what you do. Do whatever you like, within reason.*
Noeline	*Just get some common sense into the whole thing. Don't … don't talk in riddles or try to … y'know … wave it away as if it doesn't matter. It **does** matter.* [169]

The striking feature of this exchange is the complete failure of Laurie and Noeline to take up Michael's irony, either because they fail to recognise it or because they deliberately ignore it. For Michael, 'the twist and the bop and the shimmy shimmy' are clearly part of a frame for parties in the 1960s, contrasting sharply with his frame for parties in the 1990s. But for Noeline and Laurie this contrast seems much less salient, so that the irony simply passes them by. Michael is 'talking in riddles'—a move which is interpreted as an indicator of a lack of 'common sense', as an attempt to contemptuously dismiss the issue.

We see here just one small example in which frame discrepancies operating at various levels serve to produce the kind of misalignments on which many arguments feed.

11.3 Radial categories

11.3.1 Example: *leave*

The notion of radial category structure also has significant implications for discourse analysis. At one level this is an uncontroversial point. If a particular word is polysemous, then there is an obvious possibility that a speaker may intend the word in one sense and a hearer interpret it in another. A Cognitive Linguistics perspective on radiality has more subtle implications than this, however, since different uses of a word may involve different members of a radial category but not different meanings in the usual sense.

In illustration of this point consider an incident from E. M. Forster's novel *A Passage to India*. The novel is set in the time of the British occupation of India. Ronny is a British administrator whose fiancée, Adela, has recently arrived from England. Adela is anxious to see India and learn about the local culture. She has expressed interest in seeing a local school and a visit has been arranged by two Indians whom she has befriended, Dr Aziz and Professor Godbole.

When she arrives at the school with Aziz, Godbole, and Mrs Moore (Ronny's mother), Adela is met by Fielding, the headmaster. Mrs Moore accepts Fielding's offer to show them around but Adela decides to sit and rest in the courtyard, in the company of Aziz and Godbole. Suddenly, Ronny arrives and is shocked to find Adela smoking in the company of two Indians. When Fielding returns, Ronny quietly takes him to one side and admonishes him by remarking, 'I think, perhaps you oughtn't to have left Miss Quested alone' (Forster 1936: 75–6).

Quite apart from the issue of whether Adela was 'alone' when in the company of Aziz and Godbole, there is the interesting question of whether Fielding can be fairly accused of 'leaving' Adela. In one sense he clearly can. The group of people had been together in the courtyard when they were deciding what to do. At the end of the discussion, Fielding and Mrs Moore walked away to inspect the buildings. In this sense, it is undeniable that Fielding 'left' Adela. However, Fielding clearly feels that the accusation is unjust. Why should this be? In part it obviously has to do with what we normally refer to as the 'connotations' of the word *leave*, involving the notion of abandonment. Fielding wishes to reject the idea that Adela was abandoned. But the question is: does *leave* have a different meaning in an utterance where the speaker intends to convey the idea of abandonment (or when the hearer constructs such a meaning) from the meaning it has when no such meaning is intended? If one tried to adopt this position, one would have to argue that an utterance such as *John left Mary last week* (said of a situation where a married couple split up) is ambiguous. If Mary felt abandoned, *leave* would have one meaning; if she felt a sense of freedom, it would have the other. But such a claim is clearly problematic. What if she had mixed feelings? What if she felt abandoned on the day he left, but liberated the following day?

The point is that there is nothing unusual in a word being used to refer to many different situations and situation types. The word *eat* in *John is eating a biscuit* and *John is eating an orange* refers to two rather different processes. Nevertheless, the similarity between the two activities is such that few people would claim that the word *eat* has different meanings here. But the notion of similarity is a matter of degree, so the question is: at what point do two situations diverge sufficiently for two distinct meanings to be recognised? Does *ride* have different meanings in such examples as *ride a horse* and *ride a bicycle*? Does *read* have different meanings in *read a book*, *read a situation*, *read a film*? The fact that language use inevitably involves situational diversity means that radial categories are inherently fuzzy.

In the family argument cited above we see several indications of the way in which radial slippage of this kind plays a role in the interaction. We will look at three examples.

11.3.2 Example: *you*

Consider the following speech by Noeline.

(6) **Noeline** *But when they walk down the side and they're not meant to be here, can't you walk up and say, 'Listen mate you can't stay here'? Can't you do that? Isn't that what you normally do? If someone came to my front door to a party that weren't ... wasn't meant to be here, I'd go and say 'You can't come in'. Can't you do that?* [169]

The *you* of Noeline's *Isn't that what you normally do?* carries a potential ambiguity. On the most salient reading it is the indefinite *you*, pointing to the fact that in Noeline's view there is a set of regulated behaviours for private people's parties that 'you' (people in general) normally observe. On the other hand, the fact that this utterance immediately follows *Can't you do that?*, where *you* seems to refer to Michael, produces a potentially 'mystificatory' effect (Fowler & Kress 1979: 38), carrying the implication that it is perhaps Michael who 'normally does that' (conforms to her frame), so that his orientation on this occasion could be seen to be anomalous. In other words, Noeline appears to be (unconsciously) exploiting the potential ambiguity associated with *you* for specific rhetorical purposes.

The situation is complicated somewhat by the fact that the first *you* can have either reading. Although *Can't you do that?* is most obviously read as a question addressed to Michael, it can alternatively be read as meaning: 'When this situation arises, isn't one allowed to do that?' (ask gatecrashers to leave). As in other cases we have discussed in previous chapters, it is not a question of having to choose between these readings. On the contrary, the fact that they can both be in play explains how *you* can have both meanings and how slippage of this kind can happen below the level of participants' conscious awareness.

11.3.3 Example: *warn*

A further example of radial slippage occurs in the following exchange.

(7) **Noeline** (Banging photo album) *Right. We'll keep an orderly party for Saturday night ... All right?*
     Michael *I just warned you.*
     Noeline *I don't like the warning, I don't even like what I heard. So don't tell me any more.* [128]

In general, the word *warn* can be used to refer to two quite different types of situation, illustrated in (8) and (9).

(8) *I warn you that I'll sack you, if you do it again.*

(9) *I warn you that Mary will sack you, if you do it again.*

The common factor here is that the speaker predicts that something harmful to the addressee will happen if a certain condition is met. The difference is that in (8) the warning is a threat, since the relevant action is one that the speaker will carry out. In (9), the relevant action is outside the control of the speaker (let us assume). These are two very different uses of the word (so that we are certainly dealing with radiality in some sense), but there is some doubt as to whether it would be appropriate to regard these as different meanings, given the considerable degree of semantic overlap.

The above exchange between Noeline and Michael involves each of these elements. Michael's *I just warned you* involves the non-threat reading—the eventuality that he predicts is not under his control; in fact, his suggestion that there should be someone at the gate is specifically designed to forestall this eventuality. But the nature of Noeline's reply (*I don't like the warning, I don't even like what I heard so don't tell me any more*) suggests that she has chosen to interpret Michael's warning as a threat.

One further aspect of this exchange needs to be considered. There are two possible explanations for the nature of Noeline's reaction. The first is that it strengthens her rhetorical position. Since the current frame of talk is clearly argument, any move that constructs Michael's utterance as a threat can potentially weaken his rhetorical stance. On this reading Noeline is exploiting radiality for rhetorical ends.

Alternatively, it may be that Noeline is naturally led to construct this interpretation from the frame of talk in which they are operating—that is, Noeline may have been led to choose the threat element in the warning network as a result of the fact that they are involved in argument. In other words, the fact that the frame of talk in which they are engaged involves conflict may itself help to foreground meanings that are lurking in the semantic network—meanings that are associated with positional polarisation but that would tend to remain inactivated in some other frame of talk. In either case, there is again a strong connection between social factors concerning the type of talk within which the interaction is framed and cognitive factors involving the activation of elements in the relevant semantic network.

11.3.4 Example: *live*

As a final example of radial slippage, consider the verb *live* in the following exchange.

(10) **Michael**   *You guys are livin' in the past, I think.*
    Noeline   *We're living in our home.*
    Laurie   *We're living in our time, right here and now.*
    Noeline   *We're living in our home. We're living in our home, Michael.*
    Laurie   *We're not living in the past.*   [174]

There are clearly two rather distinct senses of *live* in play here. In Michael's expression *living in the past* and Laurie's *living in our time*, the word *live* is synonymous with *be alive*. Noeline, however, performs a transition to the sense of *live* as *dwell* with her utterance *We're living in our home*. In a cognitive framework these must be treated as different elements within the same radial network. There is in fact a generalisation to be made here in that the 'be alive' reading emerges from the collocation of *live* with temporal concepts ('living in the past', 'living in our time') and the locative reading from the collocation with spatial concepts ('living in our home').

Part of the explanation for the transition here seems to have to do once again with the way in which it achieves Noeline's rhetorical purposes. In particular, it constitutes an effective counter to Michael, since it shifts the issue from the problematic one of whether their frame for 'party' is or is not out of date to one where her claim cannot be challenged, since it expresses a proposition that is irrefutably true (*We're living in our home*). Moreover, in spite of the fact that Noeline's response does not address directly the issue raised by Michael, it appears to do so by virtue of the fact that it pivots on the same lexical item. Its relevance is also established by the fact that it is concerned with what has undoubtedly become the major theme of the argument by this stage—the possibility of damage to the home. In other words, Noeline exploits the potential for radial slippage in order to shift the focus of the disagreement from an issue that is problematic from her perspective to one that is not. The effectiveness of the move is based on the assumption that all participants are committed to avoiding damage to the home, while at the same time positioning Michael as one whose actions are likely to produce such damage. Ironically, from Michael's point of view, his proposal was clearly intended to avoid this, whereas their stance has every chance of producing it. But by this stage the frame misalignment and the complexity of the dynamics of the interaction, including the kind of radial slippage illustrated here, make the transition to a resolution impossible.

11.4 Conclusion

In traditional approaches, the argument between Michael and Noeline over the arrangements for the birthday party would have been interpreted as having nothing to do with the meaning of the word *party* as such. The assumption would have been that the word had the same meaning for both of them and that the disagreement was concerned with the pragmatic question of how this particular party was to be organised. On this view, the main function of language is simply to convey meanings from speaker to hearer, with meanings conceived as object-like entities associated with linguistic forms.

The alternative view adopted by cognitive linguists is to see words as causing language users to access specific areas of their 'knowledge base' (Moore & Carling 1982: 149–75) in such a way that certain linguistic forms may invoke clusters of meanings (frames) for one person that are quite different from those evoked for another—such framings being a function of the particular experience of the individual language user. It also suggests that radiality is not only a source of misunderstanding but is sometimes exploited (consciously or unconsciously) to achieve particular rhetorical ends.

In general, there are indications here that Cognitive Linguistics has the potential to offer a coherent and elaborated theory that can be applied not only to linguistic structures but also to the discursive dimension of language. This theme is pursued in the next chapter.

Exercises

1 'Australia was discovered by James Cook.' Is this statement true or false?

2 There is an obvious apparent contradiction in the sentence *He left me alone with Fred*. Why is this sentence not in fact contradictory?

3 Why has the word *spinster* more or less disappeared from current use?

4 The expressions *fathering a child* and *mothering a child* are often interpreted in quite different ways. Explain. How does this difference raise issues related to the concept of frame?

5 Below is a passage from William Golding's novel *The Inheritors*. The novel is set in neolithic times and is about a band of Neanderthalers who come into contact with a group of our own ancestors (*Homo sapiens*) and are eventually wiped out by them. The events of the novel are seen through the eyes of the Neanderthalers. In the incident reported in the passage below, one of the Neanderthalers, Lok, is shot at by a man with a bow and arrow (Golding 1961: 106).

> *A stick rose upright ... The stick began to grow shorter at both ends. Then it shot out to full length again. The dead tree by Lok's ear acquired a voice. 'Clop!' By his face there had grown a twig: a twig that smelt of other and of goose and of the bitter berries that Lok's stomach told him he must not eat.*

What features of this text are a reflex of the fact that Lok has no understanding of tools and tool-making?

6 Consider the passage below from a Sherlock Holmes story by Conan Doyle (Doyle 1928: 598). Holmes is talking to Dr Watson.

Finally, having drawn every other cover and picked up no scent, I tried my luck with the housekeeper. Mrs Lexington is her name, a little, dark, silent person, with suspicious and sidelong eyes. She could tell us something if she would—I am convinced of it. But she was as close as wax. Yes, she had let Mr McFarlane in at half-past nine. She wished her hand had withered before she had done so. She had gone to bed at half-past ten. Her room was at the other end of the house and she could hear nothing of what passed. Mr McFarlane had left his hat and, to the best of her belief, his stick in the hall. She had been awakened by the alarm of fire. Her poor, dear master had certainly been murdered. Had he any enemies? Well, every man had enemies, but Mr Oldacre kept himself very much to himself.

This text contains several different 'voices'. The main voice is that of Holmes talking to Watson, but from time to time we also hear the voice of Mrs Lexington talking to Holmes (and at one point, perhaps, also the voice of Holmes talking to Mrs Lexington). What kind of frame knowledge do readers bring to this text that enables them to interpret the text in this way? In other words, how do we know that certain parts of the text are the voice of Mrs Lexington rather than that of Holmes? And what changes have been made to the original voice in order to incorporate it into the narrative?

7 Below is the opening sentence of Jane Austen's novel *Emma*.

Emma Woodhouse, handsome, clever, and rich, with a comfortable home and happy disposition, seemed to unite some of the best blessings of existence; and had lived nearly twenty-one years in the world with very little to distress or vex her.

Which word here indicates that some of these judgments concerning Emma might be those of an observer other than the narrator? What is the effect of the construction of such an observer?

Further reading

Dressler, W. U. 1992, 'Between grammar and discourse', in M. Pütz (ed.), *Thirty Years of Linguistic Evolution*, John Benjamins, Amsterdam, pp. 149–99.

Lee, D. A. 1997, 'Frame conflicts and competing construals in family argument', *Journal of Pragmatics* 27: 339–60.

Rubba, J. 1996, 'Alternate grounds in the interpretation of deictic expressions', in G. Fauconnier & E. Sweetser (eds), *Spaces, Worlds and Grammar*, University of Chicago Press, Chicago, pp. 227–61.

Sanders, J. & Redeker G. 1996, 'Perspective and the representation of speech and thought in narrative discourse', in G. Fauconnier & E. Sweetser (eds), *Spaces, Worlds and Grammar*, University of Chicago Press, Chicago, pp. 290–317.

Tsuyoshi, O. & Thompson S. A. 1996, 'The dynamic nature of conceptual structure building: evidence from conversation', in A. E. Goldberg (ed.), *Conceptual Structure and Language*, CSLI Publications, Stanford, pp. 391–9.

Note

1   Numbers in square brackets refer to the line number in the transcript where the extract begins (see Appendix). Transcriptions have been somewhat simplified; in particular, for ease of reading overlap has not been marked.

12

CONSTRUCTIVIST PROCESSES IN DISCOURSE

12.1 Introduction

Having attempted in the previous chapter to investigate the application of concepts such as frame and radiality to discourse analysis, we focus here on the relationship between the notion of construal and that of 'constructivism', as it has emerged from approaches to discourse analysis such as Critical Linguistics (Fowler & Kress 1979), Critical Discourse Analysis (Fairclough 1989, 1992a, 1992b, 2000; Chouliaraki & Fairclough 1999), Conversation Analysis (Heritage 1984a), and Discursive Psychology (Edwards 1997). The discussion explores further the potential of Cognitive Linguistics for discourse analysis.

12.2 Constructivism

The notion of 'constructivism' is taken principally from Conversation Analysis. The central idea of Conversation Analysis is that everyday conversation is the primary medium through which we enact our culture and that the turn-by-turn nature of conversational interaction involves the ongoing construction of social reality. Conversational participants respond in creative yet highly structured ways to the continuously evolving context of the interaction. Since the key point about constructivism is that speakers of a language are not working with objective, ready-made social categories and meanings that are simply mapped onto language, there is an obvious connection with the notion of construal in Cognitive Linguistics.

One important aspect of constructivism is category assignment. As was noted in earlier chapters, language is first and foremost an instrument of categorisation: even the most commonplace utterances involve categorisation. In many cases the process is unproblematic, since there is a wide measure of agreement across speakers with respect to the way phenomena and situations are to be assigned to categories in their language. However, there are also many situations where alternative schemas of categorisation are available. For example, even as mundane an activity as 'watching television' could be alternatively categorised as 'resting', 'relaxing', 'catching up with the news', 'wasting (your) time', 'avoiding mowing the lawn', and so on.

In some cases, competing categorisations derive from differences between the knowledge bases and perspectives of participants. For example, consider once again the incident in *A Passage to India* discussed in the previous chapter. When Ronny says, *I think perhaps you oughtn't to have left Miss Quested alone*, he is constructing (or construing) the event in question as a member of the category of 'leaving'. In so doing, he constructs Fielding as an Agent (that is, as the person who bears full responsibility for creating the situation) and Adela as a Patient or victim (as someone who is 'left'). For Fielding, however, this fails to take into account the fact that Adela was actively involved in producing the situation.

One reason for this discrepancy between Ronny's and Fielding's perspective has to do with the fact that Fielding knows more than Ronny does about exactly how the situation came about. But there are also other differences in play. Only Ronny sees Adela as being 'alone' when in the company of Aziz and Godbole. And whereas Ronny feels that Fielding should have made sure that this did not happen—whatever Adela might have said or wished—Fielding clearly feels that he is not responsible for her in that sense. There are quite different assumptions here about local cultural conventions, including the respective roles of men and women. In other words, there are specific differences involving the local situation and general differences of orientation (perspective) at work, all of which underlie Ronny's coding of the situation. Lurking behind this is the more general system of social categorisation that obtained in British India. In all of this we see some of the intricacies in the relationship between frames and category construction.

12.3 Prototype theory and constructivism

Another reason why category construction is sometimes problematic has to do with the nature of categories themselves—specifically, the fact that categories have peripheral as well as central members. It is well known that people sometimes disagree about colours, for example, particularly with respect to differences such as those between blue and green, red and orange, or red and pink (not to mention brown and beige, purple and lilac, and so on). This is partly because the colour spectrum is a continuum. Since there is no sharp boundary between the blue range and the green range, there are certain hues that people find difficult to assign to one or the other category because they are at the periphery. On the other hand, people generally agree that the sky is blue, that blood is red, and that grass is green, because these hues are prototypical members of the relevant category (see Taylor 1995: 1–20 for a discussion of colour categories).

Another example of this point involves different ways of referring to the European colonisation of Australia. In traditional Australian discourses, this process is referred to as 'European settlement', but many Australians now refer to it as the 'European invasion'. One of the reasons why these two terms are in competition is that the event in question is arguably a prototypical member of neither the 'settlement' category nor the 'invasion' category. It is not a central member of the 'settlement' category because the concept 'settle' (defined by the *Concise Oxford Dictionary* as 'becoming established in more or less permanent abode or place or way of life') carries no hint of the military conflict, mass killings, and dispossession of territory that characterised the occupation of Australia. And some people might argue that it is not a central member of the 'invasion' category either, because it did not take the form of an all-out military attack on a nation state (in the Western sense of that term).

The ideological implications of the discursive competition between the terms *settlement* and *invasion* and the relevance of the prototype theory of categorisation to its rhetorical dimensions are nicely illustrated by a passage in the book *A Land Half-Won* by the Australian historian Geoffrey Blainey. At one point in his discussion, Blainey observes that in the course of Aboriginal history there were no doubt occasions on which groups of Aboriginal people were driven by drought and other circumstances to expand into the territories of other Aboriginal groups, and he refers to such incidents as 'black invasions' (Blainey 1980: 88–9).[1] The use of the expression *black invasions* here is a constructive move, creating a conceptual link between Aboriginal incursions, the European colonisation of Australia, and 'invasions' in general. It operates through 'nomination'—that is, the link is constructed simply by naming Aboriginal incursions 'black invasions'. The rhetorical intention, of course, is to undermine the moral censure implied by the use of the term *European invasion*.

Again, there are several layers of categorisation here. Underlying the question of how the various events are to be named is the issue of how the participants are to be categorised. *European invasion* sets up a category of invaders (Europeans) and a category of those who were invaded (Aboriginal people); *black invasions* challenges this dichotomy by assimilating Aboriginal people into the category of 'invaders' as well as those who were invaded.

Of particular relevance to category theory in Cognitive Linguistics is the fact that the rhetorical dimension of constructivist categorisation involves an interesting paradox. The whole point of referring to the European colonisation of Australia (or an Aboriginal incursion into a neighbour's territory) as an *invasion* is to invoke the kind of moral judgments that are normally applied to prototypical invasions (such as the German invasion of Poland in 1939). Thus newly assimilated members of the category seem to assume immediately a fully fledged status in the sense that the aim of the speaker is to cause readers to react to them as they would to prototypical members. In this respect it is as if the Objectivist theory of categories applied, such that all members of a category have equal status by virtue of possessing the set of necessary and sufficient conditions that define the category.

Yet Objectivist theory cannot explain another important dimension of the rhetorical dimension of categorisation: the fact that categories are open-ended. That is, it cannot explain the creative nature of the move made by the first user of the term *European invasion* (nor, for that matter, the creativity that Blainey displays with his term *black invasions*) in recategorising an existing phenomenon. If category membership were determined by a specific set of necessary and sufficient conditions, then categorisation could not be used as a constructive process. Nor would it have the required rhetorical effect. In order to explain the presence in one category of such disparate phenomena as the German invasion of Poland, the European colonisation of Australia, and Aboriginal incursions (not to mention such phenomena as tourist invasions, invasions of privacy, and so on), we would need to assume a very sparse set of defining features, mainly involving movement into a new territory. None of these phenomena would have any special status in the category and there would therefore be no rhetorical effects of the kind noted above in relation to such terms as *European invasion* and *black invasions.*

Prototype theory provides an elegant resolution of this paradox. It accounts for the rhetorical power of categorisation by assuming that prototypical members of a category have particular salience, so that the judgments that are typically applied to them percolate to all members of the category, including newly assimilated ones. On the other hand, it accounts for the open-ended, constructive nature of the process by assuming that motivation need only be partial. In other words, phenomena can be assimilated to a category on the basis of some perceived similarity to an existing member (core or peripheral), without assuming a specific set of necessary and sufficient conditions shared by all.

12.4 Constructive categorisation
in conversation

Let me now attempt to show that constructivist moves of the kind illustrated above occur not only in written texts but also in spoken texts. The following conversational extract is taken from an informal interview conducted by Margaret Wetherell in New Zealand in the course of a research project (Wetherell & Potter 1992). The two participants are discussing the European colonisation of New Zealand.

(1) **FR**   *And the Maori like to forget that they came and ... ate the Moriori.*
     I   *Yeah.*
     FR   *They ... they put that into the back of their minds. They seem ...*

I	*Yeah.*
FR	*... to think that they were the first here.*
I	*Yes.*
FR	*But really ... I wonder if perhaps when we came here we should have done what any other ... uhm invading country would do and that's wipe out ...*
I	*Yes.*
FR	*... the lot!*
I	*Yes.*
FR	*Which is what they did.[2]*

Like the Blainey example, this text constructs a connection between (alleged) events in Aboriginal history and the arrival of the Europeans. In both cases the motivation for this move is clear—it subverts interpretations of the colonial invasion as a unique historical event, to which special moral censure can be applied.

There are certain features that distinguish this extract from the Blainey text. Here, the process of category construction is enacted not through lexicalisation (*invasion*) but through topic structure: the speaker introduces the eating of the Moriori in the general context of the discussion of the European incursion. This mode of category construction is less overt than the process of nomination used by Blainey. Nevertheless, there are significant similarities between the two processes. By discursively linking the alleged treatment of the Moriori by the Maori to the European presence in New Zealand and by identifying the former episode as something that 'the Maori like to forget', this informant reifies the constructed categorial relationship. The effect of this process is to position the hearer as someone who shares this construction, just as Blainey's term *black invasions* positions the reader as one for whom such a category is unproblematic.

The two texts discussed in this section are manifestations of a quite general discursive strategy. If I am attacked for doing something, there are a number of defensive options open to me. I can claim that I did not do it, or that it was not as bad as my attackers claim, or that I did not mean it. But a particularly effective defence is to show that my attackers have done exactly the same thing (or something like it), since it implicitly places them and me in the same category, thereby challenging the moral basis of their critique.

12.5 The construction of agency

As we have noted above (and in chapters 10 and 11), the assignment of causation is a constructivist process *par excellence*. Most events in the real world are the result of the interplay of many causal factors, so that agency becomes a prime site for interpretation and contestation. Langacker (1990: 214) makes the point in the following terms, linking the construction of agency to the fact that selectivity is one of the central features of the linguistic production of meaning.

> Linguistic coding is highly selective. Typically, a conceived event comprises an intricate web of interactions involving numerous entities with the potential to be construed as participants, yet only a few of these interactions and participants are made explicit, and fewer still are rendered prominent. An example that should make this graphically apparent is the following, not at all implausible scenario: Floyd's little sister, Andrea, has been teasing him mercilessly all morning. Angry and desirous of revenge, Floyd picks up a hammer, swings it, and shatters Andrea's favourite drinking glass. The shards fly in all directions; one of them hits Andrea on the arm and cuts it, drawing blood. Hearing the commotion, their mother comes in and asks what happened. In response, Andrea utters these immortal words: *Floyd broke the glass.*

One issue that arose in Margaret Wetherell's interviews with her New Zealand informants had to do with the social disadvantage of Maori people. A striking feature of these conversations is that, almost without exception, informants identify the attributes of individual human beings as the sole causative factor involved in both social disadvantage and social success.

(2) **F**   *Uh ... ya'know I think they do have a lot of opportunities that ... that ... that we haven't got and if they can't make the most of them ...*

    I   *It's really their problem I s'pose.*

    F   *Yes.*

(3) **F**   *But the ones who ... who ... who want to get on do! That .... that's ...*

    I   *Mm hm.*

    F   *I mean there's some ... some ... terrific statesmen an' and ... Maoris who've done ya'know great jobs.*

(4) **M**   *And there are some ... these two guys that I know, they ... one's a Samoan an' one's a Maori, an' they're really nice guys.*

    I   *Yeah ... mm hmm.*

    M   *Ya'know he's ... whenever they are out they're always clean, they're tidy ...*

    I   *Mm hmm.*

    M   *... well-presented, well-dressed, they ... ya'know, they've got ...*

    I   *Mm hmm.*

    M   *... brains.*

    I   *Mm hmm.*

    M   *If they can do it ... so can the others.*

    I   *Yeah.*

    M   *It's just that they want to.*

(5) **M**   *But there's ... If you've got a real clever ...*
    I   *Mm hmm.*
    M   *... person I think ... born in the back end of Otara ...*
    I   *Yeah!*
    M   *... the ah ya'know ... they could ... still finish up ...*
    I   *Yes ... yeah.*
    M   *... eh you know a Rhodes scholar or anything ...*
    I   *Mm hmm.*
    M   *... because there ... there's opportunity there ...*
    I   *Yes. Mm hmm.*
    M   *... for them.*

(6) **M**   *But then you have got the misfits that don't fit in.*

(7) **I**   *So do you think ... do you think there's any racial prejudice in New Zealand?*
    M   *Yes, a lot. But I think ... I think you ... they ask for it.*

(8) **M**   *And ... here ... eh you make your own ... class.*

(9) **F**   *The Maoris who want to get on and do things do it.*
    I   *Yeah.*
    F   *They are a lazy race most of them.*

(10) **F**   *But if you're going to try and keep to em ... an integrated ...*
    I   *Yeah.*
    F   *... society .... they shouldn't have Maori seats.*
    I   *Right, yes.*
    F   *When someone such as Ben Couch can go ahead and become an MP in his own right.*

There is a striking similarity here with Labov's (1972a: 208–9) observations that the relative lack of success of Black children in the American educational system is often attributed to the personal deficiencies of the children themselves (and hence of their race) rather than to structural factors—even by 'experts' in the field (for example, educational psychologists).

> If Operation Headstart fails, the interpretations that we will receive will be from the same educationalists who designed this program. The fault will be found not in the data, the theory, nor in the methods used, but rather in the children who have failed to respond to the opportunities offered to them.

This tendency to identify the prime cause of complex social situations as the individual human agent (as opposed to social structures and social processes) is so pervasive that it requires some explanation. Part of this explanation must have to do with the obvious salience of personal agency in human cognition. Linguistic reflexes of this fact are (a) the universality across human languages of the notion of 'Agent' in the form of morphological or syntactic marking, and (b) the grammatical salience of the relevant markers. In English, for example, this manifests itself in the syntactic prominence of the grammatical subject, an element that almost every English sentence must possess.[3] In other languages the relevant grammatical marker may not be quite as salient as this (particularly if it is a morphological marker) but it always ranks as one of the most frequent formatives and (more significantly) one of the earliest acquired by children. Crucially, however, the concept of Agent is not only salient but it is also subject to prototypicality effects. The prototypical agentive situation involves an individual human agent applying some kind of force to a typically inanimate object, as Langacker (1990: 210) notes.

> The archetypical 'agent' role is that of a person who volitionally carries out physical activity which results in contact with some external object and transmission of energy to that object.

In other words, several interrelated factors have a powerful influence on human interpretive strategies in the area of causation. These are (a) the inherent cognitive salience of the notion of agency, (b) the fact that the prototypical agent is an individual human actor, and (c) the salience of the corresponding grammatical markers in discourse. This is not to adopt an extreme Whorfian position—it would clearly be absurd to claim that language does not allow us to deal with complex causalities. However, it may be that these factors lead language users to look in the first instance to the individual human actor (rather than more abstract social structures) as the primary causative force.

It might be argued that the nature of local discursive practices offers a better explanation for these data than the cognitive explanation advanced above. The informants in these interviews must have participated in many previous discussions of this topic and have therefore heard (and produced) the kind of ideas they express here on many occasions.

However, these two explanations are not incompatible. The widespread distribution and persistence of explanatory strategies of disadvantage based on individual human agency itself requires explanation and it is at this level that the cognitive factors indicated above have explanatory relevance. The point is that the notion of 'frame' in Cognitive Linguistics needs to take account of the fact that previous discursive experiences are part of the general knowledge base that speakers bring to a conversational encounter, so that these are as much part of the resources that speakers have available to them as is the 'cognitive' knowledge that the notion of frame in Cognitive Linguistics normally suggests. Moreover, such discursive experiences are subject to the same processes of schematisation and abstraction that apply to other forms of experiential knowledge. This shows up in the fact that, when informants draw upon these discursive experiences, they do not use them in a mechanical fashion—they do not use the material verbatim, for example.

This is clear from the fact that, although similar ideas are expressed in each of the examples cited above (we could say that there is a general 'discourse of equality of opportunity'), there is nevertheless a good deal of variability in the detail of their responses. This suggests that speakers are using these resources creatively, adapting them to the local context as it evolves from one moment to the next in ongoing interaction.

12.6 Counterdiscourses

It was noted above that the application of Cognitive Linguistics to discourse analysis suggests that the cognitivist concept of 'frame' needs to be extended to include speakers' discursive experiences. One interesting feature of informants' behaviour in these interviews is that they draw on the full range of discursive resources in their local sociocultural context. In this section, we consider ways in which they use discourses that run counter to their point of view in order to explain and elaborate their position. As part of this process speakers often apply specific constructivist practices relating to the form as well as the content of their discourse.

Consider the following examples.

(11) I   *Uhm ... what are the things that you value about living in New Zealand ... things that ... really appeal to you about life here or ... that you see as the most positive aspects?*

F   *Well we're not poor ... none of us are ...*

I   *Yes.*

F   *... and ...*

I   *Mm hmm.*

F   *... you might think, 'Oh that's okay for her she's on a farm' ... but we're not ... I mean we're only employed ...*

I   *Mm hmm.*

F   *... ya'know ... uhm ... but there's no need for anyone in New Zealand ... to be poor ...*

I   *Mm hmm.*

F   *... and ... there's still plenty of room ... in New Zealand ya'know ... and ... if you want to live in the country you can ... even if that means going and renting a place you can do it.*

Having expressed the view that no New Zealanders are poor, the informant introduces a 'counterdiscourse' (arrowed), suggesting that (according to some people) her view is possibly distorted by the fact that she has a privileged situation (*You might think 'Oh, that's okay for her, she's on a farm ...'*). This gives her the rhetorical opportunity to rebut the objection and develop her position further. Thus the very process of making her point (*We're not poor ... none of us are*) activates for her a dissenting voice. In incorporating this voice into her discourse, the speaker creates a counterpoint that reflects tensions in the local discursive context.

A feature that gives this move a strongly interactive character is that it is introduced by the discourse marker *oh*. As Heritage (1984b: 300) has observed, the normal function of *oh* is to mark a change-of-state reaction to an immediately preceding 'informing' by a conversational partner. At the surface level this is not the case here, since *oh* occurs within a speaker's turn. And yet—at a deeper level—it clearly is such a move. It is the reaction of a (constructed) conversational participant, challenging the speaker's claim that nobody in New Zealand is poor. In this way, the speaker constructs a fragmentary dialogue in the middle of an essentially monologic turn.

This strategy of introducing a counterdiscourse with a discourse marker is quite general. Consider the following further examples.

(12) **M**   *Ya'know it says ... it says ... in the Bible that uhm ... you're to honour the government because the government's ...*

   I   *Yeah.*

   M   *... been put there by God*

   I   *Mm hmm.*

→   **M**   *And sure okay ... what the government ... may do may not be right but you have to honour what the government says.*

→ (13) **M**   *And ... so I think ... the majority of ... yeah aw'right ... the majority of the pro-tour people ...*

   I   *Mm hmm.*

   M   *... basically just wanted to go an' watch the rugby.*

In (12) the speaker uses the discourse marker *sure okay* to introduce a counterdiscourse (CD), constructing an implicit conversational interaction of the following kind.

(14) **M**   *You have to honour the government because it has been put there by God.*

   CD   *But what the government may do may not be right.*

   M   *Sure okay but you have to honour what the government says.*

In (13) the expression *yeah aw'right* has a rather more complex character. The underlying sequence here can be reconstructed as follows.

(15) **M**   *I think the majority of [New Zealanders just wanted to watch the rugby.*

   CD   *It wasn't the majority of New Zealanders who wanted to watch the rugby.]*

   M   *Yeah aw'right—the majority of the pro-tour people wanted to watch it.*

In this case only the first few words of the first move (up to the square bracket) are expressed and the whole of the counterdiscourse is implicit. But its content is clearly signalled by the nature of the speaker's 'response', introduced by the discourse marker *yeah aw'right*.

These extracts tell us something about the nature of the frames that are active in current talk but they also shed further light on radiality. What they show is that radiality applies as much to discourse markers such as *oh*, *yeah*, *okay*, *sure*, as it does to 'ordinary' lexical items. However, the radial networks associated with discourse markers are rather different from those associated with lexical words, in that they straddle two different domains—the semantic and the pragmatic (or interactive). Consider the following (constructed) examples involving *sure*.

(16) *I'm sure that John will fail.*

(17) *That John will fail is sure.*

(18) (a) *John's a genius.*

    (b) *Sure.*

(19) (a) *Could you pass the salt?*

    (b) *Sure.*

(20) (a) *Would you like to come?*

    (b) *Sure.*

In (16) *sure* refers to a person's mental state (certainty concerning the truth of a particular proposition). In (17) 'sureness' is construed primarily as a property of the proposition itself and only secondarily as a property of a human being's mental state (that of the speaker). In (18) the notion of certainty is still present to some degree ('what you say is certainly true') but the interactional function of expressing agreement is rather more salient here than the semantics of the word itself. In (19) and (20) this functional aspect becomes even more salient, with the notion of certainty being downgraded to the relatively minor role of modalising the associated speech act (acceding to a request in (19), accepting an invitation in (20)). In other words, in (16) and (17) *sure* has a primarily semantic (or predicational) function, whereas in (18), (19), and (20) its role is largely pragmatic (or interactional).[4]

The kind of usages illustrated in the New Zealand interviews represent a further extension. Since these forms occur within a speaker's turn, their primary function here is to introduce a concession rather than express agreement. In general the point of making this concession is to enable speakers to develop their position in more detail and to enhance their status— for example, by showing that they have taken account of opposing views in arriving at their (considered) position (Antaki & Wetherell 1999). This function is, of course, present implicitly in many cases in which these markers are used to express agreement in ordinary conversational interaction—note the tendency for *sure* to be followed by *but* in exchanges such as (18)—but in (11)–(15) this concessive function has become primary.

The various functions illustrated above are connected by a number of cognitive and pragmatic factors. The connection between propositional certainty and agreement derives straightforwardly from conversational interaction in that the most straightforward way of expressing agreement is to confirm that a proposition expressed by an interlocutor in a prior turn is indeed true. Furthermore, the link between agreement to a proposition and such speech acts as accepting an invitation or signalling accedence to a request is transparent. The link with concession is somewhat more indirect, having to do with the fact that the expression of agreement with a previous utterance is often followed by some qualification. More accurately, if one wishes to make a point that is inconsistent to some degree with a prior utterance, consideration of one's interlocutor's 'face' (Brown & Levinson 1987) leads one first (and often paradoxically) to indicate acceptance. This phenomenon also shows up in the widespread use of *certainly* in written language to introduce concessions to a constructed counterargument before elaborating further one's own argument.

12.7 Conclusion

In this chapter we have considered the relationship between concepts in Cognitive Linguistics and Discourse Analysis from both angles. On the one hand, I have attempted to show the relevance of prototype-based category theory to the rhetorical aspects of both written and conversational texts. On the other hand, I have used fragments of discourse to explore further such concepts as frame and radiality, adding to each a discursive and functional dimension that complements the cognitive dimension. The constructivist processes discussed here show how speakers and writers exploit creatively the fact that categories are characterised by prototype structure. They also show that the process of constructivist characterisation is strongly associated with such related processes as selectivity, foregrounding, framing, and perspectivisation. The final chapter will focus specifically on the general question of creativity in language use.

Exercises

1 If I tell my boss that I'll resign if she adopts a particular course of action, why might we disagree over the issue of whether this is or is not an 'ultimatum'?

2 In a meeting someone says, *Of course, the problem with Tom's argument is ...* Comment on the significance of the expression *of course* in this context and on the role of the definite article in *the problem with*

Tom's argument.

3   Listen to a radio or television interview with a politician to see if there are any examples of contrasting construals involving such parameters as perspective, framing, categorisation. Were there any cases where the politician gave an answer that modified the nature of the question in some way? Alternatively, examine the transcript of a court case (or a radio or television court case) with these issues in mind.

4   Why is it not always a straightforward matter to determine whether a particular incident was a 'demonstration' or a 'riot'? Who might have an interest in this question?

5   Below are some examples of the use of *then*, *just*, and *well* in discourse (examples involving *then* and *well* are mostly from Schiffrin 1987). Comment on the range of meanings or discourse functions associated with each item.

then

(a)   *John left in a hurry,* **then** *Mary left.*

(b)   *John and Mary were at school together and they really liked each other* **then**.

(c)   *If John needs one,* **then** *he should buy one.*

(d)   A: *John really likes Mary.*
      B: **Then** *why doesn't he propose?*

(e)   *I'll throw the brick,* **then** *you run like hell.*

just

(a)   *That's to be used if you get a high fever; if you've* **just** *got a cold, there's no point in using it.*

(b)   **Just** *hop up on the bed.*

(c)   *I* **just** *notice it when I get like this.*

(d)   **Just** *in one heel it lifted but now it's back in both again.*

(e)   *It happened* **just** *after midnight.*

(f)   *That idea was* **just** *brilliant.*

(g)   *I was* **just** *about to leave.*

(h)   *It's* **just** *so hard to find that money.*

well

(a)   *Look at Bob's father and mother; they didn't approve of what he was doing—* **well** *his father didn't anyway.*

(b)   A   *They just get two years. But she hasn't gotten anything yet cause they don't know if they want to approve it.*

      B   *Why not?*

A *They did last year.* **Well** *'cause they say that more than likely she'll go back to work in September.*

(c) *So we'd been living in Pittsburgh for about ten years ... **well** near there anyway ... and so we decided ...*

(d) A *Are you from Philadelphia?*

B **Well**, *I grew up in the suburbs. And then I lived for about seven years in upstate New York. And then I came back here to go to college.*

(e) A *What does your daughter call you?*

B **Well**, *that's a sore spot. My older daughter-in-law does call me Mom. My younger daughter-in-law right now ... calls me er ... nothing.*

(f) A *Do you think there'll ever be a time when colour doesn't make a difference?*

B *In this country?*

A *Yeah.*

B **Well** *of course there will.*

(g) A *What language did your parents speak?*

B *Uh Jewish*

A *Yeah but you didn't learn it.*

B **Well** *I understand 'em but I couldn't speak it.*

(h) A *Are there any topics that you like in particular about school ... or none?*

B **Well** ... *gym.*

(i) A *Yeah I bet that there'd be a lot more competition if they were a boy and a girl.*

B *Hmm ... I don't know ...* **Well** *right now they're okay.*

Further reading

Hopper, P. 1988, 'Discourse analysis: grammar and critical theory on the 1980s', *Profession* 88: 19–26.

Kress, G. 1989, 'History and language: towards a social account of linguistic change', *Journal of Pragmatics* 13: 445–66.

Lakoff, G. 1992, 'Metaphors and war: the metaphor system used to justify war in the gulf', in M. Pütz (ed.), *Thirty Years of Linguistic Evolution*, John Benjamins, Philadelphia, pp. 463–81.

Lee, D. A. 1992, *Competing Discourses: Perspective and Ideology in Language*, Longman, Harlow, chapter 4 (part): 'Metaphor in Nukespeak', pp. 83–90, and chapter 5: 'Language, perspective, ideology', pp. 91–108.

——forthcoming, 'Constructivist processes in discourse', in H. van den Berg & H. Houtkoop (eds), *Analysing Interviews on Racial Issues: Multidisciplinary*

Approaches to Discourse, Cambridge University Press, Cambridge.

Notes

1 This text is also discussed by Kress (1989: 459).
2 In these transcripts 'I' identifies the interviewer, 'F' identifies a female informant, 'M' identifies a male informant.
3 By syntactic prominence I have in mind not only the fact that almost every sentence must have a subject but also the large number of features that define the grammatical subject in English. I do not assume that the grammatical subject invariably expresses an Agent.
4 In these cases, *sure* could in fact be replaced by an explicit performative: *I agree*, *I will*, or *I would*.

13

CREATIVITY AND THE NATURE OF MEANING

13.1 Introduction

Linguists often claim that the everyday use of language involves a high degree of creativity. Take any arbitrary sentence from a book or newspaper, the argument goes, and you will find that you have probably never encountered that particular sequence of words in your life before. Yet you have no difficulty in understanding it. Therefore, it is suggested, not only was the act of producing that sentence highly creative, but so was the act of interpretation. In the normal course of your daily life, whether you are taking part in a conversation, reading a book or a newspaper, listening to the radio, watching television or a film, you supposedly perform such creative acts hundreds—perhaps thousands—of times a day.

There are a number of ways in which one might challenge this claim. For example, it could be argued that, although the written language tends to be creative in this sense, everyday conversation is not. Consider, for example, such conversational exchanges as the following (based on an example from Heritage 1984b: 306).

(1) **A** *How is your mother by the way?*
     B *Well, she's a bit better.*
     A *Mm.*
     B *She came down on Saturday evening ...*
     A *Oh, did she?*
     B *... for the first time.*
     A *Yes.*
     B *Yes ... I don't know whether she came I ...*
     A *Oh.*

It would be difficult to argue that there is a great deal of creativity here.

But there are more serious problems for this argument. For example, the fact that a particular sentence has never been produced before does not necessarily mean that a significant degree of creativity was involved in its production. Consider a sentence such as *The Maori forget that they ate the Moriori* (a slightly simplified variant of an utterance discussed in the previous chapter). Now, it may well be that the speaker had never produced this precise sentence before and it is a fairly safe bet that no reader of this book has ever encountered it before. Yet how significant is this observation?

This sentence consists of a subject noun phrase (*The Maori*) followed by a verb (*forget*) followed by a subordinate clause, consisting in turn of a subject pronoun (*they*), a verb (*ate*) and a direct object noun phrase (*the Moriori*). We have all heard and produced sentences with precisely this structure on many occasions. Examples such as *The women said that they knew the answer, The boss knew that we needed a break*, and countless other familiar sentences all fit this pattern.

Even the fact that there is an unlimited number of possible sentences in a language does not in itself prove that the language capacity is highly creative. For example, consider the following sentences.

(2) (a) *This is the cat.*

     (b) *This is the cat that chased the rat.*

     (c) *This is the cat that chased the rat that ate the corn.*

     (d) *This is the cat that chased the rat that ate the corn that grew in the field.*

     (e) *This is the cat that chased the rat that ate the corn that grew in the field that bordered the road.*

The fact that it would be possible to extend this structure *ad infinitum* shows that there is in principle no limit to the number of possible English sentences. However, it would be an extremely simple task to program a computer to churn out sentences of this kind in such a way that it never produced the same sentence twice. All that is needed is a program that contains a limited set of words, appropriately classified, and two straightforward 'recursive' rules that allow for (a) a clause to contain a noun phrase and (b) a relative clause to be attached to a noun phrase. Yet it would be difficult to argue that such a computer was demonstrating a significant degree of creativity as it continuously produced new sentences.

Moreover, it has been noted that speakers of a language clearly have a prodigiously large mental store of set phrases and expressions. Jackendoff (1994) has pointed out that television quiz games that require participants to identify a phrase or expression from limited clues exploit this capacity and that the supply of such phrases seems enormous. So, again, relatively simple rules of combination applying to such 'chunks' may account for most of the sentences actually produced.

However, there is a deeper problem with this whole way of conceptualising the issue. The arguments outlined above (both for and against the notion that the everyday use of language involves a significant degree of creativity) are based on the idea that creativity has to do with the way in which the syntactic resources of the language are used. (Chomsky (1966) in particular emphasised the significance of the recursive properties of the syntactic component of the grammar.) But, as I have just indicated, neither the property of recursion nor the fact that the number of well-formed English sentences is infinite tells us a great deal about creativity. In fact, I will argue here that true creativity in language essentially has little to do with syntax and a great deal to do with cognition.

13.2 Mental spaces

One of the primary mechanisms for creativity in language involves the perception and construction of conceptual correspondences across mental spaces. Consider, for example, an expression such as *rumour mill*.

From the point of view of the grammar of the language, there is nothing remarkable about this expression, since there are thousands of such noun compounds in English. But whoever produced this expression for the first time demonstrated a good deal of creativity. The move was clearly motivated by the perception of similarities between the process whereby a mill produces flour (or timber or steel) and the 'production' of rumour in social talk. The expression sets up two mental spaces: a 'mill' space (M) and a 'social talk' space (ST). Correspondences are perceived (or constructed) between:

(a)   the mill in M and people who gossip in ST

(b)   the process of industrial production in M and the activity of talk in ST

(c)   the product in M and 'rumour' in ST

(d)   the notion of distribution of the product in M and that of the spread of rumour in ST.

It seems unlikely that such correspondences had been noted before the coining of this expression, so that the creativity manifested in this move is entirely cognitive in nature—the form of the linguistic expression follows straightforwardly from the cognitive event. As for the person who hears the expression for the first time, syntactic processing (that is, recognising the phrase as a noun compound) is also straightforward. The challenging part of the task is to construct the relevant conceptual correspondences—a process that depends heavily on frame knowledge and on creative exploitation of those frames.

Some creative moves have both a cognitive and a linguistic dimension. Consider, for example, the word *workaholic*, which has entered the language relatively recently. Clearly, there must have been an occasion on which a particular individual produced this word for the first time. It was motivated by the perception of similarities between addiction to alcohol and 'addiction' to work. This was a creative event, since in many respects working hard and drinking heavily are activities that have very little in common. People work to earn money but drink for pleasure. Working hard is generally perceived as socially virtuous, whereas drinking heavily is not. Normally, therefore, it is a compliment to describe someone as 'a hard worker' but not to call them 'a heavy drinker'.

Again, it is useful to invoke the concept of mental spaces to explicate this move. Let us call the domain of work mental space 'W' and the domain of drink mental space 'D'. (Each of these domains is a frame in the sense in which I have used it in this book.) We can then characterise the conceptual correspondences on which the coining of *workaholic* was based as follows.

(a)   A person (X) in W corresponds to a person (Y) in D.

(b)   The process of working in W corresponds to that of drinking in D.

(c)   The amount of work performed by X in W corresponds to the quantity of alcohol consumed by Y in D.

(d)   The amount of time X spends working in W corresponds to the amount of time Y spends drinking in D.

(e)   The harmful effects of the activity in W correspond to the harmful effects of the activity in D (effects on health, family life, social life, and so on).

These correspondences are cognitive rather than linguistic in nature, but in this case there is also a significant linguistic dimension to the creative process. It is in fact possible that similarities between alcohol addiction and hard work had been noted by other people before the coining of the word *workaholic*— similarities that could perhaps have been captured by a phrase such as *addiction to work*. However, in what amounts to a flash of insight, somebody suddenly saw that the word *alcoholic* could be manipulated to convey this idea in a way that was both succinct and striking. Moreover, in coining *workaholic*, the innovator not only created a new meaning, but also created a new morpheme in the English language. For, whereas the word *alcoholic* consists of the stem *alcohol* followed by the suffix *-ic* (which also occurs in such words as *demonic, moronic, philanthropic*, and so on), the word *workaholic* has a quite different morphological structure. It consists of the stem *work* followed by the suffix *-aholic*, a new linguistic element with its own meaning (associated with the notion of addiction). This establishes a new linguistic pattern, which can then be exploited in further creative acts. Words such as *chocaholic* and *webaholic* have been constructed using this new morpheme. These coinings in turn construct correspondences from the domains of drink and work (linked by the words *alcoholic* and *workaholic*) to other domains of experience—that is, to other mental spaces.

Other examples involving the creation of new morphemes are (a) words such as *beefburger, cheeseburger, baconburger,* and (b) words such as *spellathon, skipathon, readathon* (there are doubtless many others). As far as the examples in (a) are concerned, the source word *hamburger* consisted originally of a stem *Hamburg* and a suffix *-er.* Whoever first coined the word *beefburger* (assuming that this was the first of the words in (a) to appear on the scene) in effect re-analysed *hamburger* as a noun compound (*ham + burger*), thereby inventing the new morpheme *burger.* This paved the way for subsequent coinings such as *cheeseburger* and *baconburger,* and indeed for the emergence of *burger* as a 'free' morpheme—that is, as a word that could stand on its own.

Similarly, the coining of a word such as *spellathon* created the new morpheme *-athon* (the source word *marathon* being monomorphemic), paving the way for the creation of other words using this element.

13.3 Radiality

Linguistically creative acts based on the perception of correspondences across mental spaces are not always as spectacular as the coining of a new word or a new expression. More typical are examples in which a word that is associated with one mental space is applied to a new space. When this happens, the word typically undergoes semantic extension—that is, it acquires a radial network. Consider, for example, the word *read.* This word applies primarily to the process of interpreting written text. In recent years, it has begun to develop a quite extensive radial network. For example, the verb is often used by sports commentators in such expressions as *He reads the game well* and *He read that pass beautifully* (typically uttered in a situation where a player intercepts a pass made by someone on the opposing team). Extended uses are also found in examples such as *I can read your mind, How do you read this situation?, I find John difficult to read.* Although such utterances are no longer creative, there must of course have been an occasion on which each was used for the first time. Following the initial creative act, the process of uptake by other members of the community (conventionalisation) produces a network of related senses.

Such extensions are sometimes not particularly easy to explain without considering the nature of the semantic network as a whole. For example, there is only a very tenuous link between the process of deciphering written text and the interception of a pass by a soccer player. The connection seems to be mediated by examples such as *I can read your mind.* In reading a book or newspaper, we feel we are in communication with the mind of the writer. This provides an obvious basis for describing the process of understanding someone else's thoughts and intentions directly as 'reading' their mind. Once this usage is established, the extension to the soccer situation is more transparent. A player who intercepts a pass seems to have understood the mind (intention) of the opposing player.

Again the extension to a new usage has consequences that are sometimes described as 'linguistic'. A soccer commentator who says *He read that pass beautifully* is unlikely to apply the epithet *beautifully* to the process of reading a book or a newspaper. In other words the collocation of the verb *read* with the adverb *beautifully* occurs only in certain contexts. But this is much more than a question of combining words. The reason why someone can say *He read that pass beautifully* but not ?*He read that newspaper beautifully* has to do with the qualitative differences between the two situations. Whereas the interception of a pass can be aesthetically pleasing to an observer, this is not generally true of the process of deciphering a written text. Collocational patterns are cognitive rather than 'linguistic' in the narrow sense.

13.4 Frames

The process of establishing correspondences between two or more mental spaces that plays such an important role in creativity is part of the more general process of 'framing'. Consider the following example. Recently, I was listening to a radio documentary about the history of soccer, when I heard the statement *In the 1960s Yugoslavia was the Brazil of Europe*. I had never heard this sentence before, yet I immediately understood it (or at least assigned an interpretation to it). My interpretation was based on the following items of frame knowledge.

(a)   Yugoslavia is a country in Europe.

(b)   Brazil is a country in South America.

(c)   In the 1960s Brazil had (and still has) one of the best soccer teams in the world.

(d)   The Brazilian team has a characteristic (and exciting) style of play.

(e)   This style is associated to some extent with South American teams in general but is displayed best by Brazil.

I therefore interpreted the sentence to mean that in the 1960s Yugoslavia was the most exciting of all the European teams to watch and that its style of play was closest of all the European teams to that of Brazil. (The cumbersome nature of this paraphrase contrasts markedly with the conciseness of the original.)

However, if the sentence had been produced in a different frame, I would have assigned a different interpretation to it. For example, if the relevant frame had been economics, I might have taken it to mean that, of all the European countries, Yugoslavia's economy in the 1960s was closest to being in crisis. In other contexts, I might have taken it to mean that Yugoslavians were the most carefree of all the European peoples or that Yugoslavia was the most popular country with tourists, or that it had the greatest degree of ethnic diversity—and so on. In principle, the number of possible interpretations that such a sentence could produce is infinite, since the number of frames in which it could occur is also infinite. In this sense the acts of production and interpretation have the potential for infinite creativity in the sense that a given sentence can be exploited to produce an infinite range of meanings. But, clearly, this has nothing to do with the syntax of English.

A possible counterargument to this claim is that the sentence *Yugoslavia was the Brazil of Europe* has a meaning that is common to the various interpretations outlined above and that this schematic meaning is its 'real' or intrinsic meaning. On this view the meaning of the sentence is determined solely by the syntax of the sentence in combination with the meanings of the words that it contains—that is, the meaning of a text can be isolated from the more general elements of 'meaning' (in a wider sense) contributed by the relevant frame.

However, there are serious problems with this argument. If we were to attempt to characterise this schematic meaning for the sentence in question, we would probably express it in something like the following terms:

Yugoslavia was to Europe as Brazil was to South America

or (if we felt it necessary to be somewhat more explicit)

The relationship between Yugoslavia and other European countries was similar to that between Brazil and other South American countries.

But there is no way in which we could construct even this schematic meaning without access to frame knowledge. After all, at the syntactic level, the sentence in question consists of the form

A was the B of C

and this is a sentence type that is used not only to express propositions of the form

A was to B as C was to D

but also propositions of the form

A was the B that belongs to C

(for example, *This painting was the work of van Gogh, Geneva was the headquarters of the League of Nations*, and so on). So, in order to assign even the beginnings of an appropriate meaning to *Yugoslavia was the Brazil of Europe*, it is necessary to know that the words *Yugoslavia* and *Brazil* are the names of countries, that *Europe* is the name of a continent, that Yugoslavia is in Europe, that Brazil is not in Europe—and one also needs to know what 'countries' and 'continents' are. Since there is no principled boundary between these items of frame knowledge and those indicated in (a)–(e) above, there can be no principled boundary between the schematic meaning 'Yugoslavia was to Europe as Brazil is to South America' and the more specific meanings indicated above.

13.5 The nature of meaning

The above discussion raises a number of issues concerning the nature of meaning. There is a widespread view of language and communication that has a profound influence on our ways of talking and thinking about meaning. According to this view the process of communication is conceptualised in terms of transport. Meanings exist as object-like entities in the minds of individuals. They are 'inserted' into language in the form of speech or writing, and the role of the hearer or listener is to 'extract' these meanings from the text. In other words, language acts as a vehicle for transferring meanings from the speaker to the addressee. The meanings that are transferred in this way have essentially the same form in the minds of both transmitter and receiver when communication has taken place. This view of language and communication is generally known as the 'conduit metaphor' (Reddy 1979; Lakoff & Johnson 1980: 11–13; Moore & Carling 1982: 149–75; Lakoff 1987: 67–74). It is deeply embedded in our culture in the way that we both think and talk about language and communication, manifesting itself in such expressions as the following.

(3)   *It's hard to get that idea across to her.*

(4)   *It's difficult to put this idea into words.*

(5)   *I don't think I'm getting through to her.*

(6)   *I'm not getting any ideas out of this text.*

(7)   *Why don't you put that idea on paper?*

(8)   *I didn't get anything from that lecture.*

(9)   *I just can't take in what he's saying.*

However, the conduit metaphor is misleading in many respects. Throughout this book I have emphasised the idea that meanings are not properties of words or sentences but the product of interactional processes occurring in the mind of the conceptualiser. Specifically, a human being's knowledge base plays as great a role in the production of meaning as do the words of the utterance or sentence on the page. For example, a word such as *party* 'means' different things to different speakers, according to their personal experiences of the events that they call 'parties'. An utterance such as *Yugoslavia was the Brazil of Europe* is virtually meaningless until it is brought into interaction with some particular mental frame.

Of course, words 'have' meanings in the sense that they activate relatively specific areas of a person's knowledge base. These meanings are independent of individuals to the extent that a particular word activates similar experiential knowledge in different people. But to assume that there is a well-defined 'concept' corresponding to each word in a language is to ignore the crucial role of the individual mind in the production of meaning. And it ultimately fails to explain the extraordinary flexibility of meaning that makes language a perfect instrument for adapting to new circumstances (as illustrated by the notion of radiality) but for which we sometimes pay a price in the form of imperfect communication.

One corollary of this argument is that it divorces the notion of meaning from that of speaker intention. Consider the following example. Your car is running badly and you take it to a service station. The mechanic inspects the engine briefly and then says *It's a distributor problem*. Now, such a 'text' will mean different things to different people. Someone who knows nothing about car mechanics will assign a fairly sketchy interpretation to it. They will infer that there is some component in the engine called a 'distributor' and that this particular distributor is faulty but they will have no idea about the exact nature of the problem. Someone who knows a little more will know that the role of the distributor is to send an electric current to the spark plugs in order to generate a spark at the right moment. They might also guess that the problem can be fixed relatively easily but have only a rough idea about how this might be done. By contrast someone who knows a lot about cars will produce a much richer interpretation. They will visualise the distributor in precise terms—the points, the rotor arm, the condenser, and so on—and also envisage the kind of actions that will need to be taken to fix the problem— cleaning or replacing the points, for example. But since different interpreters produce a range of different interpretations, even in this very simple case, it is inappropriate to ask, 'What is the meaning of this text?', as if there is some essential meaning common to all the potential readings that hearers might produce.

Some scholars (for example, Knapp & Michaels 1987) have argued from within the conduit metaphor that texts do indeed 'have' meaning, specifically that they mean 'what their authors intend them to mean'. But what precisely does this **mean**? We could certainly ask the automechanic in the case cited above exactly what he meant. After all, he has just performed a close inspection of the distributor and has a good idea of the state of the points, the rotor arm, the condenser, the wiring, and so on. But how much of this information, if any, did he intend to 'convey' when he said 'It's a distributor problem'?

It would be absurd (and also perhaps inadvisable) to seek an answer to this question from the speaker himself, by asking him, for example, how detailed a picture of the distributor he expected the interpreter to construct, whether he intended to produce an image of the unit as seen in its assembled condition, or in terms of its component parts, and so on.

Nor do the words of the utterance itself provide any more helpful clues in this respect. The general point is that any utterance grossly underspecifies the situation on which it reports. Such underspecification is essential, since the task of encoding all the features of a given situation is simply not feasible, nor is it one in which either the speaker or the addressee has any interest. Underspecification is effective because of the fact that the addressee's knowledge base performs a major part of the task of meaning construction.

An inevitable corollary of this process is that meaning escapes the control of speaker intention.

This claim should not obscure the relevance of the conceptual orientation of the speaker to the construction of text. The choices available to speakers will be determined by their own conceptual structures and these in turn will derive from their experience of language and general processes of socialisation. Particular selections within that overall system of choices will result from speaker judgments concerning the interaction between linguistic factors and contextual factors, including the knowledge base of the addressee. In abandoning the conduit metaphor, however, we have to reject the idea that speakers simply select those sentences that carry meanings corresponding to those in their minds. Rather, texts are the product of a complex interaction between social, psychological, and linguistic factors impinging on the producer of a text at a particular time in a particular situation.

Although this seems a rather arcane issue at first sight, in fact it has a good deal of relevance to the real world. For example, a few years ago a rift developed between the political leaders of Australia and Malaysia as a result of a comment by the Australian prime minister of the time, Paul Keating, concerning the Malaysian leader, Dr Mahathir. After a series of difficult negotiations concerning trade between the two countries, Mr Keating described Dr Mahathir as 'recalcitrant'. Dr Mahathir took this as a serious personal insult. This clearly surprised Mr Keating, who claimed that in his view the term was inoffensive.

Now, if texts mean what their author intends them to mean, then Dr Mahathir ought to have been satisfied with this explanation from Mr Keating. But he clearly was not. Moreover, nobody was surprised by this. In this particular case and in others like it, users of a language do not accept that a speaker or writer has the power to dictate the meaning of his or her text.

This issue arises in many areas of our everyday life. How often has an argument between two people arisen from a remark that has been 'taken the wrong way' (from the speaker's perspective)? Moreover, consider the traditional practice of using masculine gender terms to refer to groups of people that include women. In a discussion of this issue some years ago, one academic wrote an article defending the practice, claiming that the use of generic male terminology does not involve any intention to exclude women (Gerson 1985). Again, this defence is based on the assumption that author intention is the sole determinant of meaning. But there would be few who would accept this defence. Examples such as the following are relevant to this issue, since they demonstrate how easy it is to slip from the use of generic male terms (which are supposedly gender-neutral) to male-only uses.

(10) *Man can do several things that the animal cannot do ... his vital interests are life, food and access to females.* (Erich Fromm, cited in Silveira 1980: 169)

(11) (Of 'Man' in the generic sense) *His back aches, he ruptures easily, his women have difficulties in childbirth.* (Loren Eisley, cited in Graham 1975: 62)

There is, in fact, a good deal of experimental evidence to support the view that the use of male terms produces male images (Miller & Swift 1988: 170), whatever users of such terms may claim about what they 'meant'.

One of the main objections to the doctrine that a text means what its author intends it to mean is that it is a dangerous claim. In effect, it provides the author with an excuse for disclaiming responsibility for the meanings which his or her text produces. This may not be problematic in the domain of literature—one could hardly hold Jane Austen responsible for all the meanings that her texts have already produced or may do so in the future in contexts that she could never have anticipated. In certain situations, however, the question of author responsibility is crucial. Studies in the area of the ethnography of communication show that there are countless situations in which an intended meaning misfires—an utterance intended as a question is interpreted as an insult, a ritualistic utterance is taken to be a substantive offer or enquiry. The fundamental point is that in most communicative situations there is an onus on the initiator to show sensitivity with respect to the way in which his or her text will interact with the knowledge base of the addressee. The claim of authorial control over meaning is dangerous in that it provides the producer of a text with grounds for attempting to evade this responsibility.

13.6 Conclusion

The famous German linguist and scholar Wilhelm von Humboldt once said that language makes infinite use of finite means. But the question arises: are the 'means' with which language works in fact finite? This book suggests that there is a sense in which even as basic an item as a word is not a finite entity. Since the word *read*, for example, possesses a semantic network that is potentially open and accessible to new meanings, it has—at least in principle—infinite potential. Who could have predicted forty years ago the kind of meanings that words such as *bug, save, write, disk, program, screen, virus,* and thousands of others would acquire as a result of the computer revolution? Given the infinite variability of human experience and the infinite capacity of human beings to construct the kind of conceptual mappings that we call perceptions of similarity, there is a very clear sense in which even the basic components of language are not in fact finite. The process of putting together linguistic units cannot be divorced from the process of putting together conceptual units, and the ways in which such conceptual combinations produce meaning is infinitely variable. In this sense we have to conclude that the reason why language is able to cope with the infinite variability and open-endedness of human experience is precisely the fact that it does not make use of finite means. This view is tenable only if we see language and cognition as inextricably interwoven.

Exercises

1 Listen to a sports commentary and note any creative expressions, any metaphors, or examples of words used in an extended sense. Comment on each of the examples below (from a tennis commentary).

   (a)   *This is a pivotal game.*

   (b)   *There's some really solid hitting in this game.*

   (c)   *The match was a real slugfest.*

   (d)   *She can't afford to lose another game.*

   (e)   *That was a really deep serve.*

   (f)   *His game is beginning to crack.*

   (g)   *There's a forest of photographers over there.*

   (h)   *He really unloaded on that backhand.*

   (i)   *She nailed that one down the line.*

   (j)   *Jones won in straight sets.*

2 Comment on each of the following expressions.

   (a)   *gene jockeys* (referring to scientists involved in human genetic research)

   (b)   *pay lip service to*

   (c)   *I have wall-to-wall meetings all day.*

   (d)   *The car was totalled.*

   (e)   *They are trying to white-ant our program.*

   (f)   *Some of the golfers had difficulty reading the greens.*

3 There is a developing tendency in English for new verbs to be created from nouns by the morphological process of conversion (that is, by simply using a noun as a verb without a change in form). Historically, the following verbs are all derived in this way: *chair* (*Who's going to chair the meeting?*), *table* (*The student tabled a motion*), *floor* (*That floored me completely*). Give an example in which each of the following nouns could be used as a verb: *workshop, summit, surface, screen, interface, wheelbarrow, bus.*

4   In what way did the title of the film *A Bridge Too Far* involve a novel use of the expression *too far*? As a result, it is now possible to envisage further creative extensions of this kind. For example, in what kind of situation might I use the expression *a beer too far*? Give some other examples of your own.

5   In Australia the word *Clayton's* underwent creative extension as the result of a television commercial for a non-alcoholic drink called 'Clayton's'. The commercial contained the slogan: *Clayton's: the drink you have when you're not having a drink*. The term then came to be applied to a wide variety of situations. For example, if the government made a promise that it later broke, this came to be known as a 'Clayton's promise'. What was the basis for this extension? Give some examples of your own where there is a potential for the term *Clayton's* to be applied in this way.

6   Comment on the expression *This is the Rolls Royce of computers*. What other expressions of this kind are you familiar with? Is it possible to coin new expressions following this model?

Further reading

Johnson, M. 1987, *The Body in the Mind*, chapter 7: 'The nature of meaning', University of Chicago Press, Chicago, pp. 173–93.

Köveces, Z. 1993, 'Minimal and full definitions of meaning', in R. A. Geiger & B. Rudzka-Ostyn (eds), *Conceptualizations in Mental Processing in Language*, Mouton, Berlin, pp. 247–66.

Lee, D. A. 1990, 'Text, meaning and author intention', *Journal of Literary Semantics* 19: 166–86.

Moore, T. & Carling, C. 1982, *Understanding Language: Towards a Post-Chomskyan Linguistics*, Macmillan, London.

Reddy M. J. 1979, 'The conduit metaphor—a case frame conflict in our language about language', in A. Ortony (ed.), *Metaphor and Thought*, Cambridge University Press, Cambridge, pp. 284–324.

Sinha, C. 1993, 'On representing and referring', in R. A. Geiger & B. Rudzka-Ostyn (eds), *Conceptualizations in Mental Processing in Language*, Mouton, Berlin, pp. 227–46.

APPENDIX

TRANSCRIPT OF FAMILY ARGUMENT

Note: Square brackets in this transcript mark overlapping speech.

	Michael	And … can I have a DJ too, is that okay?
	Noeline	Laurie?
	Laurie	What? (Looks up briefly, then down at a magazine.)
	Noeline	Can he have a DJ … a DJ?
5	**Michael**	Cause you won't be spending much money on food, so I thought …
	Laurie	Well, how much does a DJ cost?
	Michael	Yeah, I've gotta find out.
	Noeline	(To Michael) The DJ why d'you have to have a DJ? What does he do? Just plays records all night?
10	**Michael**	Yeah.
	Noeline	(To Laurie) What d'you think about the DJ, is that okay with you?
	Laurie	I just wanna know how much it is, first.
	Noeline	(To Michael) Right, that's what you've gotta do first, right?
	Michael	I'm gonna have to get Paul to come over, too.
15	**Noeline**	Why?
	Michael	So people don't crash the party.
	Noeline	They won't crash the party, sweetheart, you [can easily put them …
	Michael	[Oh yeah, yeah, maybe twenty years ago, Mum, you know today … if … there'd be easy
20		another forty people if you didn't have a person at the gate.
	Laurie	Bullshit.
	Michael	Look, I don't want [to be embarrassed, you know.
	Noeline	[But … Don't you think it's a little bit dramatic saying you've gotta have a bouncer at a private [person's party?
25	**Michael**	[Okay … Fine … We'll leave the gate open. We'll leave the pontoon there, and you see you just see. You … you think I'm so stupid. But if you … you look around and open your eyes, you'll see. We'll wait till the night.
	Noeline	I think we'll just have a nice orderly party, thank you … All right?
30	**Michael**	I'm just warning you, that's all. I'm just saying … either … either Laurie's at the gate or someone's gotta be there.

Noeline	*Laurie can be at the gate then.* (Placating tone) *What's the password?* (Laughs.)
Michael	(Looks down, picks at hairs on hand.)

♦ ♦ ♦

35   (A little later, Noeline and Laurie alone)

Noeline	*I hope you're gonna put that magazine down and give me a bit of a hand in a minute.*
Laurie	*Bit of a hand with what?*
Noeline	*It won't be a party like that.*
40 **Laurie**	*I just said 'Who's coming?' … Has he … has he give you the list? How many people's coming?*
Noeline	*Well he wrote the invitations yesterday.*
Laurie	*Well how many's he invited?*
Noeline	*I don't know.*
45 **Laurie**	*Well find out how many he's invited for a start, before we go any further.*
Noeline	*Will we need a bouncer?*
Laurie	*Well, we'll have to find out how many's comin'. We might have to knock a few on the head. There might be that many comin'. We*
50	*mightn't have the room for that …*
Noeline	*Well you've just said 'Yes' to the boy.*
Laurie	*Well I've just realised y'd have to have, y'd … it's crazy, having a DJ here.*
Noeline	(Loud) *But you keep doing this, you say 'Yes' one minute and then*
55	*you say 'No' when he's gone.*

♦ ♦ ♦

(Michael comes in, puts container in freezer.)

Noeline	*We **will** have an orderly party, Michael, thank you. Without thuggeries. So any thugs that might be comin', just tell them not to come to the street.*
60 **Laurie**	*How many blokes have you invited?*
Michael	*There's the rugby tour guys.*
Noeline	*Where do they live? Mainly over the other side?*
Michael	*Yeah.*
Noeline	*So a hell of a lot of 'em won't come.*
65 **Laurie**	*How many have you invited?*
Michael	*About thirty-five rugby guys and about seven others … other guys.*
Laurie	*Jeez, it's a lot of people. I don't know where we're gonna put 'em all. Christ Almighty.*
Noeline	*Two-thirds of 'em won't come, Laurie.*

70	**Laurie**	*Well, I hope they don't all come. It's … forty. It's a lot of people. This is our home. We're certainly not going to start bloody having fights or bloody well trouble in this joint.*
	Michael	(Quietly) *Righto.*
	Laurie	*If there's any idea that we're gonna the whole thing's off. Forget it.*
75	**Michael**	(Quietly) *I can't [believe some of the shit you come out with.*
	Laurie	[*Because the cops'll only come here once or twice. Then they'll leave you on your own, if you keep ringing them, if there's trouble here.*
	Noeline	*What?*
80	**Laurie**	*The cops'll …*
	Noeline	(Loud) *Well, there's not going [to be any trouble.*
	Laurie	(Loud) [*Well, Michael seems to think there is.*
	Michael	*Oh yeah, there's gonna be gang warfare in my back yard is there?*
	Laurie	(To Noeline) *Michael seems to think there'll be trouble if we've got*
85		*no bouncers here.*
	Noeline	*Why do you need a bouncer at the gate? Come on.*
	Michael	*I'm just saying, well say I invite three guys, they bring a friend along. He's … he's a guy that I don't like …*
	Noeline	*Well [tell them …*
90	**Laurie**	[*Well tell them not to bring friends, you've invited them.*
	Noeline	*Tell them not to bring friends.*
	Michael	*Oh, how'm I gonna do that?*
	Laurie	[*Of course you are.*
	Noeline	[*It's by invitation only.*
95	**Laurie**	(Loud) *We've only … we've only got room for thirty people here, maximum, so if you've invited thirty-seven and they're all going to bring friends, we haven't got enough room, have we? Common sense.*
	Michael	(Quietly) *Forget about it, man. [You're an idiot man.*
	Noeline	[*Michael you can sit right down.*
100	**Laurie**	(Loud) *All I'm saying is, if you invited thirty-seven people and … they're all going to bring friends, you can't bring friends.*
	Noeline	(Shouting, to Michael) *You can cut it out right now, [right this minute.*
	Michael	[*Don't give me this shit.*
105	**Noeline**	(To Michael, shouting) *You sit right down now.*
	Michael	(Walks out of kitchen) *Forget about it.*
	Noeline	(To Laurie, shouting) *For God's sake, he **can** have a bloody birthday party.*
	Laurie	(Shouting) *Of course he can. But he's just saying, if there's gonna be*
110		*bloody a million people here, we haven't got the room.*
	Noeline	(Shouting) *Of course we haven't got the room. He's not stupid.*
	Laurie	(Quietly) *Well he … you heard what he just said, Noeline.*

Noeline	(Loud) *Gawdstruth Laurie, one of these days I'll pack me bloody bags and I'm goin' outa here. Truly. It's more drama living in this house than out of it.*
115	
Laurie	(Quietly) *I don't know why.*
Noeline	(Loud) *I don't know why.*
Laurie	(Shrugs) *Wouldn't have a clue.*
Noeline	*Did you ever have a birthday party as a child?*
120 **Laurie**	*Course I did.*
Noeline	*How many parties did you have as a child?*
Laurie	*I would have had two or three when I was a [kid ... teenager*
Noeline	*[Did you have one when you were sixteen?*
125 **Laurie**	*I can't remember.*
Noeline	*But sixteen's an age.*
Laurie	*I can't remember whether I had a party. I probably did.*

◆ ◆ ◆

Noeline	(Banging photo album) *Right. We'll keep an orderly party for Saturday night ... alright?*
130 **Michael**	*I just warned you.*
Noeline	*I don't like the warning, I don't even like what I heard. So don't tell me any [more.*
Michael	*[I just ... D'you ... d'you think I'm stupid or something?*
Noeline	(Loud) *I don't think you're stupid, I just don't think it's bloody*
135	*necessary.*
Michael	*Settle down.*
Noeline	*I had a twenty-first and no ... we didn't have any gate crashers.*
Michael	(Shakes head. Looks away from Noeline.)
Noeline	*We had your damn party over at the park. We didn't have gate*
140	*crashers.*
Michael	*Party over at the park, how old was I Mum? Eight?*
Noeline	*Six. What are you going to say to Laurie? Eh? When something is ripped on Saturday night? Because if you're inviting these sort of people I don't want them in my home.*
145 **Laurie**	*That's exactly what's in my mind.*
Michael	*Who's coming in the house?*
Noeline	*I thought they were Newington boys.*
Michael	*Who's coming in the house?*
Noeline	*No one's com' ... What if they wreck the outside of the house?*
150 **Michael**	*Well that's why you put all the furniture down the side, so there's nothing that people can wreck.*
Noeline	*But we're not going to have fights.*

Michael		I said, I never said a fight. This is a figment of someone's imagination.
		Laurie's come up ... oh yeah there's gonna be a brawl in my back
155		yard. All I said is that you got to have someone at the gate to stop
		people I don't want comin' in here coming in here. That's all I said. I
		never said anything about fights.
Laurie		If there's gonna be people here you don't want, we don't have any.
Michael		Fine. Forget about it.

♦ ♦ ♦

160	**Noeline**	You are being a smart arse Michael.
	Michael	You reckon? You really think so?
	Laurie	Well, if you've got any idea that there's gonna be trouble here ...
		then we don't want trouble.
	Michael	Ah, here we go again!
165	**Michael**	I didn't ... Are you thick or somethin'? Is there somethin' wrong?
		I said there wasn't gonna be fighting in the back yard. I just said
		people that I don't want coming in should be stopped from coming
		in. Is there something wrong with that?
	Noeline	But when they walk down the side and they're not meant to be here,
170		can't you walk up and say, 'Listen mate you can't stay here'? Can't
		you do that? Isn't that what you normally do? If someone came to my
		front door to a party that weren't ... wasn't meant to be here, I'd go
		and say, 'You can't come in'. Can't you do that?
	Michael	You guys are livin' in the past, I think.
175	**Laurie**	No we're not. No we're not.
	Noeline	We're living in our home.
	Laurie	We're living in our time, right here and now.
	Noeline	We're living in our home. We're living in our home, Michael.
	Laurie	We're not living in the past.
180	**Michael**	Right, so we get out there and we do the twist and the bop and the
		shimmy shimmy and whatever, [do we?
	Laurie	[Don't know what you do. Do
		whatever you like, within reason.
	Noeline	Just get some common sense into the whole thing. Don't ... don't talk
185		in riddles or try to ... you know ... wave it away as if it doesn't
		matter. It does matter.
	Michael	Well, so that if ... forget it.
	Laurie	And we can't have any more than forty people here.
	Michael	Forget [it.
190	**Noeline**	[Write down your guests, Michael.
	Laurie	We're not having any more than forty people here. Simple as that.

Noeline	*You are being … a sixteen-year-old little twit. Sit down and write down your [guests.*
Michael	*[It's a joke. It's a joke. I might as well laugh at it.*
195 **Noeline**	*It's [not …*
Laurie	*[It's not a joke. You think it's a joke, we don't think it's a joke. If you wanna have a party here, forty people is the limit. Simple as that.*
Michael	(Writing the word no-one on a piece of paper) *No-one. There we go … It's all over … No more screaming.* (Walks out.)

REFERENCES

Antaki, C. & Wetherell, M. 1999, 'Show concessions', *Discourse Studies* 1: 7–28.

Aske, J. 1989, 'Motion predicates in English and Spanish: a closer look', *Proceedings of the Berkley Linguistics Society* 15: 1–40.

Beedham, C. 1983, 'Language, indoctrination and nuclear arms', *University of East Anglia Papers in Linguistics* 19: 15–31.

Blainey, G. 1980, *A Land Half-Won*, Macmillan, Melbourne.

Blom, J.–P. & Gumperz, J. J. 1986, 'Social meaning in linguistic structures', in J. J. Gumperz & D. Hymes (eds), *Directions in Sociolinguistics*, 2nd edition, Holt Rinehart & Winston, New York, pp. 407–34.

Bransford J. D. & Johnson, M. K. 1972, 'Contextual prerequisites for understanding: some investigations of comprehension and recall', *Journal of Verbal Learning and Verbal Behavior* 11: 717–26.

Brown, P. & Levinson, S. C. 1987, *Politeness: Some Universals in Language, Usage*, Cambridge University Press, Cambridge.

Bryant, P. 1985, 'Regional variation in the Australian English lexicon', Australian Journal of Linguistics 5: 55–66.

Burton-Roberts, N. 1992, 'Prepositions, adverbs and adverbials', in I. Tieken-Boon van Ostade & J. Frankis (eds), *Language Usage and Description*, Rodopi, Amsterdam, pp. 159–72.

Chafe, W. 2000, 'Loci of diversity and convergence in thought and language', in M. Pütz & M. H. Verspoor (eds), *Explorations in Linguistic Relativity*, John Benjamins, Amsterdam, pp. 101–23.

Chomsky, N. 1966, *Cartesian Linguistics*, Harper & Row, New York.

Chouliaraki, L. & Fairclough, N. 1999, *Discourse in Late Modernity: Rethinking, Critical Discourse Analysis*, Edinburgh University Press, Edinburgh.

Clark, H. H. & Clark, E. V. 1977, *Psychology and Language*, Harcourt Brace, New York.

Clyne, M. 1994, *Inter-Cultural Communication at Work*, Cambridge University Press, Cambridge.

Coates, J. 1983, *The Semantics of the Modal Auxiliaries*, Croom Helm, London.

Cruse, D. A. 1986, *Lexical Semantics*, Cambridge University Press, Cambridge.

Crystal, D. 1997, *Dictionary of Linguistics and Phonetics*, 4th edn, Blackwell, Oxford.

Denison, D. 1993, *English Historical Syntax: Verbal Constructions*, Longman, London.

Dixon, R. M. 1972, *The Dyirbal Language of North Queensland*, Cambridge University Press, Cambridge.

Doyle, A. C. 1928, *Sherlock Holmes: The Complete Short Stories*, John Murray, London.

Eades, D. 1982, 'You gotta know how to talk: information-seeking in South-East Queensland Aboriginal Society', *Australian Journal of Linguistics* 2: 61–80.

Edwards, D. 1997, *Discourse and Cognition*, Sage, London.

Fairclough, N. 1989, *Language and Power*, Longman, London.

——(ed.) 1992a, *Critical Language Awareness*, Longman, London.

——1992b, *Discourse and Social Change*, Polity Press, Cambridge.

218   **References**

——2000, *New Labour, New Language?*, Routledge, London.
Fauconnier, G. 1994, *Mental Spaces*, Cambridge University Press, Cambridge.
——& Sweetser E. (eds) 1996, *Spaces, Worlds and Grammar*, University of Chicago Press, Chicago.
Fillmore, C. J. 1968, 'The case for case', in E. Bach & R. T. Harms (eds), *Universals in Linguistic Theory*, Holt, Rinehart, London, pp. 1–88.
——1977, 'The case for case reopened', in P. Cole & J. M. Sadock (eds), *Syntax and Semantics*, vol.8, Academic Press, New York, pp. 59–81.
——1982, 'Frame semantics', in Linguistic Society of Korea (ed.), pp. 111–37.
Forster, E. M. 1936 (1912), *A Passage to India*, Penguin, Harmondsworth.
Fowler, R. & Kress G. R. 1979, 'Critical linguistics', in R. Fowler & G. R. Kress (eds), *Language and Control*, Routledge & Kegan Paul, London, pp. 185–213.
Gerson, S. 1985, 'Tongue-tied by sexist language', *Courier-Mail*, Brisbane, 4 June 1985.
Gleason, H. A. 1961, *An Introduction to Descriptive Linguistics*, University of Chicago Press, Holt, Rinehart & Winston, Chicago & London.
Goldberg, A. E. 1995, *Constructions: A Construction Grammar Approach to Argument Structure*, University of Chicago Press, Chicago.
Golding, W. 1961, *The Inheritors*, Faber & Faber, London.
Goodenough, W. 1956, 'Componential analysis and the study of meaning', *Language* 32: 195–216.
Graham, A. 1975, 'The making of a non-sexist dictionary', in B. Thorne & N. Henley (eds), *Language and Sex: Difference and Dominance*, Newbury House, Rowley, MA, pp. 57–63.
Gumperz, J. J. 1982, *Language and Social Identity*, Cambridge University Press, Cambridge.
Haiman, J. 1985, *Iconicity in Syntax*, John Benjamins, Amsterdam.
Heritage, J. 1984a, *Garfinkel and Ethnomethodolgy*, Polity Press, Cambridge.
——1984b, 'A change of state token and aspects of its sequential placement', in J. M. Atkinson & J. Heritage (eds), *Structures of Social Action: Studies in Conversation Analysis*, Cambridge University Press, Cambridge, pp. 299–345.
Herskovits, A. 1986, *Language and Spatial Cognition: An Interdisciplinary Study of the Prepositions in English*, Cambridge University Press, Cambridge.
Hopper, P. J. & Thompson, S. A. 1980, 'Transitivity in grammar and discourse', *Language* 56: 251–99.
——& 1985, 'The iconicity of the universal categories "Noun" and "Verb" ', in J. Haiman (ed.), pp. 151–83.
Huddleston, R. D. 1984, *Introduction to the Grammar of English*, Cambridge University Press, Cambridge.
Ikegami, Y., 1985, ' "Activity"—"accomplishment"—"achievement": a language that can't say "I burned it, but it didn't burn" and one that can', in A. Makkai & A. K. Melby (eds), *Linguistics and Philosophy: Essays in Honor of Rulon Wells*, John Benjamins, Amsterdam, pp. 266–304.
Ingram, J. 1989, 'Connected speech processes in Australian English', *Australian Journal of Linguistics* 9: 21–49.
Jackendoff, R. 1994, The boundaries of the lexicon, manuscript, Brandeis University, Waltham, MA.
Johnson, M. 1987, *The Body in the Mind: The Bodily Basis of Meaning, Imagination, and Reason*, University of Chicago Press, Chicago.

King, R. T. 1988, 'Spatial metaphor in German causative constructions', in B. Rudzka-Ostyn (ed.), pp. 555–85.

Knapp, S. & Michaels, W. B. 1987, 'Against theory 2: hermeneutics and deconstruction', *Critical Inquiry* 14: 49–68.

Kress, G. R. 1985, 'Discourses, texts, readers and the pro-nuclear arguments', in P. Chilton (ed.), *Language and the Nuclear Arms Debate*, London, Frances Pinter, pp. 65–87.

——1989, 'History and language: towards a social account of linguistic change', *Journal of Pragmatics* 13: 445–66.

Labov, W. 1972a, 'The logic of non-standard English', in P. P. Giglioli (ed.), *Language and Social Context*, Penguin, Harmondsworth, pp. 179–215.

——1972b, *Sociolinguistic Patterns*, Blackwell, Oxford.

Lakoff, G. 1972, 'Hedges: a study in meaning criteria and the logic of fuzzy concepts', *Papers from the 8th Regional Meeting of the Chicago Linguistics Society* 13: 183–208.

——1977, 'Linguistic Gestalts', *Papers from the 13th Regional Meeting of the Chicago Linguistics Society*: 236–86.

——1987, *Women, Fire and Dangerous Things: What Categories Reveal About the Mind*, Chicago University Press, Chicago.

——1996, 'Sorry, I'm not myself today: the metaphor system for conceptualizing the self', in Gilles Fauconnier & Eve Sweetser (eds), pp. 91–123.

——& Johnson, M. 1980, *Metaphors We Live By*, Chicago University Press, Chicago.

Langacker, R. W. 1982, 'Remarks on English aspect', in P. J. Hopper (ed.), *Tense-Aspect: Between Semantics and Pragmatics*, John Benjamins, Amsterdam.

——1987, *Foundations of Cognitive Grammar*, vol. 1, *Theoretical Prerequisites*, Stanford University Press, Stanford.

——1988a, 'An overview of cognitive grammar', in B. Rudzka-Ostyn (ed.), pp. 3–48.

——1988b, 'A view of linguistic semantics', in B. Rudzka-Ostyn (ed.), pp. 49–51.

——1988c, 'The nature of grammatical valence', in B. Rudzka-Ostyn (ed.), pp. 91–125.

——1990, *Concept, Image and Symbol: The Cognitive Basis of Grammar*, Mouton, Berlin.

——1995, 'Raising and transparency', *Language* 71: 1–62.

Lee, D. A. 1989, 'Sociolinguistic variation in the speech of Brisbane adolescents', *Australian Journal of Linguistics* 9: 51–72.

——1992, *Competing Discourses: Perspective and Ideology in Language*, Longman, London.

——1999, 'Intransitive prepositions: are they viable?', in P. Collins and D. A. Lee (eds), *The Clause in English*, John Benjamins, Amsterdam, pp. 133–47.

Levin, B. & Rappaport Hovav, M. 1991, 'Wiping the slate clean: a lexical semantic exploration', *Cognition* 41: 123–51.

Lindner, S. 1982, 'What goes up doesn't necessarily come down: the ins and outs of opposites', *Papers from the 18th Regional Meeting of the Chicago Linguistics Society*, pp. 305–23.

Linguistic Society of Korea (ed.) 1982, *Linguistics in the Morning Calm*, Hanshin, Seoul.

Lounsbury, F. G. 1956, 'A semantic analysis of the Pawnee kinship usage', *Language* 32: 158–94.

Miller, C. & Swift, K. 1988, *The Handbook of Non-sexist Writing*, 2nd edn, Harper & Row, New York.

Milroy, J. 1992, *Linguistic Variation and Change*, Blackwell, Oxford.

Moore, T. & Carling, C. 1982, *Understanding Language: Towards a Post-Chomskyan Linguistics*, Macmillan, London.

Moorman, C. (ed.) 1977, The Works of the *Gawain*-Poet, University Press of Mississippi, Jackson MI.

Nishimura, Y. 1993, 'Agentivity in cognitive grammar', in R. A. Geiger & B. Rudzka-Ostyn (eds), *Conceptualizations and Mental Processing in Language*, Mouton, Berlin, pp. 487–530.

Nunberg, G. 1979, 'The non-uniqueness of semantic solutions', *Linguistics and Philosophy* 3: 143–84.

Piaget, J. [1936] 1952, *The Origins of Intelligence in Children*, trans. M. Cook, International Universities Press, New York.

Radden, G. 1992, 'The cognitive approach to natural language', in M. Pütz (ed.) *Thirty years of linguistic evolution*, John Benjamins, Amsterdam, pp. 513–41.

Reddy, M. J. 1979, 'The conduit metaphor—a case frame conflict in our language about language', in A. Ortony (ed.), *Metaphor and Thought*, Cambridge University Press, Cambridge. pp. 284–324.

Romney, A. K. & d'Andrade, R. G. 1964, 'Cognitive aspects of English kin terms', in A. Kimball Romney & R. G. d'Andrade (eds), *Transcultural Studies in Cognition*, *American Anthropologist* 66, special publication, vol. 3, part 2, pp.146–70.

Rosch, E. 1975, 'Cognitive representations of semantic categories', *Journal of Experimental Psychology: General* 104: 192–233.

Rudzka-Ostyn, B. (ed.) 1988, *Topics in Cognitive Linguistics*, John Benjamins, Amsterdam.

Sands, S. J. 1996, The verb *turn* and its semantic interaction with its complements: a cognitive analysis, manuscript, University of Queensland, St Lucia.

Saussure, F. de [1915] 1974, *Course in General Linguistics*, trans. by W. Baskin, Fontana/Collins, London.

Schiffrin, D. 1987, *Discourse Markers*, Cambridge University Press, Cambridge.

Scollon, R. & Wong Scollon, S. 1995, *Intercultural Communication: A Discourse, Approach*, Blackwell, Oxford.

Silveira, J. 1980, 'Generic masculine words and thinking', *Women's Studies International Quarterly* 3: 165–78.

Swan, M. 1980, *Practical English Usage*, Oxford University Press, Oxford.

Sweetser, E. 1988, 'Grammaticalization and semantic bleaching', *Proceedings of the Berkeley Linguistics Society* 14: 389–405.

——1996, 'Role and individual interpretations of change predicates', in J. Nuyts & E. Pedersen (eds), *Language and Conceptualization*, Cambridge University Press, Cambridge, pp. 116–36.

Talmy, L. 1988, 'Force dynamics in language and thought', *Cognitive Science* 12: 49–100.

Tannen, D. 1982, 'Ethnic style in male–female conversation', in J. J. Gumperz (ed.), pp. 217–31.

Taylor, J. 1995, *Linguistic Categorization*, 2nd edn, Clarendon Press, Oxford.

Traugott, E. C. 1993, 'The conflict promises/threatens to escalate into war', *Proceedings of the Berkeley Linguistics Society* 19: 347–58.

Ware, R. X. 1979, 'Some bits and pieces', in F. J. Pelletier (ed.), *Mass Terms: Some Philosophical Problems*, D. Reidel, Dordrecht, pp. 15–29.

Wetherell, M. & Potter, J. 1992, *Mapping the Language of Racism*, Harvester Wheatsheaf, Hemel Hempstead.

Whorf, B. L. [1945] 1971, 'Grammatical categories', in J. B. Carroll (ed.), *Language, Thought and Reality*, MIT Press, Cambridge MA, pp. 87–101.

Wierzbicka, A. 1985, 'Oats and wheat: the fallacy of arbitrariness', in J. Haiman (ed.), *Iconicity in Syntax*, John Benjamins, Amsterdam, pp. 311–42.

Wilkins, D. 1996, 'Semantic change and the search for cognates', in M. Durie & M. Ross (eds), *The Comparative Method Reviewed: Regularity and Irregularity in Language Change*, Oxford University Press, New York, pp. 265–304.

INDEX